WOMEN'S ROLES IN THE MIDDLE AGES

WOMEN'S ROLES IN THE MIDDLE AGES

Sandy Bardsley

Women's Roles through History

GREENWOOD PRESS
Westport, Conn. London

Library of Congress Cataloging-in-Publication Data

Bardsley, Sandy.
   Women's roles in the Middle Ages / by Sandy Bardsley.
      p. cm. — (Women's roles through history, ISSN: 1553–5088)
   Includes bibliographical references and index.
   ISBN-13: 978–0–313–33635–5 (alk. paper)
   ISBN-10: 0–313–33635–0 (alk. paper)
  1. Women—History—Middle Ages, 500–1500. 2. Sex role—Europe—
History. 3. Social role—Europe—History. 4. Social change—
Europe—History. 5. Europe—Social conditions. I. Title.
   HQ1147.E85B37   2007
   305.42094'0902—dc22   2007009620

British Library Cataloguing in Publication Data is available.

Library of Congress Catalog Card Number: 2007009620

ISBN-13: 978–0–313–33635–5
ISBN-10: 0–313–33635–0
ISSN: 1553–5088

First published in 2007

Greenwood Press, 88 Post Road West, Westport, CT 06881
An imprint of Greenwood Publishing Group, Inc.
www.greenwood.com

Printed in the United States of America

The paper used in this book complies with the
Permanent Paper Standard issued by the National
Information Standards Organization (Z39.48–1984).

10 9 8 7 6 5 4 3 2 1

*For Marianne, who was there throughout, and Cai,
who arrived halfway through.*

Contents

Series Foreword

Women's history is still being reclaimed. The geographical and chrono-logical scope of the Women's Roles through History series contributes to our understanding of the many facets of women's lives. Indeed, with this series, a content-rich survey of women's lives through history and around the world is available for the first time for high school students to the general public.

The impetus for the series came from the success of Greenwood's 1999 reference *Women's Roles in Ancient Civilizations,* edited by Bella Vivante. Librarians noted the need for new treatments of women's history, and women's roles are an important part of the history curriculum in every era. Thus, this series intensely covers women's roles in Europe and the United States, with volumes by the century or by era, and one volume each is de-voted to the major populated areas of the globe—Africa, the Middle East, Asia, and Latin America and the Caribbean.

Each volume provides essay chapters on major topics such as

- Family Life
- Marriage and Childbearing
- Religion
- Public Life
- Lives of Ordinary Women
- Women and the Economy
- Political Status
- Legal Status
- Arts

Country and regional differences are discussed as necessary.
Other elements include

- Introduction, providing historical context
- chronology
- glossary
- bibliography
- period illustrations

The volumes, written by historians, offer sound scholarship in an accessible manner. A wealth of disparate material is conveniently synthesized in one source. As well, the insight provided into daily life, which readers find intriguing, further helps to bring knowledge of women's struggles, duties, contributions, pleasures, and more to a wide audience.

Acknowledgments

I am especially grateful to Judith Bennett, Marianne Cutler, Kit French, and Janet Loengard, who read parts of this manuscript and gave me sage advice. Remaining errors are very much my own responsibility. Kit, Judith, Janet, and Maryanne Kowaleski also helped with specific questions and citations. I particularly valued the support and understanding of Wendi Schnaufer, the series editor for Women's Roles through History at Greenwood Press. Nancy Strobel and Debbie Gaspar of Moravian College's Reeves Library ordered hundreds of books and articles on interlibrary loan with impressive efficiency and good humor. I am very grateful to Margaret Schaus for the excellent bibliographical resource she provides on the Internet: Feminae (http://www.haverford.edu/library/reference/mschaus/mfi/mfi.html) is a terrific starting point for anyone researching the history of medieval women. Bev Beaver, Rachel Colancecco, and Michelle Squiccimara helped find resources and compile the chronology and bibliography. Dianne Bardsley, Judith Bennett, John Black, Jack Custy, Marianne Cutler, Mark Del Franco, Kit French, Dennis Glew, Janet Loengard, Bob Mayer, Jan Muzyczka, and Jamie Paxton provided moral support and encouragement, for which I am very grateful. Much-needed distraction was provided by Caedwyn Bardsley-Cutler, who inherits a world in some ways quite different from—and in other ways eerily similar to—that of her medieval foremothers.

Chronology

c. 30   Crucifixion of Jesus of Nazareth

313   The Roman Emperor Constantine issues the Edict of Toleration, meaning that it is no longer illegal to be a Christian within the Roman Empire

327   Death of Helena, mother of Constantine and patron of religious houses

c. 340   Birth of the influential Christian writer Jerome in Dalmatia

c. 347   Birth of Paula, a Roman ascetic, pilgrim, and founder of religious communities for women and men in Bethlehem

c. 354   Birth of the influential Christian writer Augustine in North Africa

370s   Melania the Elder travels from Rome to Egypt to found a monastery and convent

c. 390   Birth of Galla Placidia, daughter, sister, half-sister, mother, and regent of various Roman Emperors

391   Christianity becomes the official religion of the Roman Empire

410   Visigoths sack the city of Rome

412   Christians murder the famous pagan philosopher Hypatia in Alexandria, Egypt

438   Eudocia, a Byzantine Empress and poet, makes a pilgrimage to Jerusalem and returns with the relics of St. Stephen

470   Birth of Clotild (Clotilda, Chrotilda), who becomes Queen of the Franks and converts her husband, Clovis, to Christianity

476	Last Roman Emperor in Western Europe is deposed
c. 480	Birth of St. Scholastica, sister of St. Benedict, who heads a nunnery in central Italy
c. 497	Birth of Theodora I, Byzantine Empress
early sixth century	Caesarius of Arles establishes a convent for his sister, Caesaria
c. 518	Birth of St. Radegund, runaway wife of the Frankish king Clothar and founder of an important convent at Poitiers (France)
526	Amalasuntha becomes regent of Ostrogothic Italy for eight years on behalf of her son
c. 530	Birth of Sophia, Byzantine Empress
c. 595	Prophet Muhammad marries Khadija, his first wife
c. 610	Baudonivia, a nun, writes the first female-authored saint's life, a biography of St. Radegund
613	Death of Brunhild, queen of the Franks and important political figure
626	Birth of St. Gertrude of Nivelles, Frankish princess, founder of a double monastery, abbess, and ascetic
c. 639	Birth of St. Aldegund, Frankish abbess and autobiographer
664	Abbess Hild (Hilda) oversees the Synod of Whitby, at which differences between Roman and Irish forms of Christianity are resolved
673	St. Æthelthryth founds an important double monastery at Ely in the English kingdom of East Anglia
c. 700	Burginda, a Frankish nun, copies manuscripts and writes commentaries
748	Leoba, an Anglo-Saxon nun, arrives in Germany to assist the monk Boniface in converting Pagans to Christianity
793	Viking invasions begin
797	Irene, the Byzantine Empress, blinds her son, deposes him, and rules alone
800	Charlemagne, King of the Franks, is crowned "Holy Roman Emperor" by Pope Leo III
c. 801	Death of Rābi'a al-'Adawiyya, an Islamic Sufi and poet of Basra (modern Iraq)
820s–40s	Kassia, a Byzantine nun, composes chants and hymns

841–43	Dhuoda, a Frankish noblewoman, writes *Liber Manualis* for her son William
847	The Council of Mainz condemns and punishes Theoda, a German prophet, for preaching that the end of the world is about to come
870	Vikings burn the convent of Barking (England)
870	Vikings attack Coldingham (Scotland); the nuns of Coldingham cut off their noses and upper lips to try to prevent sexual assault
871	Vikings attack the English convent of Ely
910	Æthelflæd becomes effective ruler of the Anglo-Saxon kingdom of Mercia after her husband is incapacitated
c. 910	Jórunn Skáldmær composes poetry in Norway
914	Zoe Karbounopsina becomes regent of the Byzantine Empire
c. 935	Birth of abbess, dramatist, and author Hrotswita of Gandersheim
994	Birth of Wallāda, poet, sponsor of poets, and daughter of Caliph al-Mustakfi of Cordoba
c. 999	Steinunn Refsdóttir composes poetry in Iceland
late tenth century	Birth of Aasta of Norway, future mother and advisor to King Oláf
c. 1047	Birth of St. Margaret of Scotland, queen, and patron and reformer of the church
1052	Death of Queen Emma of England, wife to both an Anglo-Saxon king and a Viking king of England
c. 1056	Bertha of Vilich, a German nun, begins writing the biography of St. Adelheid
1066	The Normans conquer England
c. 1067	Death of the real Lady Godiva (Godgifu), a generous patron of the church (but probably not a naked horse rider) in England
c. 1067	Birth of Adela of Blois, strong ruler of areas of central France in her husband's absence and important literary patron
1077	Emperor Henry IV seeks the forgiveness of Pope Gregory VII at the castle of Matilda of Tuscany at Canossa
1095	Pope Urban II calls for the first crusade

1096	Crusaders en route to the Holy Land attack Jews in Europe; women like Rachel, wife of Rabbi Judah of Mainz, sacrifice their children to prevent them being converted to Christianity
c. 1096	Birth of Christina of Markyate (England), recluse and steadfast virgin
1098	Birth of the German abbess, author, and composer Hildegard of Bingen
1100	Matilda of Scotland marries Henry I of England, enabling her to become patron of English musicians, scholars, poets, and the church
c. 1101	Birth of Heloise, lover of Peter Abelard, abbess of the Paraclete, and author of passionate letters
1112	The Blessed Jutta of Disibodenberg is enclosed within an anchorhold, along with her pupil Hildegard of Bingen
1115	Petronilla of Chemillé becomes the first abbess of Fontevraut, an important abbey, and its daughter houses
1117	Queen Urraca of Léon-Castile conquers the Northern Spanish cities of Siguenza, Atienza, and Medinaceli from the Muslims
1118	Anna Comnena, daughter of a Byzantine Empress, conspires unsuccessfully to have her husband succeed the throne in place of her brother; she then withdraws to a convent and writes the *Alexiad,* a history of her father's reign
1122	Birth of Eleanor of Aquitaine, sponsor of poets, queen of France, queen of England, and a force to be reckoned with
c. 1127	Death of the recluse Frau Ava, the first woman known by name to have composed in German
1129	Birth of St. Elisabeth of Schönau, a German mystic, visionary, and author
c. 1130	Death of Diemud (Diemoth) of Wessobrun, a German nun, who spent much of her life copying by hand more than 40 manuscripts
1134	Ermengarde of Narbonne, future patron of troubadours, succeeds her father to become viscountess of Narbonne
1135	King Henry I of England dies; barons in England elect Stephen, his nephew, over Matilda, his daughter, thus prompting nearly twenty years of civil war
1145	Queen Melisende of Jerusalem, regent of the Kingdom of Jerusalem on behalf of her son, refuses to cede power to him once he comes of age and rules alone for another seven years
1145	Birth of Marie de Champagne, daughter of Eleanor of Aquitaine and sponsor of troubadours

1150	Birth of Christina Mirabilis (Christina the Astonishing), a Flemish mystic known for miracles, extreme visions, and levitation
1158	Birth of Yvette of Huy, a Dutch anchoress who has herself bricked into an enclosure attached to the wall of a leper colony
1159	Herrad of Hohenburg (Herrad of Landsberg) begins work on compiling her *Hortus deliciarum* (*Garden of Delights*), a collection of theological and secular texts
c. 1165	Birth of Gualdarada de' Ravignani, a Florentine noblewoman renowned for political activity
1177	Birth of Marie d' Oignies, a foundational figure in the Beguine movement
1193	Ingeborg of Denmark is married to Philip Augustus of France; after Philip rejects her a few days later, Ingeborg begins a long campaign of letter writing to popes to enlist their support in making Philip stand by the marriage
c. 1193	Birth of St. Clare of Assisi, friend of St. Francis and founder of the "Poor Clares"
1196	Death of Dulce of Worms, teacher and leader of prayers among Jewish women
late twelfth century	Marie de France, the best-known female troubadour, composes her lyrics
	Trota of Salerno, a southern Italian healer, records some of her remedies and medical advice
1200	Birth of Agnes of Prague (St. Agnes of Bohemia), a princess of Bohemia, who refuses marriage to the German Emperor Frederick II in favor of her religious vocation
1201	On her husband's death, Blanche of Navarre assumes the regency of the county of Champagne for the next 21 years
1202	Hedwig, wife of Duke Henry I of Silesia, persuades her husband to found a convent at Trebnitz
c. 1207	Birth of Mechthild of Magdeburg, German mystic, Beguine, and visionary
1214	Berenguela of Castile begins serving as regent for her brother, Henry I of Castile
1215	The 4th Lateran Council meets in Rome and passes new rules about marriage and clerical celibacy

1215	The English barons force King John to sign Magna Carta
c. 1225	Composition of the English *Ancrene Riwle* (or *Ancrene Wisse*), a guide for anchoresses (women who enclose themselves in buildings or parts of buildings in order to live holy lives)
1226	Blanche of Castile becomes regent of France
1230s	Guillaume de Lorris composes the original *Roman de la Rose,* a poem of about 4,000 lines
1231	Death of Elisabeth of Hungary, mystic and servant of the poor; within four years of her death she is made a saint
c. 1240	Douceline of Digne, a rich townswoman and mystic, founds a beguinage
1247	Birth of Margaret of Cortona, who becomes the mistress of an Italian nobleman; she later regrets her ways and becomes a Franciscan tertiary, visionary, and caretaker of the sick
c. 1248	Birth of Angela of Foligno, Italian mystic
1260	Death of Hadewijch, Belgian mystic and Beguine
1261	Gertrude of Helfta (Gertrude the Great) is sent to a convent at the age of five; she will become a renowned mystic and author
1260s–70s	Jean de Meun adds 17,000 lines to Guillaume de Lorris's *Roman de la Rose,* giving the poem a misogynist spin
1268	Death of Beatrice of Nazareth, nun and mystic
1272	Nicole of Rubercy, a laundress in Paris, suffers a stroke and is taken by her friends to the tomb of St. Louis at St.-Denis in hope of a miracle
1290	Death of Eleanor of Castile, Queen of England; her husband King Edward I is so distraught that he orders crosses to be erected at each place her body rests overnight on its journey to London
c. 1295	Birth of Cecilia Penifader, a peasant woman, on the English manor of Brigstock
late thirteenth century	Na Bieris de Roman, a female troubadour, composes her lyrics

1310	Marguerite Porete is burned at the stake for the heretical ideas in her book, *The Mirror of Simple Souls*
1317	Worst year of the Great Famine; many starve to death
1324	Alice Kyteler is accused and convicted of witchcraft in Ireland as part of a property dispute
1325	Na Prous Bonetta, French Beguine and religious freethinker, confesses to heretical beliefs and is burned at the stake
1326	Isabella of France, wife of the English King Edward II, conspires with her lover Roger Mortimer to overthrow her husband
1342	Birth of Julian of Norwich, important English mystic and author
1346	St. Brigid (Birgitta) of Sweden, renowned mystic and visionary, founds the Brigittine order of nuns
1347	Birth of St. Catherine of Siena, a Dominican tertiary, mystic, author, and servant of the poor
1347	The Black Death enters Europe
1347	The besieged French city of Calais surrenders to Edward III of England; according to stories, Queen Philippa persuades her husband Edward to spare the lives of its burghers
1353	Bourgot, a female illuminator, is employed by Yolande of Flanders, countess of Bar
1353	Birth of Margaret of Denmark, Queen of Norway and effective ruler of all of Scandinavia
1355	Inés de Castro is assassinated by her father-in-law, Alfonso IV of Portugal, who considers her an unfit match for his son
1358	Rebellion of the Jacquerie (peasants) in France
1360	Death of Elizabeth de Burgh of Clare, wealthy widow and patron of culture, education, and the church
c. 1362	Giovanni Boccaccio begins his *De claris mulieribus* (*Famous Women*), a companion to his volume on famous men
c. 1373	Birth of Margery Kempe, pilgrim and author of the first autobiography in English
1375	A tournament is held in honor of Alice Perrers, mistress of Edward III of England; in parliament the following year, English nobles officially protest her prominent position
1381	The English Peasants' Revolt
1382	Mary of Hungary becomes the Hungarian queen
1384	Jadwiga of Hungary, sister of Mary of Hungary, becomes queen of Poland

1385	Death of Joan of Kent, princess of Wales, mother of the English king Richard II, and protector of the heretical scholar John Wycliffe
c. 1386	Anne of Bohemia, wife of Richard II of England, encourages Geoffrey Chaucer to write his *Legend of Good Women*
1389	Christine de Pisan, newly widowed, begins her literary career
1394	John Rykener, a cross-dressing prostitute going by the name "Eleanor," is arrested in London
1394	Death of Dorothea of Montau, German mystic and recluse
c. 1412	Leonor López of Córdoba begins her *Memorias,* a memoir of her family and its political misfortunes
1418	Birth of Isotta Nogarola, scholar of Latin and Greek, translator, and poet
1425	Birth of Lucrezia Tornabuoni de'Medici, political advisor to her husband Piero de'Medici (ruler of Florence), composer of religious hymns, and patron of art and literature
1426	Margery del Mulne, a brewster and baker from the town of Middlewich, England, is fined 12 pence for "scolding" a neighbor
c. 1426	Birth of Margaret Paston, prolific letter writer and member of the English gentry
1431	Joan of Arc is burned at the stake
1436	Alessandra Macinghi Strozzi of Florence becomes a widow; for the next 35 years she runs the family estates and communicates by letter with her exiled sons
1440	Johannes Gutenberg invents the printing press with movable type; the first bibles are printed in 1455
1446	Birth of Margaret of York, duchess of Burgundy, political figure, and patron of the printer William Caxton
c. 1451	Alijt Bake, prioress of a Dutch Augustinian convent, writes her autobiography
1453	Constantinople is captured by the Turks
c. 1453–60	Teresa de Cartagena, a Spanish nun deaf since childhood, writes treatises on physical infirmities and spiritual growth
1455	Margaret Beaufort, at the age of thirteen, gives birth to the future Henry VII of England
1463	Birth of Caterina Sforza, countess of Forli, regent for her son, and participant in Italian political intrigues and battles

1469	Isabella of Castile marries Ferdinand of Aragon, uniting their two countries and providing the foundation for the modern Spanish state
c. 1469	The English gentlewoman Margery Paston horrifies her family by marrying their bailiff, Richard Calle, rather than someone of higher social status
1486	Publication of *Malleus maleficarum* (*The Hammer of Witches*), a virulently anti-female treatise, by the German friars Heinrich Kramer and James Sprenger
1490	St. Catherine of Genoa, pious noblewoman and visionary, becomes director of Genoa's Pammatone hospital for the poor
c. 1495	Death of Margery Brews Paston, English letter-writer
1499	Isabella d'Este, marquessa of Mantua and patron of authors and artists, persuades Leonardo da Vinci to sketch her

Introduction: Medieval Women

Discussing medieval women as a group implies that they saw they had something in common. Yet chances were that a medieval noblewoman or a queen saw little, if any, connection between herself and a peasant woman, and that a Christian woman and a Jewish woman regarded themselves as having little in common. Medieval women were divided from one another in many ways: by their social class, their religion, their age, their marital status, and by the place and the period in which they lived. Yet, as historians look back at the experiences of medieval women, they cannot help but see common patterns that transcend barriers of class, religion, age, time, and place. Two patterns in particular emerge in this study of medieval women. First, women as a group were virtually always viewed as inferior to men as a group. In other words, medieval societies—like those that preceded and followed them—were patriarchal. Second, individual women could sometimes overcome this inferior status and break the rules assigned to their sex. The fact that some women were able to break these rules did not, however, mean that all women were able to do so.

How did medieval women differ from one another? When a medieval person thought about his or her identity, class status may often have been more important than gender. The life of a medieval noblewoman was certainly different from that of a nobleman in terms of work, responsibilities, and behavioral expectations, but it was arguably less different than the gap between a noblewoman and a peasant woman. Class changed over time and place, too: in some regions of Europe in the early Middle Ages, class distinctions were less entrenched. In later periods, people became acutely conscious of social class and strove to improve their families' places in the social hierarchy. Women became important in their families' class strategies, whether as potential marriage partners, useful in forging alliances, or as more active participants in gift giving, fostering of children, and exchanges of favors.

Social class separated the lives of medieval women from one another, but so too did factors such as religion, age, and marital status. Most Europeans were Christian, although it took several centuries before it was clear what this really meant. For many, the conversion from Paganism to Christianity was a gradual, rather than an abrupt, process. Stories attest to the role of women, such as the sixth-century Clotild (discussed in chapter 1), in converting their families to the new religion. It also took several centuries before Christianity became centralized and organized. In the early Middle Ages, Celtic Christianity differed from Roman Christianity (many of these differences were resolved at a church council of 664), Byzantine and Western Christianity drew further apart, and Arian Christianity (the belief that Jesus was more human than divine and thus not a full member of the trinity) persisted in many areas. Women practicing Celtic, Byzantine, or Arian forms of Christianity may well have perceived themselves as different from women practicing Roman Christianity. In the high and late Middle Ages, Christian women and men whose beliefs differed from those of the mainstream church were condemned as heretics, with consequences ranging from cautious disregard to outright persecution. Jews, too, experienced a variety of attitudes from mainstream Christian society: in the early Middle Ages, Jews were seldom persecuted, but this changed from the end of the eleventh century onward. Thereafter, Jews were intermittently attacked and blamed for a range of social ills. Jewish women faced many of the same strictures as their Christian counterparts, such as their banishment from important religious or public positions. But some norms differed, too: for example, Jewish communities tended to be far less tolerant of wife-beating than Christian communities were. Just as Christians sometimes accepted and sometimes persecuted Jews, so too their attitudes toward Muslims were ambivalent. Much of Spain was under Islamic control from the eighth century onward. The term *medieval women* includes Islamic women living in Spain, yet their experiences were certainly different from those of Christian or Jewish women. Like social class, then, religion separated women from one another.

Age and marital status also affected the lives and roles of women in important ways. Behavioral expectations and social norms for girls and maidens, for instance, were quite different from those of married women and widows. A minority of women remained single throughout their lives. Others saw themselves as married to God and thus do not fit neatly into any marital category.

Medieval women can easily be separated into the various groups outlined above: noblewomen, townswomen, or peasant women; Christian women, Jewish women, or Islamic women; girls, maidens, wives, widows, or lifelong single women. What, then, did these various groups have in common? What justifies our regarding them as a distinctive category? In each case, the main thing that these women had in common was their relationship to men. Whether Jewish, Islamic, Christian, noble, peasant, single, married, widowed, old, or young, women were regarded as inferior to men of the same category. A noblewoman could trump a peasant man in terms of social power, but medieval society understood that she was almost certainly subject to a man who occupied the same social status as she did. Medieval societies—whether Frankish courts, Jewish ghettoes, peasant manors, or one of many other subcultures—were patriarchal. Although each society contained women who were able to transcend the generally inferior role assigned to their sex, the majority of women were kept firmly in their place by a network of expectations and attitudes.

PRIMARY SOURCES ON MEDIEVAL WOMEN

The subordinate status of medieval women is quickly apparent when one looks at surviving primary sources. Finding sources for any aspect of medieval life can be a challenge: especially in the early Middle Ages, few people were literate, and those who were tended to be more concerned with making records for immediate needs than for posterity. Medieval historians thus need to be skilled at reading between the lines and teasing details from terse accounts. Such skills are even more necessary when one studies medieval women, since most of the surviving documents deal exclusively with men. Yet historians of medieval women have done an impressive job of scouring the records for information and analyzing it in thoughtful ways. The following survey illustrates just a few of the many types of sources used by historians of medieval women.

Sources written or dictated *by* women are some of the most valuable in giving insight into how women thought and felt. As one might expect, most female-authored works survive from women of higher social status, since women of lower status were almost never taught to read or write. Religious women, for instance, might recount their visions, advice, or instructions, particularly for the edification of other women. The twelfth-century Hildegard of Bingen, for example, was a prolific writer who did not hesitate to record her messages to the nuns under her care. In a letter to the nuns at her convent of Rupertsburg, she wrote:

And therefore, daughters of God, I advise you and I have advised you from my youth that you love one another, so that because of your goodwill towards others you might be like the angels as a bright shining light strong in your powers...May the Holy Spirit grant you its gifts, for after my death you will no longer hear my voice. But may my voice never fall into forgetfulness among you; may it rather be heard often in your midst in love.

Hildegard's words show a strong self-consciousness of her own spiritual power; they also demonstrate the power she attributes to the written word, since her "voice" will survive largely through her writings. Earlier in the same letter she stipulates that the nunnery was granted to her through a "written contract in a legal codex," emphasizing to the sisters of the convent, both of her time and in the future, the legality of their foundation.[1] Hildegard was among the most articulate and most literary of medieval women, using the written word both to protect and guide her community. St. Clare of Assisi attempted to do the same through the list of rules she compiled for her nuns in the thirteenth century. Clare's Rule, in fact, acknowledges that only some of her nuns were literate: those who could read were responsible for reading the religious services aloud; those who could not were given extra prayers to say instead. Indeed, Clare did not think it worthwhile to teach nuns to read: instead, everyone should work and worship according to the talents and skills they possessed. Clare's Rule emphasized obedience and humility, exhorting her nuns to wear cheap clothing, speak seldom, and obey their abbess.[2] Documents such as those of Hildegard and Clare lend insight into the everyday lives of religious women and the relationships among them. Other sources authored by religious women (including others by both Hildegard and Clare) provide insight into their spiritual lives. One of Hildegard's visions uses a distinctively female metaphor in casting the church as a mother:

Her [the church's] womb is pierced like a net with many openings, with a huge multitude of people running in and out; that is, she displays her maternal kindness, which is so clever at capturing faithful souls by diverse goads of virtue, and in which the trusting peoples devoutly lead their lives by the faith of their true belief.[3]

Hildegard walked a narrow line: she and fellow visionaries had to avoid carefully any claim of spiritual authority over men. Consequently, much visionary literature and much advice literature written by women was specifically directed toward other women. As chapter 5 explains, women were also among the authors of poems and plays, although few of these survive.

Letters written by medieval women provide another important female-authored source. Noblewomen often wrote or dictated letters to be sent to their husbands when the latter were away from home in order to keep them updated on matters of family business. They also used letters to family members and friends as part of their participation in family politics. Such was the case in a letter written by Joan, princess of Wales, to her half-brother Henry III of England in the early thirteenth century. Joan's letter shows her intervening in the relationship between her half-brother and her husband, the Welsh prince Llewellyn the Great:

> To her most excellent lord and dearest brother, Henry, by the grace of God, King of England, Lord of Ireland, Duke of Normandy and Aquitaine and Count of Anjou, Joan sends her own greetings.
>
> Know, lord, that I am grieved beyond measure, that I can by no means express, that our enemies have succeeded in sowing discord between my husband and you. I grieve no less on account of you than on account of my husband, especially since I know what genuine fondness my husband used to have, and still has, for you, and how useless and dangerous it is for us, with due respect, to lose true friends and have enemies instead. Thus on bended knee and shedding tears, I beg your highness to alter your decision, as you may easily do, and do not fail to be reconciled to those who are joined to you by an unbreakable bond and learn both to love friends and oppress enemies.[4]

As Joan's letter demonstrates, she occupied a vital role in the relationship between these two important men, and she did not hesitate to use emotive writing to try and achieve peace between them. Llewellyn the Great might have found it undignified or unmanly to appeal to Henry III "on bended knee and shedding tears," but Joan had no such scruples. Letters such as these tell historians about the important role played by women in politics (a topic discussed further in chapter 6) and about women's use of rhetoric (discussed in chapter 5).

Another source that might be considered female-authored is that of wills. Women did not typically write wills with their own hands; instead, they dictated them to scribes who wrote them up in the style of the day. Yet while they might not have governed the format of the documents, women were, at least, responsible for their contents, and historians have used these sources to good effect. For the most part, only widows had wills; married women could usually make wills only with the consent of their husbands, and their property was regarded as belonging to their husbands. Wills written by widows reveal interesting data about their emotional, social, and religious connections, as well as the property available for their disposal. For example, a particularly detailed will written by the Anglo-Saxon woman Wynflæd in c. 950 bequeathed money, offering-cloths, a cross, and silver cups to her local church, along with further sums of money to various religious houses. To her daughter Æthelflæd, she left land and jewelry, and to her son Eadmær, she left lands. Wynflæd also freed various of her enslaved servants in her will, although some of these servants were directed to go and serve her daughter. Her son, daughter, grandson, and other relatives also received various precious cups, but Wynflæd expressed in her will her hope that they might in turn give some of their own cups to the church. Linen, gowns, chests, and tapestries were also parceled out among her heirs.[5] Wynflæd's will typifies a trend that some historians have noted in which women tended to be more specific and particular than men in disposing of their possessions. Later female wills were similarly detailed and continued to demonstrate the importance of the church. Katherine Peverel's will of 1375, for instance, left bequests of money to no fewer than 17 religious houses and hospitals. The 1405 will of Beatrice Roos showed similar concern: in addition to endowing various religious houses, she left 100 marks (a considerable sum) to pay "for as many masses as can profitably be celebrated after my death for my soul and the souls of my husbands, ancestors and parents, and all the faithful departed, at York, and in divers monasteries, abbeys, priories, convents of mendicant friars, hospitals, parish churches, and chapels in Yorkshire." In addition, she paid for masses in specific places: £50 for two chaplains in the parish church of Helmsley to celebrate mass twice daily for five years; £20 for one chaplain in the chapel of Storthwaite for four years; £6 for four masses to be celebrated as soon as possible after her death, and £10 for a series of masses of St. Gregory to be celebrated within a year of her death. Beatrice dispersed her material goods with similar specificity: Thomas de Rolleston, rector of Kirby Misperton, was to receive a silver goblet with a cover marked on the knob with two *b*'s, while her servant Robert de Hoton was given a covered silver goblet decorated with branches and leaves of yew.[6] Wills like those of Wynflæd, Katherine Peverel, and Beatrice Roos can thus reveal much to historians about the religious and social networks in which these women lived. One major disadvantage to using wills as a source, however, is their availability: only a relatively small number survive, and those that do are limited mostly to noble widows. Peasant women and poorer townswomen did not make wills, and married and single women made them only seldom.

Texts written by women are thus relatively scarce. Only very occasionally do historians and literary scholars encounter documents in which women self-consciously reflect on their lives. One such document, for example, is the fifteenth-century *Book of Margery Kempe*, the first autobiography to be written in English. Margery's *Book*, dictated to scribes, recounts her efforts to live a holy life.[7] Indeed, Margery faced considerable difficulty in finding a scribe who was willing and able to record her words as she wanted. Other particularly useful texts include the works of Christine de Pisan, a fifteenth-century Italian noblewoman living in France. Christine's *Book of the City of Ladies*, and its sequel, *Treasure of the City of Ladies*, provide advice for women of all social statuses and give

Christine an opportunity to reflect on the ways in which women were maligned in contemporary texts.[8] Works such as these, discussed further in chapter 5, are invaluable to historians. Yet one must note, once again, that female-authored texts were written by a very small fraction of the medieval female population.

Thus historians must look to other sources. Comments by male authors on the lives, nature, and status of women convey much useful information, yet these comments must—as with any other source—be taken with a grain of salt. St. Paul's first letter to the Corinthians, for instance, insists that women should be silent in the churches and subordinate to their husbands. Yet elsewhere he greeted and acknowledged female leaders within the church. St. Jerome insisted that virginity was the worthiest state for a woman, yet clearly most of his contemporaries disagreed, or the population would have died

Christine de Pisan (c.1364–c.1430) writing at her desk, from a Parisian manuscript of c.1410–15. © British Library, London, UK/ © British Library Board. All Rights Reserved/ The Bridgeman Art Library

out. Comments on the nature and status of women are frequently misogynist, but this does not necessarily mean that all medieval men hated women.

Conversely, positive depictions of women did not mean that they were necessarily admired. Chivalric literature of the high and late Middle Ages that placed women on a pedestal did not translate to idealization of real women, for instance. The chaste, beautiful, and remote "lady in the tower" served as an object of devotion for fictional knights, who admired her from afar. Yet little evidence exists that such attitudes were carried over to real noblewomen, who remained hardheaded household managers. Glimpses of strong female characters can also be found in Scandinavian tales: the Danish Alvild, for example, becomes a pirate, although she is ultimately tamed by her suitor; Sigrid the Strong-Minded of Sweden (perhaps a real queen, though one whose legends were distorted by time) was renowned for wisdom and defiance against the bullying of King Olaf of Norway. Yet real Scandinavian women were seldom allowed such license.

Other documents written by men also touch upon the lives of women, although historians must be prepared to read between the lines. For instance, a document such as a court roll from a medieval manor or town can reveal a great deal about women's work, their marital status, their participation in public life, their familial and friendship networks, the crimes they were most likely to commit, and their ownership of land. Take, for example, the following excerpts from court records of the small town of Middlewich (England) in 1424–25:

"Great Court" held at Middlewich, 10 October 1424

John Baylly, William Dicky, Henry le Vernon, and Richard Busshell are elected by the whole community of the town of Middlewich and the jurors of the court to oversee and govern the craft of salt boiling and to see that the rules are not broken and that the lord King gets the proper taxes.

John Baylly comes before the court and pays a fee of 13 shillings and 4 pence for a license to boil salt with 6 saltpans. Guaranteed by William de Erdeley.

William de Erdeley pays 13 shillings and 4 pence for 6 saltpans. Guaranteed by John Baylly.

[13 more payments, ranging from 3 shillings and 8 pence to 26 shillings and 8 pence, are listed in the same format as above. Of the fifteen payments for salt boiling, 13 are made by men and two (from Katherine de Halghton and Agnes Cause) by women.]

"Great Court" held at Middlewich, 3 July 1425

The members of the jury—Robert Page, William Croucher, Robert Waryhull, Henry le Vernon, Richard Busshell, Thomas Batesson, Robert Wyche, Richard

Burgess, Hugh Hicson, Roger Ruskin, William Dicky, and Richard Wilkyn-
son—swear upon their oath that:

Agnes wife of Roger Croxton, Margery wife of Thomas del Mulne, Eleanor
wife of William Rolde, Agnes wife of Thomas le Taylor, and Agnes Cause
are common bakers and owe money for the right to bake bread. [Agnes
Croxton and Margery pay 6 pence; Eleanor pays 4 pence; Agnes Taylor and
Agnes Cause pay 3 pence.]

And the members of the jury state that:

Agnes wife of Roger Croxton, Margery wife of Thomas del Mulne, Margery
Benefet, Richard Clerk, and Matilda wife of Henry le Vernon are common brewers and owe fees for the right to practice their trade [each pays
3 shillings and 11 pence]

And the members of the jury state that:

Agnes le Merton, Isotta de Buycroft, Edmund del Crosse, Joan le Warner,
Cecilia wife of Richard Turner, Alice Haynesson, Katherine de Whytemore,
Alice wife of Ralph Rowley, Joan wife of William de Erdeley, Joan Halfmark,
Agnes le Nurse, Cecilia wife of John de Cotton, Isabel Thycope, Whyrle wife
of John Sawyer, Matilda wife of William Barber, and Christina le Huersa are
common food sellers [Alice Haynesson, Agnes le Nurse, and Whirle Sawyer
pay 4 pence; Agnes le Merton, Katherine de Whytemore, Alice Rowley, and
Christina le Huersa pay 3 pence; the rest all pay 2 pence]

And the members of the jury state that:

Richard Busshell, Edmund del Crosse, Hugh Hicson, Robert del Okes, John
Smallwood, Thomas Rothelonde, David del Okes, and John Norley are common butchers and owe fees for the right to practice their trade [Richard,
Edmund, Hugh, Robert, and John Smallwood each pay 12 pence; Thomas
and David each pay 8 pence; John Norley pays 6 pence][9]

In these short extracts alone, one can already detect several important
patterns: first, the major industry in the town (salt-boiling) was one in
which men owned almost all the assets (in this case, salt pans). Yet it is also
important to note that there were exceptions to this rule, as in the cases
of Katherine de Halghton and Agnes Cause. In other words, women were
not necessarily excluded from owning important town assets, but they
were far less likely to do so than men. The fees paid for licenses to brew
ale, bake bread, butcher meat, and carry foodstuffs are also revealing. Only
two of these trades (butchery and baking) were exclusive to one gender in
fifteenth-century Middlewich. The higher fees paid by butchers, however,
suggest that this trade was more lucrative, and the low fees paid by food
sellers indicate that this was a low-status trade. The occupational pattern

suggested by these sources, therefore, is one in which women were mostly clustered in lower-status occupations and men were mostly clustered in higher-status occupations. The boundaries between the two were, however, permeable, and a few women could make their living by owning salt pans, while a few men (such as Richard Clerk and Edmund del Crosse) had to rely on food selling and brewing.

The court record also gives important information about marital status. Women were generally identified by their relationship to men (as wives, daughters, or widows), although there were again some exceptions to this rule (as in the case of Agnes Cause). Men, however, were very seldom identified in documents through their relationships to women. Marital status also correlates with occupation: brewing and baking in Middlewich (as elsewhere) were mostly, though not exclusively, carried out by married women.

The public life of Middlewich can also be glimpsed through these records. All of the appointees to official roles—here governors of salt boiling and jurors—were men, and this too reflects a broader pattern seen throughout most of medieval Europe. Whereas work boundaries were somewhat permeable, boundaries of public authority were far less so. Despite the fact that Katherine de Halghton ran a salt house with six salt pans, she was never appointed to the position of governor of salt boiling, nor was she made a juror, a bailiff, or a chamberlain. Instead, these positions, in Middlewich as elsewhere, were held by men.

More information about the town of Middlewich and the role of women in the town can be gleaned by examining a longer series of court records and building up a database to collect information on each individual. For example, if one examines all surviving fifteenth-century court records, one learns that Margery del Mulne, mentioned here among the ale brewers and the bakers, brewed ale on at least 60 occasions between 1421 and 1434, aided by a servant. Margery and her husband Thomas owned an inn, and Thomas also worked as a salt boiler. Thomas was, in fact, one of the wealthiest salt boilers, using 12 salt pans and paying 26 shillings and 8 pence in fees. After Thomas died sometime in the mid- to late-1430s, Margery continued to bake bread for commercial sale, and she actively used the courts to pursue debts owed to her. In 1439, she also acted as a guarantor for a man who had failed to appear before the court in a debt case, an unusual role for a woman. Court records also show that Margery was once charged as a "scold," a person who engaged in loud, inappropriate public arguments. Information about Margery is thus mentioned in the chapters on law and on work that follow. Building up databases about individuals like Margery is known as *prosopography.* Prosopography, or collective biography, is a particularly useful method to derive information about women and men of lower social status, those who would not normally appear in documents authored by the nobility.

Records of borough courts and rural manor courts are terrific sources for approaching the lives of ordinary people, but other court records are useful too. Church courts operated throughout much of Europe, and as the Middle Ages proceeded they dealt with an increasing amount of business. In particular, they were concerned with issues of marriage and morality. People accused of adultery, bigamy, or desertion of their spouses might find themselves accused before such courts. Conflicts over marriage (especially whether or not a marriage had been properly conducted and hence counted as a true marriage) were also heard by the church courts.

Laws themselves, as outlined in chapter 4, provide other helpful information on the position of women. Interpretation of such laws, however, can be ambiguous. In some places, for instance, the clothing of both women and men was regulated in order to prevent people from wearing clothes inappropriate to their social station or clothes of excessive wealth. According to Venetian laws of 1299, women were not to wear strings of pearls in their hair and could be fined heavily if caught doing so.[10] This regulation might be interpreted in various ways: on the one hand, it might be seen to limit a woman's self-expression, yet on the other it might imply that men were using women as clotheshorses in order to display their own wealth and status. Similarly, the thirteenth-century Sicilian law that punished men who raped prostitutes might, on the one hand, be interpreted as protecting women, yet the very existence of such a law—and the fact that prostitutes were mentioned separately from other women—suggests that rape of prostitutes was a problem in medieval Sicily.[11] Moreover, we have no way to know how well many medieval laws were enforced.

Other kinds of legal documents are useful, too: charters recording the transfer of land, for instance, sometimes reveal female ownership. Women's legal right to property is a complex issue, explored in more detail in chapter 4. Widows had more rights than married women (whose property typically belonged to their husbands), yet even widows faced restrictions in disposing of property since they were often prevented from disinheriting their husband's heirs. Nonetheless, some women were able to control property in their own right. Others were occasionally listed alongside their husbands in documents recording pious donations to monasteries, nunneries, or other religious foundations. Powerful women might possess their own seals, metal engravings that would be pressed into wax to signify a document's authenticity. Such seals sent important messages about a woman's authority, particularly when they depicted her seated on a throne or accompanied by coats of arms or other symbols of power.

Account rolls are sometimes a helpful source for finding out about women, too, although these tend to favor the noble classes. The thirteenth-century household roll of Joan de Valence of England, for instance, contains careful records of the amounts spent on wine, ale, meat, eggs, and milk. It also details the costs of feeding horses and buying salve for them, and paying wages to the 43 grooms.[12] Such account rolls point to the complexity involved in running a medieval household. A noblewoman such as Joan de Valence was required to anticipate expenses and manage a large staff. Account rolls often record visits from fellow nobles, since these visits required extra expenditure. In addition, they sometimes record meals given to paupers as charity. Historians can thus use account rolls to learn about the social and charitable networks of noblewomen.

Written sources are vital to the study of medieval women, but non-written sources can be important too. Archaeology and artwork provide important clues about women's lives. For instance, we know from the analysis of bones found in medieval cemeteries that the work of men and women in the countryside tended to be very physical. Both male and female skeletons from rural areas show evidence of upper arm development, although the work they did was different: men worked in the fields (though women helped out on occasion), women hauled water, scrubbed laundry, carried children, and more. In the towns, however, male skeletons show more signs of heavy labor than female skeletons, suggesting that the division of labor for townspeople was quite different from that of their country cousins.[13] Manuscript illustrations can provide further information about work: peasant women are depicted feeding chickens, washing sheep, and spinning yarn using a distaff and spindle.

Many different types of primary sources can thus be found to shed light on the lives of medieval women, but these sources often require careful interpretation. Because the lives of women, especially those at the lower end of the social scale, were often poorly documented, historians have had to be particularly creative and careful in their approach to these sources. The large majority of medieval women have disappeared without a trace: not even their names survive. But by extrapolating from surviving records, we can at least get some clues into what the lives of these missing women may have been like.

AN OVERVIEW OF THE MIDDLE AGES

The term *Middle Ages* refers to the period between the disintegration of the Roman Empire in the fourth and fifth centuries and the beginnings of the early modern era in the fifteenth to sixteenth centuries. These dates are necessarily vague and arbitrary, because it is difficult to say where one era leaves off and the next begins. Did the deposition of the last Roman Emperor in 476 mark a watershed for Europeans? Not really, since he was merely a figurehead and many were unaware that he had even been deposed. Did the accession of King Henry VIII of England in 1509 signify a transformation in the lives of Europeans? Probably not. Certainly it made little impact on those outside of England, and even in England few men or women saw themselves in 1509 on the brink of a new era. Furthermore, the Middle Ages are traditionally divided into three main periods, separated by equally arbitrary dates: the early Middle Ages, from about 500 to 1000, the high Middle Ages, from about 1000–1300, and the late Middle Ages, from about 1300 to 1500.

The Early Middle Ages

The early Middle Ages were a period of struggle and accommodation, as three cultures gradually merged with one another to create a new and distinctive one. The first of these cultures was that of the Celts, who had lived throughout much of Western Europe prior to Roman expansion. Although few sources give direct evidence about real Celtic women, those that survive suggest that their status was seldom high. For instance, stories emphasize that women were typically banned from participating in warfare, the most prestigious activity in Celtic society. Exceptions to the rule, such as the beautiful Queen Medb who battles the warrior Cúchulainn in the Irish *Táin Bó Cúailnge*, were brought low by their own biological makeup: Medb, who is menstruating during the decisive chariot battle, is forced to squat to "relieve herself" and is thus captured by Cúchulainn.[14] Medb was almost certainly fictional, but historical Celtic women warriors fared little better. Queen Boudicca led a revolt of the Iceni against the Romans in the first century C.E., but she was also defeated. The preferred role for women was that of loyal wife and bearer of children. Yet religion offered some esteem for such roles in Celtic society. Mother-goddesses were well-known in Celtic culture, and female deities were often associated with wells, springs, and other life-giving places. Scholars debate the extent and the nature of Celtic goddesses' power, and they also debate whether esteem for goddesses translated into esteem for real women. Scraps of surviving evidence, however, suggest that Celtic society was probably just as patriarchal as any other.

As Romans spread into areas formerly peopled by the Celts, they brought different ideas about women, although they certainly shared the notion that women were inferior to men. By the second century C.E., the Roman Empire was vast, stretching from as far as Britain in the west to North Africa in the south to the area around modern Israel/Palestine in the east. By the fourth century, however, it was overwhelmed by problems: the population had declined, due to plagues and constant warfare; the political situation was unstable and coups were frequent; and the economy was in disarray. Roman society retained, however, a strong hierarchy in which people seldom moved from the social class into which they were born. Many Romans could read and write, and they looked back to the so-called golden age of the first to second centuries C.E. in which much of their literature had been written and many of their aqueducts, temples, and public edifices had been built. In spite of their political difficulties, Romans valued law and order, and their laws were usually written down and carefully elaborated. Roman society was also, despite its decline, based around cities and urban life. Compared with women in other ancient societies, Roman women usually had more rights and privileges. They were not confined to the home (as some Greek women had been), and—under particular circumstances—had the right to a divorce. They also had rights, albeit limited, to control their own property. Roman society was patriarchal—each household was dominated by the father, who had considerable power over both his wife and his children—yet Roman women fared better than many.

So too, perhaps, did Germanic women, although far less is known about Germanic societies prior to their movement into the Roman Empire. Some Germanic peoples used runes for recording inscriptions, but writing was not a regular nor important aspect of life, so primary sources on Germanic society are scarce. In fact, Germanic peoples were quite unlike the Romans: they lived in much smaller-scale settlements—villages, rather than cities—and their economy was based around agriculture and metalwork. Germanic tribes were governed individually and separately, not by a central emperor. And Germanic society was somewhat more egalitarian than Roman society: although there were still some distinctions of class and status, the divisions between them were more permeable, and it was possible to rise and fall in status. In particular, a family's status might rise if it contained a particularly good warrior. Women seem to have been valued particularly for their childbearing abilities and for creating kinship networks among men. They also, according to Roman commentators, played an important backup role on the battlefield by calling encouragement to men, bringing them food and supplies, and tending the wounded. Women also took responsibility for spinning, weaving, and sewing. Yet, as chapter 4 explains, Germanic laws suggest that women were seen largely as possessions, under men's control and traded between men at the time of their marriage.

From the fourth century onward, Germanic tribes that had lived in the area north of the Roman Empire took the opportunity of Roman weakness to move across the border and carve out territory for themselves. The first to move were the Visigoths, spurred by invasions from the Huns to the east. In the late fourth and early fifth centuries, the Visigoths traveled throughout much of southern Europe in search of a territory that they could settle. They were followed by many other tribes: the Vandals, who settled in North Africa, the Franks and Burgundians, who ended up in parts of modern-day France, the Ostrogoths and Lombards, who attempted to rule parts of the Italian peninsula, the Angles, Saxons, and Jutes, who settled Britain, and others.

The early Middle Ages saw the gradual merging of these three cultures—Celtic, Roman, and Germanic—into one society. This involved reconciliation of some major differences: Who would rule each region? Which languages would dominate? Would literacy prevail? Whose laws would be followed? Whose religion? Which social structure? And what would all this mean for the position of women? Different regions within Europe found different answers for these questions. For example, in the kingdom of the Franks (arguably the most successful of the new kingdoms), the Germanic rulers established the Merovingian dynasty. They took their Germanic laws, previously passed on orally from one generation to the next, and recorded them in writing, a Roman convention. Gradually, the social structures of the various cultures merged, too, to form a social structure unique to the Middle Ages: at the top was the aristocracy, then the free peasantry, then the unfree peasantry, then slaves. Unfree peasants (known as serfs) were tied to the land on which they were born and were required to work several days per week for their local nobles. In return for this labor and other services, they received a small plot of land sufficient to grow their own food. This system, whereby serfs and free peasants rented land from nobles and repaid them with a variety of obligations, was known as *manorialism.* The number of serfs increased considerably during the early Middle Ages, as their numbers were augmented by former slaves and by free peasants who were unable to make a living by wage labor and thus committed themselves and their descendents to serfdom in exchange for the security of a plot of land.

During the early Middle Ages, no one lived at a level that could be described as comfortable by modern standards. Even among the aristocracy, standards of living were low. Agricultural yields were meager, which meant low profits and little money available for luxury items. Indeed, many long-distance trade routes that formerly supplied luxury items shut down during this era. Nobles wore woolen clothing (remarkably itchy!) and lived in houses made of wood. For the most part, they were responsible for their own protection, since kings had little power. Indeed, the title of king often meant little in the early Middle Ages. Aside from a few exceptions, such as Charlemagne in the eighth to ninth centuries, and Otto I in the tenth century, kings were often indistinguishable from other members of the nobility in terms of their power and their standard of living. Lacking an efficient and enforceable system of taxation, they found it impossible to build up their armies or exert authority over independent-minded nobles. This situation became all the more acute toward the end of the early Middle Ages when repeated attacks from Magyars, Muslims, and Vikings further undermined central power. Nobles, recognizing that they were on their own in terms of defense, undertook responsibility for their local areas and—in consequence—came to expect that the areas they defended belonged to them.

Thus evolved the system of feudalism. Whereas the term *manorialism* describes the relationship between peasants and nobles, *feudalism* refers to relationships among members of the nobility. Men from the lesser nobility, known as knights, promised to serve members of the upper nobility, whom they referred to as their lords. In doing so, they became the lord's *vassals.* Vassals owed lords military service but, as time went on, various other dues were required as well. They had to serve in their lords' courts, house and feed their lords if the latter came visiting (often an expensive undertaking), and occasionally pay special fees, such as ransom if lords were captured. Lords, in return, promised to protect their vassals and provided them with a court system for working out their disputes with one another. Eventually, in the high Middle Ages, some kings were able to capitalize on the system of feudalism and assert themselves at the top of the feudal pyramid. In other words, a king such as the eleventh-century William the Conqueror of England allowed the major lords in his kingdom to take on as many vassals as they wished, but everyone (lords and vassals alike) had to acknowledge William's position as overlord. The system of feudalism was one that emphasized military strength and was fundamentally a male institution. Except in the rarest of circumstances, women could not become vassals because they were not permitted to fight.

For women, the decentralization and low standard of living of the early Middle Ages brought both dangers and opportunities. In the absence of a strong central authority, women were vulnerable to sexual assaults and exploitation, both by those living around them and by invaders. Yet some women also managed to carve out positions of power for themselves amidst the chaos. Abbesses, as chapter 1 will show, enjoyed a position of relative strength during the early Middle Ages, a strength that would be curtailed as the power of the church and state grew in later centuries. Some queens, too, held positions of significant influence. The persuasive power of Clotild, wife of Clovis, king of the Franks, is also documented in chapter 1. Clotild persuaded Clovis to convert to Christianity, which meant that the whole of the Frankish kingdom became Christian. Some women, like Æthelflæd, the Anglo-Saxon queen of the Mercians (discussed in chapter 6), were able to command armies. Yet the system of feudalism, which developed toward the end of the early Middle Ages, would ultimately disempower women, since it located authority within a network of obligations from which women were excluded. The gradual merging of Celtic, Germanic, and Roman traditions neither empowered women significantly nor disempowered them significantly. Instead, as the three cultures merged and produced a new, different society, so too they produced a new, different patriarchy. Women were still quite definitely inferior to men, as they had been in each previous culture, yet—as before—individual women could sometimes transcend patriarchal rules. Similarly, the impact of Christianity had an ambivalent effect: chapter 1 discusses the ways in which women were empowered by leadership roles and a notion of egalitarianism in the early centuries of Christianity, yet many of these early freedoms were already curtailed, or about to be, by the end of the early Middle Ages.

The High Middle Ages

Compared with the era from 500 to 1000, the high Middle Ages (1000–1300) were centuries of growth: growth in crop yields, in standards of living, in population, in towns and the variety of trades practiced in them, in schools and universities, in art and literature, in the power of the church and the various states, and in the power of men over women. Life became more varied and interesting—people were no longer struggling quite so desperately merely to get by—but they also became more subject to competing systems of authority. Although there were exceptions to this rule, women did not, on the whole, fare as well as they had during the early Middle Ages.

Women's lives were certainly benefited in a material sense by the so-called medieval agrarian revolution which was underway by the year 1000. New systems of farming and new technologies led to higher crop yields. Because medieval people lacked modern fertilizers, they could not plant the same crops in the same fields year after year without the soil becoming exhausted, or in other words, depleted of nutrients. Instead, they left one field fallow, or unplanted, every other year. The discovery that certain crops, especially beans, peas, and other legumes, could replenish the nitrogen in the soil meant that peasants could afford to plant each field two years out of three, instead of one out of two. New technologies such as the horseshoe and collar meant that horses, much more efficient than oxen, could be used increasingly for farm work. Windmills and watermills ground grains more finely and made for slightly less gritty and more palatable bread than flour ground by handmills. By the end of the high Middle Ages, peasants were reaping about six or seven bags of grain for every bag they sowed. This was far better than the two or three bags of grain they reaped in the early Middle Ages, and it enabled a better standard of living for everyone. Of course, the system of manorialism enabled nobles to profit most from this new efficiency: they found ways to charge peasants with a variety of fees and fines, and they profited directly from increased productivity on their own land. Yet peasants also benefited a little, as evidenced by the increased birth rate in the high Middle Ages. Female fertility is linked directly to diet, particularly the amount of iron that women receive. Women living in malnourished societies, like the early Middle Ages, have difficulty conceiving and bearing children. Clearly women in the high Middle Ages received more food and—in all likelihood—were able to eat more iron-rich foods such as red meats. In consequence, the population of Europe doubled during the high Middle Ages (and in some places, such as England, grew even faster).

Now that Europe's population was larger and the food supply was more efficient, more people could be freed up to do something other than work the land. In the early Middle Ages, almost everyone was forced to grow grain (with the exception of nobles, priests, monks, and nuns) in order to survive. But a larger surplus of crops meant that some of these former farmers could invest their labor in other trades and buy grain, instead of producing it themselves. Consequently, the towns started to grow in size, and they became more highly organized. Serfs were not allowed to leave their manors without the permission of their lords, but the tradition developed that if a serf ran away to a town and was able to survive for a year and a day without capture, then he or she was free. Runaway serfs, along with free peasants, established themselves in trades such as shoemaking, baking, candlemaking, and stonemasonry. Eventually each trade came to be organized into a local guild, which protected the interests of its members. Guilds ensured that no one could gain a monopoly on the supplies for their trade (no shoemaker, for instance, could buy up all the local leather), and they looked after their members in the case of disability or death. The widow of a guild member might expect help in paying for her husband's funeral, plus a degree of financial assistance in bringing up her children. Guilds also regulated prices for their products, ensuring that no shoemaker undercut another by offering cheaper shoes, for instance. And they exercised quality control, inspecting the work of other guild members and overseeing the apprenticeship process. As chapter 2 explains, however, women seldom belonged to guilds. Although they usually worked alongside their husbands, the public face of the family workshop was most often that of men. Single women tended to be confined to lower-status trades without guilds, such as household service or prostitution. As towns grew and asserted autonomy, women were also excluded from governance. In some towns, membership of the merchants' guild, the wealthiest of all the guilds, was a prerequisite for participation as a city councilor or mayor. Women's exclusion from the merchants' guild thus also excluded them from participation in the administration of their towns. It must be noted, however, that they were also excluded from public offices on manors. When peasants administered their communities through manorial courts, they almost never appointed women to offices such as bailiff or aletaster (see chapter 6 for further discussion).

A larger and more complex economy in the high Middle Ages opened up new educational possibilities, too. In the early Middle Ages, very few schools had existed, and even most nobles were illiterate. Early medieval scholarship was mostly confined to the monasteries, and monks and nuns focused far more on copying out manuscripts than exploring new ideas or engaging in original scholarship. The high Middle Ages, however, saw a huge expansion in the numbers of schools and the types of work they carried out. New schools were founded in towns to teach basic literacy and numeracy. Often attached to cathedrals, these schools employed resident scholars to teach local boys. By the twelfth century, some cathedral schools were becoming quite specialized and certain scholars gained reputations for particular brilliance. Peter Abelard, for example, taught at the cathedral school in Paris and was well known for his lectures on philosophy and theology. During the next few decades, cathedral schools evolved into universities. Open to male students who could read and write in Latin, these universities focused on rhetoric, grammar, and logic. Lectures were several hours long and consisted of professors reading directly from books and adding their own commentaries. (This tedium was necessitated partly by the scarcity of books: prior to the invention of the printing press at the end of the Middle Ages, books had to be copied out by hand, and were thus extremely expensive.) Despite the rather dull classroom format, students found ways to have a good time. They quickly gained reputations for excessive drinking, singing, and debauchery. Women were excluded from universities, although stories circulated of women dressing as men to attend classes. Women were also present on the margins of university life in the form of prostitutes. Rules for universities strictly forbade students from visiting prostitutes or "entertaining" any woman in their dormitory rooms, but the repeated injunctions suggest that the rules were not always followed. Expansion in education during the high Middle Ages thus had little direct impact on the lives of women.

Nor did women benefit a great deal from growth in literature and art. Expansion in the economy enabled not only the growth of schools and scholarship, but also the creation of elaborate manuscripts and buildings and the employment of professional *troubadours* (poet-musicians who often traveled from one place to another). Whereas early medieval buildings were typically made from wood, easily obtainable from local forests, a larger workforce in the high Middle Ages made it possible to build churches, cathedrals, castles, and other large buildings in stone. Wealthy nobles could pay for stone to be quarried, carted to the building site, shaped by stone masons, and arranged according to the direction of professional architects into buildings in the Romanesque or Gothic styles. They could also pay for the many expenses involved in the production of manuscripts: the multistage preparation of parchment from animal skins, the painstaking copying of texts, and the work of illustration and decoration. Nobles could also sponsor troubadours or dramatic productions, making for a richer cultural life than that of their early medieval ancestors. The portrayal of women in new literary genres of the high Middle Ages, such as the songs sung by troubadours, sometimes idealized them, but—as discussed above—this had little impact on the lives of real women. Songs survive from only a hand-ful of female poets, and little is known of female artists or musicians (see chapter 5 for further discussion). Representations of women in art were ambivalent: while saints (especially the Virgin Mary) were idealized, real women were sometimes ridiculed.

The growing power of the state and the church also did little for women. As chapter 1 explains, the church's efforts to insist on celibacy for priests and monks led them to portray women as evil temptresses. Powerful abbesses found their authority curtailed as church leaders emphasized the doctrine that women must always be under the control of men. Women were not the only ones affected by the growth in church power: Jews, heretics, lepers, homosexuals, and other minorities also found themselves subject to new strictures. Although the pope had headed the church in Western Europe for several centuries, it was during the high Middle Ages that the papacy came into its own. Popes like Innocent III wielded considerable power, more than any single king. Indeed, they could use their so-called spiritual weapons such as excommunication or *interdicts* (placing a country under an inter-dict meant that no religious services could be carried out) to force unruly monarchs to follow church commands. This power would ultimately wane, but during the high Middle Ages the papacy was stronger than any time be-fore or since. Popes were strong, but so too was popular religious sentiment. One manifestation of this fervor was in the form of monastic movements. Monasticism had been important in Europe during the early Middle Ages, especially after St. Benedict established his "Rule" (a detailed series of rules and regulations to govern the behavior of monks) in the sixth century. By the high Middle Ages, however, some monasteries had become complacent, enabling a lifestyle that was more luxurious and lazy than that envisaged by St. Benedict. The high Middle Ages thus saw a proliferation of new types of monasticism, movements seeking to get back to an ascetic, austere life-style. As chapter 1 explains, these movements often excluded women, and the monastic orders established for women alone tended to be marginal-ized. The increased power of the church and the new fervency of the high Middle Ages were not always bad for women. For instance, church courts became important as means of enforcing morality and marriage laws, and these probably helped women at least as much as they helped men. Strong central leadership meant that nobles could no longer play fast and loose with marriage laws either: when Philip Augustus of France tried to remarry by annulling his marriage to Ingeborg of Denmark in 1193, Pope Innocent III stepped in to block the annulment. (In fact, Philip did not properly rein-state Ingeborg until after the death of his subsequent wife 20 years later, so Innocent's efforts were not completely successful; nonetheless, they sent an important message to other, less powerful, nobles of the period that women could not always be discarded at will.)

Philip Augustus's efforts to overturn his marriage provide insight into the increasing power of kings in the high Middle Ages. In contrast to the relatively weak kings of the early Middle Ages, high medieval kings often exercised more power. While their success varied from place to place and from one monarch to another, they attempted to tax their subjects and assert themselves at the top of the feudal hierarchy. Ever cautious to limit the power of their nobles, kings often claimed the right to approve marriages of wealthy widows. In some places, like England, this resulted in the king basically selling off the right to marry widows to the highest bidders, a practice decried in the Magna Carta of 1215. Daughters of kings found themselves more than ever at the mercy of their fathers when it came to choosing marriage partners: a royal marriage was an opportunity to build a political alliance, and women themselves had little or no say in the matter. Although a few women, such as Eleanor of Aquitaine (c. 1122–1204), were able to exercise power, others found that the new authority of kings circumvented their autonomy.

Overall, then, the high Middle Ages represented a period in which the status of women declined somewhat relative to that of men. Women, as a group, did not experience the high Middle Ages as an era of growth in quite the same ways as their brothers and fathers. While they were directly affected by the increasing food supply and population, they did not participate equally in the growth of educational opportunities nor the increased power wielded by church and state. While they certainly flocked in large numbers to the growing towns, they found themselves excluded from the more lucrative occupations and often forced into low-status trades. And while they participated to a small degree in the burgeoning literary and artistic innovations of the high Middle Ages, they did so far less than men and they often found themselves portrayed in less than flattering ways. As life became more complex and interesting in the high Middle Ages, women—on the whole—reaped fewer of the benefits.

The Late Middle Ages

Historians used to believe that the late Middle Ages (c. 1300-1500) saw a reversal of this trend and that women in the late Middle Ages occupied something of a "golden age." Recent research, however, has largely debunked this myth. The late medieval era was one of major change—for both better and worse—but the gender order in European society proved largely impervious to this change, and there is little evidence that women's status changed significantly.

Perhaps the most dramatic change of the late Middle Ages took the form of the Black Death, or Bubonic Plague, which entered Europe in the late 1340s. Sweeping across the continent, it killed somewhere between one-third and one-half of the population. Medieval people were terrified and bewildered. Having no concept of germs, they speculated wildly as to the plague's cause and cure. Some blamed the plague on the opening of fissures in the earth's surface which were said to have released poisonous gases. Others claimed it resulted from God's anger with humankind. Others still claimed that the Jews had brought about the plague by poisoning drinking water. To avoid catching the plague, people undertook many futile measures: they wore charms around their necks or inhaled fragrant herbs, they whipped themselves as a means of trying to appease an angry God, they persecuted innocent Jews, and they locked themselves within their houses. Of course, nothing helped. The plague killed victims of all ages, religions, and social ranks, and it killed men and women alike. People living in the countryside might have been slightly less susceptible than those living in the crowded and unsanitary towns, and members of the nobility—better-fed and hence more resistant to disease—might have fared slightly better than their social inferiors, but no one was immune. Moreover, the plague recurred in several waves throughout the late fourteenth and early fifteenth centuries, finding new victims who had been born since the first onset.

The consequences of this demographic disaster were profound. In the decades immediately following the initial outbreak of plague, peasants benefited. A shortage of workers meant that wages increased, and a shrunken grain market meant that prices decreased. The nobility reacted swiftly, however: in many places, they tried to keep wages at their pre-plague levels, and they passed laws designed to limit peasants' and townspeople's opportunities to climb the social ladder. For instance, in the aftermath of the plague, laws were passed to prevent non-nobles from wearing certain fabrics that were thought to denote nobility. An English Statute of 1363 forbade those below the rank of knight from wearing any embroidered garments or silks; carters, ploughmen, cowherds, and the like were to wear garments of woolen cloth worth no more than 12 pence.[15] Adding insult to injury, late medieval governments tried to increase taxes on their citizens to make up for decreased income and pay for extra expenses. Such measures quickly led to resentment, manifested most dramatically in rebellions. In 1358, peasants around Paris revolted in what became known as the rebellion of the Jacquerie. They burned manor houses and, in some instances, slaughtered noble families. English peasants and townspeople revolted in 1381, marching on London, burning palaces and killing officials, and demanding an end to serfdom. Although caught by surprise, nobles were quickly able to reestablish the traditional social order, and the reprisals for these rebellions were in many cases far harsher than the rebellions themselves. The Black Death thus increased social tensions in the short term, but it did not result in an overthrow of the class structure. In the longer term, though, economic forces could not help but chip away at the system of manorialism, and serfdom did eventually break down. Nobles found it impossible to track down runaway serfs and were forced to offer higher wages. Some peasants were able to build up their assets by getting control of land left by those who had died without heirs; within a few generations, some families were able to hoist themselves out of the peasantry altogether and aspire to join the nobility.

Just as the Black Death caused social tensions and eventual change in the social structure, so too it facilitated changes in attitudes toward Christian practice. Leadership problems in the church had been apparent even before the plague, and late medieval popes had little hope of claiming the kind of power that high medieval popes like Innocent III had had. The Black Death further undermined the power of the papacy because the church was—understandably—powerless to halt the death and suffering. Medieval people expected the church to serve as an intermediary between themselves and God. Medieval logic argued that, whether or not he caused it, God would only have allowed the plague to continue if he were unhappy with humankind. If God were unhappy with humankind, then the church was failing in its duty as intermediary. As a result, people's experiences of Christian practice became, in many cases, more individualized and less likely to be channeled through the church. Rather than see the church as the sole focus of their religious efforts, many looked for a direct connection with God or Jesus. Church attendance continued to be compulsory, and the church continued to exercise a great deal of power, but—especially as literacy spread—the writings of mystical authors became increasingly popular. Eventually this movement toward a more individual relationship with God would fuel the Protestant Reformation that began in the early sixteenth century.

The Black Death played an important part in challenging social and religious hierarchies in medieval Europe, but it prompted no such challenge to the gender hierarchy. In an era of labor shortage, for example, it would make sense for the practice of paying women less than men to break down. Yet women continued to earn about the same percentage of male wages as they had before the plague. At a time when many local officials had died, it would make sense for women to step in as aletasters, jurors, churchwardens, or bailiffs. Yet positions of public authority continued to be dominated by men. In some areas, especially in northern and western Europe, women migrated to the towns in larger numbers than before and married at a later age than before the plague, but it is unclear whether this shift resulted in any increased autonomy for women. In other areas, especially southern Europe, women married younger and had more children, perhaps as part of a broader social concern to rebuild the population following the catastrophe of the plague. In the decades that followed, painters and sculptors emphasized the importance of motherhood in tender representations of the Virgin Mary and her son. While this may have been good for women on the one hand, imbuing their traditional role with more significance, it also implied that motherhood was the only appropriate function for women. The Black Death thus demonstrates the resilience of the patriarchal system in medieval Europe: while the plague enhanced opportunities for peasants and decreased the power of the church, it did little to alter women's status.

The late Middle Ages also saw the beginnings of the intellectual and artistic movement known as the Renaissance, although its consequences for women were similarly negligible. Traditionally, the Renaissance has been seen as a watershed in Western history, the dividing line between the Middle Ages and the early modern era, but most scholars now reject this rigid periodization. In Italy, for instance, the Renaissance was already underway by the late fourteenth century and certainly in swing by the fifteenth. But it took longer for its effects to be felt elsewhere. England, for example, was little impacted before the sixteenth century. In the 1970s, the historian Joan Kelly asked an important question: did women have a Renaissance? That is, did women experience intellectual and artistic renewal or rebirth in the same way that male scholars and artists did? For the most part, Kelly concluded, the answer was no.[16] Although some women certainly benefited from increased opportunities to exercise patronage, and a few men of the period educated their daughters alongside their sons, the Renaissance passed most women by. In some ways, in fact, it may further have confined women: the Renaissance emphasized the participation of elite men in the culture of their cities, and this public participation was only possible if their wives were to take care of the domestic details at home. Historians have since extended Kelly's question to other groups of people: Did peasants have a Renaissance? Did the urban poor have one? Again, they have concluded that the Renaissance had little impact on populations other than urban, elite men. Research into women's history has thus paved the way for a reconsideration of the Renaissance's significance.

The late Middle Ages therefore demonstrate the resilience of the gender order. Although a few women managed to lead remarkably autonomous, even influential, lives, women as a whole remained firmly subordinate to men as a whole. Despite the many changes of the time period, the overall status of women was altered remarkably little. Indeed, some historians have argued that the changes in women's lives over time are so minimal that they should not constitute the main focus of study. Rather than examine changes in women's experiences over time, they argue, historians should examine continuities.[17] In other words, historians should focus on the experiences of women and the forces shaping women's lives that remained consistent throughout the medieval period rather than placing too much emphasis on the minor changes.

This book largely subscribes to such an argument, as it is organized primarily by topics, rather than chronology. Chapter 1 examines religion, focusing on women's roles in the early Christian church, the lives of nuns and other professional religious women such as anchoresses and Beguines, the participation of Christian laywomen, and the experiences of Jewish and Islamic women in Western Europe. The second chapter examines women's work, looking in turn at the kinds of work performed by peasant women, townswomen, and noblewomen. Women's roles within the family form the subject of the third chapter. This chapter follows women throughout the typical lifecycle—from girl to widow—examining the expectations and experiences of women at each stage. Chapter 4, "Women and the Law," focuses on the ways in which laws both restricted and protected women. It also considers the crimes with which women were most often charged and surveys laws regarding marriage and widowhood. Women's roles in creative arts form the basis of the fifth chapter, "Women and Culture." This chapter examines women's roles as artists, authors, composers, and patrons, as well as investigating the ways in which women were represented in works produced by men. Finally, chapter 6 discusses women's experiences in positions of power and authority. While women as a group were typically banned from holding positions of public authority, some found ways to get around this stricture, while others were able to exercise power behind the scenes. The final chapter thus encapsulates a major theme of this book: the interplay between broader patriarchal forces that limited women's status and autonomy and the role of individuals who were able to overcome or circumvent such forces. Medieval women were, as a group, subordinate to their husbands and fathers, but certain women, under certain circumstances, evaded subordination.

NOTES

1. *Women's Lives in Medieval Europe: A Sourcebook*, ed. Emilie Amt (New York: Routledge, 1993), 233–35.

2. *Women's Lives in Medieval Europe*, 235–45.

3. *Women and Writing in Medieval Europe: A Sourcebook*, ed. Carolyne Larrington (London: Routledge, 1995), 136.

4. *Letters of Medieval Women*, ed. Anne Crawford (Stroud: Sutton, 2002), 53–54.

5. *Women's Lives in Medieval Europe*, 130–32.

6. *Women of the English Nobility and Gentry 1066–1500*, ed. Jennifer Ward (Manchester: Manchester University Press), 224–29.

7. Margery Kempe, *The Book of Margery Kempe*, ed. B. A. Windeatt (New York: Viking Penguin, 1985).

8. Christine de Pisan, *The Book of the City of Ladies*, ed. and trans. Earl Jeffrey Richards (New York: Persea, 1982); Christine de Pisan, *A Medieval Woman's Mirror of Honor: The Treasury of the City of Ladies*, trans. Charity Cannon Willard, ed. Madeleine Pelner Cosman (New York: Persea, 1989).

9. The National Archives: Public Record Office, London: SC2 156/5.

10. *Women's Lives in Medieval Europe*, 75.

11. *Women's Lives in Medieval Europe*, 60.

12. *Women of the English Nobility and Gentry*, 180.

13. Simon Mays, "Wharram Percy: The Skeletons," *Current Archaeology* 193 (2004), 45–49.

14. Bonnie S. Anderson and Judith P. Zinsser, *A History of Their Own: Women in Europe from Prehistory to the Present*, Revised edition (New York: Oxford University Press, 2000), 2 vols., v. 1, 26–38.

15. *The Black Death*, ed. and trans. Rosemary Horrox (Manchester: Manchester University Press, 1994), 340–42.

16. Joan Kelly Gadol, "Did Women Have a Renaissance?," reprinted in *Feminism and Renaissance Studies*, ed. Lorna Hutson (New York: Oxford University Press, 1999), 21–47.

17. Judith M. Bennett, "Confronting Continuity," *Journal of Women's History* 9 (1997), 73–94.

SUGGESTED READING

Bennett, Judith M. and C. Warren Hollister. *Medieval Europe: A Short History*, 10th ed. Boston: McGraw Hill, 2006.

Bitel, Lisa M. *Women in Early Medieval Europe 400–1100*. New York: Cambridge University Press, 2002.

Erler, Mary C. and Maryanne Kowaleski, eds. *Gendering the Master Narrative: Women and Power in the Middle Ages*. Ithaca: Cornell University Press, 2003.

Erler, Mary C. and Maryanne Kowaleski, eds. *Women and Power in the Middle Ages*. Athens: University of Georgia Press, 1988.

French, Katherine L. and Allyson M. Poska. *Women and Gender in the Western Past*. 2 vols., v. 1: to 1815. Boston: Houghton Mifflin, 2007.

Klapisch-Zuber, Christiane, ed. *A History of Women, Volume II: Silences of the Middle Ages*. Cambridge: Belknap Press of Harvard University Press, 1992.

Leyser, Henrietta. *Medieval Women: A Social History of Women in England 450–1500*. London: Phoenix Press, 1996.

Mitchell, Linda E., ed. *Women in Medieval Western European Culture*. New York: Garland, 1999.

Shahar, Shulamith. *The Fourth Estate: A History of Women in the Middle Ages*. London: Routledge, 1983.

Ward, Jennifer. *Women in Medieval Europe 1200–1500*. London: Longman, 2002.

1

cœœ

Women and Religion

Religion was a huge part of every medieval woman's life. In the modern West, religious beliefs and practices are often seen as matters of private conscience: religion is generally regarded as something that one chooses. For women in the Middle Ages, however, whether Christian, Islamic, or Jewish, religion was neither private nor a matter of choice. Religious practice and belief were expected of all women, no matter what their social status, and they generally took place in a public context. This chapter examines some of the forms that religious beliefs and practices took, surveying the religious lives of early Christian church leaders, nuns, mystics, heretics, and laywomen. Because the vast majority of women in Western Europe were Christian, this study focuses on Christianity, but it will also consider briefly the practices and opportunities open to Islamic and Jewish women within their own faith communities. Religion both confined women and offered them opportunities for leadership, respect, and autonomy. These confinements and opportunities varied over the course of the Middle Ages. While early medieval noblewomen might use religion as a source of authority in both the family and the nunnery, many of these opportunities were restricted during the high Middle Ages. In the late Middle Ages, women's religious prospects expanded once more, as women became eager participants in a broad range of new devotional practices.

WOMEN AND THE CHURCH IN THE EARLY MIDDLE AGES

The Christian Bible gives conflicting evidence about the role of women in church leadership in the first centuries after the life of Jesus of Nazareth. On the one hand, the letters of St. Paul praise women such as Junia and Phoebe for carrying out the work of Christianity. On the other hand, Paul insists that women should be silent in church, have no right to preach, and ought to remain subordinate to their husbands.[1] Scholars of the early Christian church generally believe that women enjoyed expanded opportunities in the century or so following the death of Jesus but that these opportunities were curtailed as Christianity spread. In the earliest years of Christianity, congregations were small and consisted of small gatherings of people in someone's home, led by a member of the laity. Evidence from the Bible such as Paul's praise of Junia and Phoebe suggests that these informal leaders were sometimes women (indeed, Phoebe is referred to as a deacon). As the new faith became more popular and gained more adherents, one home was no longer big enough to fit the new, large congregations. By the fourth century, purpose-built churches were being constructed, staffed by religious professionals who became known as priests. These priests were all male. This meant that women were effectively excluded from the hierarchy of the Christian church throughout the Middle Ages and—in the case of most Christian denominations—well beyond the Middle Ages, because just as priests were male, so too were bishops and archbishops. When the most important of the bishops in Western Europe, the Bishop of Rome, came to be recognized as the pope in the fifth to sixth centuries, there was no question of appointing a woman to the position. The same was true in the Byzantine church (which increasingly diverged from the Western European church from the early Middle Ages onward). The chief religious official in the Byzantine Empire, known as the Patriarch of Constantinople, was male, and women did not play a large role in the Byzantine church, either.

Their exclusion from the hierarchy of the Christian church did not mean, however, that women had no role to play in medieval religion. During the early Middle Ages, as the new religion spread, noblewomen were important in helping convert their husbands and those around them to Christianity, a process which scholars have called "domestic proselytization." One of the best-known domestic proselytizers was the Frankish queen, Clotild (c. 470–c. 544). According to Bishop Gregory of Tours, who wrote an account of her famous deeds half a century later, Clotild was ultimately responsible for the conversion of the Franks, the Germanic tribe that settled in the area that now approximates modern-day France. Clotild's husband, King Clovis, was a pagan whose troops had looted Christian churches, so he was not receptive at first to her pleas that he consider converting to the new religion. Clovis reluctantly allowed the couple's first son to be baptized, but when the child died he blamed Clotild and the failure of the Christian God. When their second son was born, Clotild again had the baby baptized; on this occasion, the boy fell ill but recovered. Despite the survival of his second son and the urging of his wife, Clovis remained a pagan until he found himself in a dangerous battle situation. Clovis then prayed to the Christian God for success and, on his victory, announced his conversion. Clotild, according to Gregory of Tours, arranged for her husband to receive Christian instruction and to lead the Frankish people in becoming baptized. Through her influence over her husband, therefore, Clotild played a major role in ensuring that the Frankish kingdom became Christian, thus paving the way for a long relationship between medieval French kings and popes. It is likely that Clovis or one of his successors might have converted eventually anyway, as this was a politically expedient move in early medieval Europe. But what is most interesting about this story is the way in which Gregory of Tours and other historians of the early Middle Ages were willing to give the credit to a woman. As one anonymous biographer of Clotild put it in the late ninth or early tenth century:

> Oh happy Gaul! Rejoice and exult, praise the Lord, delight in the true God! For through the prayers of Saint Chrothilda [Clotild], the mystical embodiment of the church, your first king was chosen by the King of Heaven and torn from the cult of demons.[2]

The Frankish princess Bertha (d. 612), a great granddaughter of Clotild, was equally pivotal in the conversion of Kent, in southeast England. Pope Gregory the Great himself wrote letters to Bertha, thanking her for her support of Christian missionaries, but also encouraging her to try harder to convert her husband, Æthelbert of Kent. Bertha ultimately succeeded in converting her husband and was acknowledged locally as a saint.[3] In the early Middle Ages, therefore, women may not have been allowed to be priests, but they were still seen as powerful agents of Christianity.

VIRGINS

Even while Clotild converted her husband and—ultimately—his kingdom, Christianity was still evolving. The basic Christian text was the Hebrew Bible, with the addition of collected gospels, letters, and other material constituting what came slowly to be accepted as the New Testament. But as scholars thought about how to apply Christian teachings to everyday life, and as they tried to match up Christian philosophy with the philosophy they had inherited from the ancient Greeks and Romans, they generated new doctrines. One of the most important new beliefs was that the ideal life for a Christian—whether male or female—was one of chastity. Staying away from worldly temptations like sex was thought to enable a person to focus on a relationship with God rather than being distracted by earthly pleasures. This idea took a while to develop, and it was helped especially by two major Christian writers (known as "Church Fathers"): St. Jerome (c. 342–420) and St. Augustine (354–430). Jerome was best known for his work in translating the Christian Bible into Latin, the language in which it remained throughout the Middle Ages. In addition to his translation work, however, he also had much to say about appropriate Christian behavior for his time. Both Jerome and Augustine lived in an era immediately before the Middle Ages proper: they were part of Roman society during the crisis-ridden years in which the Roman Empire was disintegrating. Both men felt, to some extent, that their world was under threat and about to end, so both saw the need to find the ideal Christian life as a matter of urgency.

Jerome, like St. Paul, was ambivalent about women. In some of his writings he condemned them as weaker than men, while in others he was very supportive of individual women who were his friends. Jerome regarded virginity as one of the highest virtues and one of the best ways for a woman to overcome her weak and sinful nature. As far as he was concerned, the main good that came from marriage was the production of more virgins. Jerome also believed that the Virgin Mary was not only virginal before the birth of Jesus but also for the remainder of her life, an idea that became part of official church doctrine in the seventh century. His contemporary, St. Augustine, agreed that virginity was preferable to marriage, partly because it made the individuals who chose this path more like the angels. Unlike Jerome, however, Augustine was more positive about marriage and the conception of children (perhaps, in part, because he himself had had a long sexual relationship as a young man and was father to an illegitimate son). The role of women, for Augustine, was mainly to produce babies. Augustine's definition of virginity, though, was a little broader than that of Jerome: for Augustine, it was important that a virgin not only be physically pure (i.e., refraining from all sexual activity), but spiritually pure as well.

Attitudes toward virginity underwent some interesting changes throughout the Middle Ages.[4] Jerome's view of virginity as primarily a physiological state was emphasized throughout the early Middle Ages and most of the high Middle Ages, and many women went to heroic lengths to protect their virginity in the face of temptation and even attempted rape. For instance, when the parents of Christina of Markyate (c. 1096-post 1155), an English woman, wanted her to marry, they tried all kinds of tricks to make her abandon her vow of virginity. Christina was nagged, cajoled, bribed, encouraged to get drunk, locked in a room with the man whom they intended her to marry, and generally subject to every kind of pressure. In each case, however, she held true to her vow and remained a virgin. For Christina, as for others in the early and high Middle Ages, physical virginity was extremely important, and few women who were not virgins were re-garded as saints. Virgin martyrs were seen as especially holy, and many such women were celebrated during the early Middle Ages. Many medi-eval legends involving virgin martyrs from the late Roman period told of situations in which their pagan parents tried to marry them off, much as Christina's parents had tried to do. In some stories, virgins prevented mar-riage by praying for (and receiving) temporary physical deformities, such as growing a beard or being stricken with a skin disease, so that their potential husbands would reject them.

Physical virginity remained important in the centuries that followed but, scholars have suggested, the definition of virginity began to shift. From about the thirteenth century onward, religious authors came to see a wom-an's spiritual state as an important component of what it meant to truly be virginal, and mothers like Brigid of Sweden (c. 1303–73) were acknowl-edged as saints in spite of their non-virginal state. Moreover, in order to be considered a true virgin, one had to do more than refrain from sex but also be pure and modest in behavior. For instance, a story that was used in late medieval sermons to illustrate the importance of pure and chaste speech told of a nun who never broke her vow of chastity but was known for "speaking wickedness" with her friends. After the nun died, she was buried beside an altar, but soon after her death two demons appeared to beat the nun around the mouth with burning swords. The bottom half of the nun's body, which had preserved its virginity, went to heaven, while the top half was sent to hell. "For though her deeds were chaste," people were warned, "Her words were all vile and waste."[5] The story of the nun shows how the meaning of virginity had expanded beyond just chastity: the gos-siping nun could not be considered a true virgin because her speech wasn't sufficiently pure.

The concept of holy virginity—both before and after the shift in mean-ing—was empowering to some women, because it gave them a special spiritual status. Virgin martyrs remained an especially important group of saints venerated throughout the Middle Ages. St. Margaret of Antioch, for instance, was martyred in the fourth century, during the late Roman era, but she was honored by women throughout the Middle Ages. Pregnant women, and women trying to conceive, addressed prayers to Margaret in the hope that they might bear children safely. Women who preserved their physical and spiritual virginity were thus honored by their communities, but this was not an option available to all women. A peasant woman or poor townswoman who did not marry would be leaving herself economi-cally vulnerable: she would have a hard time making enough money to sup-port herself throughout the rest of her life without some help from family and friends. Certainly she would not have enough resources to spend her time in prayer and holy works and still expect to have enough to eat at the end of the day. Women from noble families had more options, so long as they were supported by their families. Many noble families, like those of Christina of Markyate, would have expected their daughters to be married in order to forge alliances with other noble families or carry on the family blood lines, and would not have been interested in supporting a daughter who could do little directly for family fortunes. Others, however, may have been more tolerant, especially if they had multiple daughters and sufficient resources, and they may have been more willing to allow their daughters to become nuns or participate in other forms of the religious life. Holy virginity offered the potential for some women to be honored and to escape the direct control of a husband, but it was not a state to which women of all classes could aspire.

NUNS

The most recognized way in which to pursue a life of holy virginity was by becoming a nun. Throughout the Middle Ages, nuns tended to come from the wealthier groups in society, as nunneries required a payment similar to a dowry before one could enter. During the early Middle Ages, women in nunneries often exercised a great deal of control over their own lives, and abbesses—the heads of nunneries—were sometimes regarded as particularly influential figures within the regional church. During the high Middle Ages, however, nunneries would become subject to increasing regulation by the church and the power of abbesses was curtailed.

Nunneries (not typically known as convents until after the Middle Ages) began to emerge at much the same time as the first monasteries for men were established. In the late Roman era, Christianity shifted from a small persecuted sect into a widely adopted and state-sponsored religion. While most Christians saw the spread of their religion as a victory, the new popularity also meant that there was no longer anything particularly special or risky about being Christian. Instead, Christianity became the mainstream religion—almost the default choice—in cities like Rome and Constantinople. For some Christians, the new mainstream religion seemed too easy. In an effort to emulate the suffering of Jesus, particularly during his 40 days in the desert, they undertook the practice of *asceticism* (depriving oneself of all luxuries, such as ample food or sleep, comfortable clothing, or sexual pleasure).

Women were among these early ascetics. Some lived in small communities, along with other virgins. When Helena (d. 327), the mother of the Roman Emperor Constantine, visited the Holy Land in the early fourth century, she visited several communities of virgins. By the fourth century, large numbers of women as well as men lived in monastic communities in the Egyptian desert. Travelers to this area remarked on communities of 400 women and more, alongside communities of men. Smaller communities thrived in towns throughout the Roman Empire. Women of means established "house monasteries," which consisted of virgins and widows living in common, often accompanied by servants. Despite his generally negative view of women, St. Jerome was a close friend of Paula (347–404), a woman who was part of a religious community in Rome. Paula's community was headed by a wealthy widow, Marcella, who turned her substantial home into a place of prayer, Christian study, and austere living. Paula, also a widow, studied with Marcella and developed a reputation for great piety. When Jerome was forced to leave Rome, she traveled with him to Egypt and the Holy Land, where they visited communities of ascetic women and men. Eventually, Paula founded several similar communities for women (and one for men) in Bethlehem, and served as their head until her death. Communities such as Paula's each had a set of rules by which all members were expected to abide, but these rules were probably fairly informal and many houses may never have written them down.

Just as early Christians needed to work out the practical realities and rules of what Christian-like behavior entailed, so too monasteries and nunneries took several centuries before their rules for proper conduct became more standardized. One of the first to write a rule for religious women was St. Augustine, who collected sets of rules from various communities and tried to integrate them into one common text. Augustine's Rule, initially composed for his sister Perpetua, who was part of a community at Hippo in North Africa, emphasized the need for obedience and for each individual nun to subordinate herself to the community as a whole. In the early sixth century, Caesarius, Bishop of Arles, wrote two sets of rules, one for women and one for men. The Rule for women, intended for his sister's community of virgins in southern France, emphasized that women should be strictly enclosed—that is to say, that they should not be allowed to leave the gates of their communities once they had entered. He also insisted on the communal nature of the religious life: women were to give up their individual property when they entered the institution, and prayer, work, eating, sleeping, and all other activities were to be shared. Religious life was becoming more structured and more separate from everyday society.

The biggest name in male monasticism of the early Middle Ages is that of St. Benedict of Nursia, who wrote a Rule for monasteries in the mid-sixth century. Benedict's Rule is important because of its emphasis on moderation. Monks were to lead lives that were still tough and somewhat ascetic, but not so tough as to be unreasonable. His Rule is long and detailed, anticipating all kinds of matters that monks might encounter (for instance, how many robes should one own and what should they be made from? Exactly how much food should each monk be allowed? Is it right for abbots to have favorites?). Throughout Western Europe, monastic communities adopted

Benedict's Rule (in the Byzantine Empire, though, monastic communities each continued to follow their own separate sets of rules). Like Augustine and Caesarius, Benedict also had a sister who was part of a community of women. Benedict's sister, St. Scholastica (c. 480–c. 543), headed a nunnery near his in central Italy and adopted a version of his Rule. Many nunneries throughout the Middle Ages also adopted a form of Benedict's Rule, and the nuns who followed Benedict's Rule, along with the monks living in monasteries using his Rule, became known as Benedictines. Like their brothers, they took vows of poverty, chastity, and obedience.

What was life like under the Benedictine Rule? Benedictine nuns were kept very busy. Seven times a day and once during the night, they gathered in the chapel to pray, sing, and listen to the readings of religious texts. They ate together in the refectory, often listening as they ate to the reading of further religious texts. If literate, they might spend some time in individual devotional reading. Nuns would also work: some might copy manuscripts; others prepared food, made or mended clothing, cared for sick or elderly nuns, taught children, worked in the garden, or oversaw community finances. As in Caesarius's Rule, nuns were expected to be strictly enclosed—that is, they were not supposed to leave the nunnery under any circumstances—although in practice, there were sometimes exceptions to this regulation.

Both monasteries and nunneries depended on economic support from members of the nobility. Kings and queens, in particular, founded religious institutions and donated land and money to institutions founded by their ancestors. This was not merely charity, because they had certain expectations in return. Nobles expected both monks and nuns to pray for them and their families. Specifically, they expected prayers for the salvation of their souls—that is, they wanted to be sure that their souls would ascend to heaven after they died, rather than being condemned to hell, and they regarded prayer as one way to help overcome their sins. Many of the prayers recited by nuns, therefore, were dedicated to particular individuals who had given resources to the nunnery. Nobles expected something else from the institutions they endowed, too: they expected that these monasteries and nunneries would house members of their own family who, for various reasons, might want to take refuge in the church. For instance, an elderly widow might sometimes be forced into a nunnery by sons eager to claim their inheritance. A child born with a serious disability might be placed in a nunnery or monastery as a way to remove him or her from public view. Families who could not easily afford to marry off all their daughters might force some of them into nunneries, since the entry fee was typically lower than that required for dowries. And families with too many sons might give some of their boys to monasteries so that they did not threaten the inheritance of their older brothers. Nunneries and monasteries thus served important social functions, along with their spiritual functions, throughout the Middle Ages.

Some women were forced into nunneries, but many entered very much of their own volition. Nunneries could be places of refuge for widows and even, sometimes, for brutalized wives. Although virginity was expected in theory, most nunneries accepted widows and even wives who had their husband's consent. Radegund (c. 518–87), the daughter-in-law of Clotild and Clovis, fled to the religious life after her husband murdered her brother. She eventually established the nunnery of Holy Cross at Poitiers, in western France, and adopted the Rule of Caesarius. More than 200 women lived at Holy Cross while Radegund was abbess, and her good works led to her eventual recognition as a saint. Abbesses like Radegund exercised a considerable degree of power in the early Middle Ages. Some ruled over communities not only of women but of men also. These so-called *double monasteries* housed women and men in separate buildings, but all were generally subject to the authority of the abbess. The abbess was responsible for the administration of her community (which typically owned and needed to gather income from various pieces of land) and the spiritual health of men and women under her command. Some abbesses were powerful figures indeed: Hild (616–80), abbess of the double monastery at Whitby (northern England) hosted an important church meeting that decided whether the church in northern England would follow the Irish or Roman form of Christianity. She also recognized the talent of Caedmon, a peasant with a gift for poetry, and persuaded him to become a monk. The early Middle Ages is sometimes known as the era of the great abbesses, a period in which abbesses enjoyed considerable control over their own institutions with little interference from church authorities.

Christianity was accepted by much of the nobility in the early Middle Ages, but it took longer to be accepted by all members of society. While King Clovis could simply declare himself and his people converted to Christianity, it took a little longer for his people to understand exactly what Christianity involved and how it differed from the paganism that they had previously followed. Nuns often played a critical role in this conversion of ordinary people, serving as missionaries. The Anglo-Saxon nun Leoba (c. 700–c. 780), for instance, accompanied St. Boniface on his mission to convert the northern Germans. Leoba, who originally belonged to a double monastery in southern England, had a dream in which a never-ending purple thread was drawn from her mouth and wound up into a ball. One of the elderly nuns interpreted this dream as meaning that God intended Leoba to teach others. When the missionary monk St. Boniface heard of Leoba's talents, he requested that her abbess allow her to help him in his conversion work. Leoba was appointed as abbess of a double monastery at Bischofsheim in Germany, where she was much admired for her patience, holiness, wisdom, and knowledge. Despite local resentment against Christianity, Leoba's reputation for miracles and holiness helped to convince the Germans to convert. Just as queens like Clotild and Bertha could facilitate conversions among the nobility, so more ordinary nuns like Leoba in the early Middle Ages could work for the conversion of pagans of ordinary status.

One other sign that the early Middle Ages was a particularly good era in which to be a nun was the flourishing of education in nunneries. Some nunneries, such as Chelles in France or Gandersheim in Germany, acquired reputations as centers of learning and scholarship. Many early medieval nunneries educated both girls and boys, as well as fostering original scholarship by talented nuns. Hrotswita of Gandersheim (c. 935–c. 975), abbess of a Benedictine nunnery, produced an impressive number of plays, poems, biographies of saints, and letters (see chapter 5 for further discussion). Her works demonstrate the depth and breadth of her education: she was obviously familiar with much literature of the Roman era as well as with a wide array of early Christian writers. Even more prolific than Hrotswita was another famous German abbess, Hildegard of Bingen (1098–1179), who lived during the first centuries of the high Middle Ages. Hildegard was a composer of music, a visionary, and an author of a wide range of texts. Hildegard's visions were well-known and respected in her own time, both by her nuns and by churchmen. She was also unusual among women in that she preached sermons to both women and men, and even went on several preaching tours. Hildegard corresponded with popes and with the foremost abbots of her day. Hrotswita and Hildegard represent abbesses' power at its peak. They, and others like them, were able to exercise a great deal of authority within their communities and freedom to practice religion as they saw fit.

Life as a nun in the early Middle Ages was not always one of autonomy, however. During the era of the Emperor Charlemagne, who ruled the areas of France, western Germany, and northern Italy in the late eighth to early ninth centuries, church councils passed rules that insisted more rigidly on nuns' enclosure and reduced their opportunities to interact with the outside world. In the turbulent ninth and tenth centuries, when Western Europeans faced repeated attacks from Viking, Muslim, and Magyar invaders, many nunneries fared badly. Viking attacks were the most long-lasting and destructive. Many Anglo-Saxon and Frankish nunneries completely disappeared in these centuries, wiped out by invasions or disbanded as invaders approached. Nunneries, poorly defended but with gold crosses and treasure there for the taking, were seen as easy targets by the invaders. Sometimes invaders did more than loot the church's treasure: they also raped the nuns. Nuns were well aware of their vulnerability, but had few ways of protecting themselves. Stories tell of nuns such as those at Coldingham, in present-day Scotland, in c. 870, who disfigured themselves to try and prevent sexual assault by Viking invaders. Following the example of their abbess St. Ebba the Younger, the nuns of Coldingham cut off their noses and upper lips. According to the chronicles, the Vikings were repulsed and did not rape the nuns, although they did set fire to the buildings. The nuns, burned alive, were subsequently acknowledged as martyrs.[6]

Life as a nun in the early Middle Ages thus provided some very real opportunities for education and leadership, but it also involved some very real risks. The situation became more restricted in the centuries that followed as nuns found themselves increasingly subject to the authority of the church as a whole. Abbesses like Hild, Hrotswita, and Hildegard had enjoyed a considerable amount of authority within their own institutions, but from about the eleventh century onward abbesses found that they were more answerable to the church administration. The church in the eleventh century was undergoing some important changes. While the political and economic situation of the early Middle Ages had meant that members of the nobility could easily control their local church, monastery, or nunnery, the church of the high Middle Ages was stronger and eager to shake off noble influence. In the early Middle Ages, men selected as bishops or archbishops were often chosen for their breeding and influence rather than their piety. During the high Middle Ages, however, members of the church worked hard to reduce the influence of kings and other important nobles over ecclesiastical policies and personnel. The monastery of Cluny, in southern France, was the first major center of reform. It was founded in the tenth century and—instead of being subject to the control of a local bishop who might be influenced by his noble relatives—it was directly under the authority of the pope. Over the following centuries, Cluniac monks secured some of the top church positions, including that of Pope, and were in a position to impose broader church reforms. Priests, bishops, and archbishops, they said, should be chosen for their piety rather than for their money or family connections. Moreover, they should all be celibate. Although priests and their superiors had been told to be celibate in earlier centuries, this decree was not well enforced during the early Middle Ages, and many priests and bishops had unofficial wives. Reformers were adamant, however, that their so-called wives should be dismissed and that the church should warn religious men against the evil temptations of women. Odo, a tenth-century abbot of Cluny, for instance, compared a woman to "a sack of dung" and argued that "the highest virtue in a woman is not to wish to be seen." For Odo, the ideal woman was one who was securely locked away out of sight and—hence—out of the way of male temptation. Other reformers of this period reminded Christians of Paul's teaching that women were not to have authority over men: hence double monasteries of the early Middle Ages that had previously been headed by an abbess were often disbanded or split into two separate institutions. Bishops inspected nunneries more closely

Manuscript illumination showing Poor Clares chanting services in church. © British Library, London, UK/© British Library Board. All Rights Reserved/The Bridgeman Art Library

and insisted that abbesses confine their authority to within their own institutions, rather than playing more important roles in their local communities. Enclosure was enforced more strictly. Nunneries that had previously educated both boys and girls were now confined to teaching girls alone. And when the first universities were founded in the twelfth and thirteenth centuries, students were required to be ordained, thus excluding women.

Yet nunneries continued to increase in number and size. During the high Middle Ages, the population of Europe was growing at a fast rate. So too were religious opportunities, especially for men. Stemming in part from the church reform movements, the high Middle Ages witnessed the emergence of many different types of monasteries. By the late thirteenth century, a nobleman intent on a religious life could choose between a traditional Benedictine monastery, a stricter and more austere Cistercian monastery, a more hermit-like existence in a Carthusian monastery, a life of preaching and holy poverty as a Franciscan or Dominican friar, or several other options. Women's opportunities expanded too, but not nearly so much, in part because of the insistence on enclosure. For instance, when St. Francis of Assisi established the Franciscan order, he resisted the wish of his friend Clare to set up a parallel organization of wandering, preaching nuns. St. Clare (c.1193–1253) was allowed to form an order (known as the "Poor Clares") but her nuns had to be strictly confined to the cloister and were not allowed to preach. They were popular nonetheless: by 1400, about 400 houses of Poor Clares had been founded, more than half of these in Italy and most of the others in Spain and France.[7] Male-dominated monastic movements, such as the Cluniacs and the Cistercians, reluctantly allowed nunneries to be associated with them, but treated them very much as second-class members. Some monastic orders, such as that of the Premonstratensians, tried to expel women from their ranks. The numbers of religious houses for women varied from one region to another: German nunneries, for instance, housed somewhere between 25,000 and 30,000 nuns by 1250, whereas English nunneries in the same era were home to only 2,500 to 5,000 nuns.[8]

While the number of nuns varied between regions of Western Europe, one thing remained constant: they were always poorer than their male counterparts. In Normandy (northwestern France) in the mid-thirteenth century, for instance, the average net worth of a monastery for men was £394. The average net worth of a nunnery, by contrast, was £60 (or 15 percent of that of a monastery). This disparity was even more marked when one takes into account that the nunneries of Normandy were slightly larger than its monasteries (each had an average of 35 nuns as opposed to 23 monks).[9] Nunneries were considerably poorer in England too: when Henry VIII closed monasteries and nunneries in the 1530s as part of the English Reformation, each nunnery possessed, on average, fewer than half the resources of the average monastery. While a few houses, like Syon Abbey, were fairly wealthy, many more were quite poor. The prayers of nuns did not attract the same kind of financial support among the laity as did the prayers of monks. In part, this may have been due to the fact that monks were sometimes ordained as priests, and the spiritual value of having an ordained priest pray for one's soul was thought to trump any prayers from nuns or from non-ordained monks. However, this cannot be the only reason that nunneries tended to make less money than monasteries, because even monasteries without large numbers of ordained priests fared better than nunneries. Throughout the Middle Ages, families tended to invest less in their daughters than in their sons.

NEW POSSIBILITIES: ANCHORESSES, VOWESSES, TERTIARIES, BEGUINES, AND MYSTICS

For a woman of means who wanted to live a religious life, becoming a nun was certainly the most accepted and expected route. But by the high and late Middle Ages, other possibilities existed too. During the period 1100 to 1400, the opportunities for a religious life expanded, and so too did the number of women who were recognized for their piety. In the eleventh century, women accounted for less than 10 percent of all those made saints; by the fifteenth century, about 28 percent of new saints were female. While women still made up less than one third of the total number of saints, the fact that their numbers almost tripled in these centuries suggests that women's spirituality may have been more recognized than it had been earlier.[10]

One new form of piety was that of the anchoress (or, the male form, anchorite). A woman of sufficient means could become an anchoress by having herself bricked into a small enclosure—sometimes a room or two, sometimes a cell too small in which to stand or stretch out fully. This anchorhold might consist of a room within a private house, part of a bridge or town wall, or a cell attached to the side of a chapel or church, sometimes with a small slanted window through which the anchoress could watch the ceremony of communion. An exterior window would enable her to receive food and pass through bodily waste. Obviously, each anchoress would need a loyal servant on the outside in order to keep her properly supplied. Anchoresses and anchorites were sealed into their cells in special ceremonies, often conducted by bishops or abbots, and they were expected to stay in their anchorholds until their deaths. Many were widows, such as the Dutch anchoress Yvette of Huy (1158–1228), who had herself enclosed into the wall of the chapel of a leper colony. Despite being physically restricted by the boundaries of their cells, anchoresses were still part of the community. Often they served as spiritual guides for local people, who would come to discuss their troubles and seek religious advice. Yvette, for instance, was visited not only by lepers but also by priests and townspeople. Some anchoresses, such as Julian of Norwich (1342–1416), gained reputations for great piety and even wrote religious texts. However, anchoresses clearly created some concern, too: one widely copied guide for anchoresses, written in the thirteenth century, warned anchoresses not to become too enmeshed in local gossip and concerns. They were not, the author warned, to give advice to men, but rather to restrict themselves to advising women.[11] Anchoresses had earned spiritual esteem, but religious authors wanted to be sure that they did not eclipse the spiritual power of priests.

A slightly less extreme form of female piety was that of the vowess. Vowesses, usually widows, differed from nuns in that they took vows of chastity, but not vows of poverty or obedience. They differed from anchoresses in that they were not confined to a particular cell but were rather free to move around. If they chose to, they might live within nunneries, renting rooms or living in free-standing buildings on nunnery grounds. Like anchoresses and nuns, vowesses were typically women of fairly high social status. Recent scholarship has shown that nuns, vowesses, and anchoresses were often very familiar with one another and shared books. In an era before printing began, a book was a very valuable object, and was often passed within networks of female piety and friendship.[12]

Similar to vowesses were tertiaries, or members of "third orders." These could be men or women (virgins, wives, or widows) who were associated with a monastic order. The Franciscans and Dominicans were especially known for encouraging tertiaries, some of whom lived with their families and others of whom lived in small attached houses with other tertiaries. Tertiaries might engage in charitable work, such as care of the sick, but they did not take the same vows as monks or nuns. One such Dominican tertiary was St. Catherine of Siena (1347–80), discussed further below, who was regarded even in her own time as an influential and very pious woman.

For a woman without the resources to support herself as an anchoress, vowess, or tertiary, another option existed, especially if she happened to live in northwestern Europe (around the modern-day Netherlands, Belgium, Germany, Switzerland, and northern France). Townswomen in these regions might choose to become Beguines, women who lived together in a convent-like setting but had no particular leader or organizational structure in the sense that nuns did. Instead, each group of Beguines was independent of the other groups and made rules that best suited its members. Beguines also differed from nuns in that they did not take lifelong vows and were free to leave the community at any time. Indeed, many went outside the community to work or to perform charity such as tending the sick. Beguinages (houses in which Beguines lived together) emerged as early as the thirteenth century, and initially they appealed to women from wealthier families, both rural and urban. As time went on, however, women of lower status were often able to become Beguines too.

Beguinages grew significantly in both number and size during the thirteenth and fourteenth centuries. In 1320, Beguines accounted for about 15 percent of the population of Cologne, and they constituted 7 to 8 percent of several late medieval northern cities. Beguinages could be quite large, too: several had over 100 members, and a few more than 1000.[13] But this growth did not mean that Beguines found it easy to make ends meet. While many nunneries struggled to get by, Beguines often had it even worse: the fact that their members typically came from lower social ranks than nuns and the fact that the church was ambivalent about Beguines meant that they struggled for enough money to keep going. The church's ambivalence about Beguines stemmed from the fact that these were communities of women outside the control of men. Whereas nuns were firmly under the control of local bishops by the late Middle Ages and expected to be strictly enclosed within their nunneries, Beguines seemed harder to define and control. Their membership shifted as individuals came and went, and their participation in the community at large made them vulnerable, in the eyes of church authorities, to temptation and sin. In some places, church opposition forced Beguinages to disband, and some Beguines, such as Marguerite Porete (d. 1310), were accused of heresy. Porete, a mystic, was burned at the stake because the ideas expressed in her book *The Mirror of Simple Souls* were thought to contradict church teachings. The Beguine movement has survived (barely) into the twenty-first century, but it is nothing like the religious force that it was in the late Middle Ages, when the Beguine movement provided an option for women to practice a professional religious life in a similar way to that of nuns, anchoresses, vowesses, and tertiaries.

The roles of nun, anchoress, vowess, tertiary, and Beguine provided religious women in the late Middle Ages with a particular set of expected behaviors. Each of these positions involved certain rituals and practices. But by the late Middle Ages, people were itching to go beyond religious practice to seek out a more intense relationship with God. For some, religion became less about what a person *did* and more about how fervently a person *believed.* In particular, some people sought a very direct experience of God: rather than go through the typical channels, such as attending mass and confession, they sought to communicate directly with God through their own prayers, visions, and mystical experiences. Mysticism—the direct, personal experience of God and (especially) Jesus—became a widely recognized and accepted form of piety during the late Middle Ages, and it was a form in which women participated even more often than men. Mystics aimed to put themselves in God's presence and even experience a kind of union with God. Mystics could be nuns (like Beatrice of Nazareth; d. 1268) or anchoresses (like Julian of Norwich) or Beguines (like Marguerite Porete), but they could also be lay women (like Catherine of Siena) who, by virtue of their circumstances, were able to devote much of their time and attention to intense prayer and meditation.

Mystics can be traced both through their own writings and through what others wrote about them. In the case of Catherine of Siena, copies survive of some of the letters that she wrote to popes and kings, and their survival suggests that she was taken seriously by them. As the following excerpt from a letter to Pope Gregory XI shows, she did not hesitate to offer spiritual advice:

> I long to see you a courageous man, free of slavish fear, learning from the good gentle Jesus, whose vicar you are. Such was his boundless love for us that he ran to the shameful death of the cross heedless of torment, shame, insult, and outrage. He suffered them all, totally free of fear, such was his hungry desire for the Father's honor and our salvation. For love had made him completely let go of himself, humanly speaking. Now this is just what I want you to do, father. Let go of yourself wherever selfish love is concerned.[14]

Julian of Norwich was less inclined than Catherine to lecture popes, but her main work, *Revelations of Divine Love,* possesses a spiritual authority that is still recognized by many Christians today. One of her more startling revelations was the idea that Jesus had a maternal side that could be of great comfort to someone seeking spiritual guidance. Julian's writings talk about "our True Mother Jesus" and compare the action of a mother breast-feeding

St. Catherine of Siena dictating her *Dialogues*. Tempera on panel, c. 1447–61 by Giovanni di Paolo di Grazia (1403–83). © The Detroit Institute of Arts, USA/ Founders Society Purchase/The Bridgeman Art Library

her child to that of Jesus feeding worshippers with the Eucharist (the bread of Communion).[15] Other mystics can be studied not through their own writings but through writings by others, particularly the priests to whom they related their visions.

As historians have pointed out, one feature common to many late medieval mystics was an obsession with food. In order to achieve union with Jesus, mystics would try to identify with his suffering on the cross (known as Christ's passion). Depriving themselves of food or eating things that were repugnant served as one way in which they might suffer and thereby achieve a union with Jesus. Angela of Foligno (c. 1248–1309), an Italian mystic, drank the water in which she had washed the feet of festering lepers. Catherine of Siena placed the diseased breast of a leprous woman in her mouth and deprived herself of ordinary food (eventually dying from starvation). Such measures seem extreme today, and it is tempting to dismiss such women as mentally disturbed. If they were, however, most of medieval society was the same way, because virtually all of Christian Europe endorsed and admired their extreme behaviors. For Angela, Catherine, and many others, eating little or eating repulsive things were means to an end, and the end was direct experience of Jesus.

When mystics achieved their goal of directly experiencing the presence of Jesus, they sometimes struggled to explain to others just how this experience felt. Angela of Foligno described herself drinking blood from the wounds in Christ's side (not an uncommon vision: several others had the same experience). Many mystics used metaphors involving food to describe what the presence of Jesus was like. Some talked about "tasting God" and having "hunger" for Jesus as a way to put words to the intensity of their visions. Some, such as Beatrice of Nazareth, consciously sacrificed their sanity in order to achieve such visions. For medieval people, especially during the intensely pious years of the late Middle Ages, religion was not merely a calm, rational, and restrained set of beliefs and practices: it was something emotional and all-encompassing, something to which they might give themselves completely and utterly, sacrificing their sanity, their health, and even their lives. In doing so, some women gained a considerable amount of both spiritual authority and secular esteem. Women were still prohibited from the priesthood, and nunneries still received significantly less financial support than monasteries, but late medieval society nonetheless recognized that some women held a special place in the eyes of God.

CHRISTIAN LAY WOMEN

For the vast majority of women, religious experience was neither so dramatic nor so well esteemed as that of nuns, anchoresses, vowesses, Beguines, and mystics. The religious lives of most women centered on their parish churches. Parish churches lay literally at the center of most communities. Each village was focused around a church, usually constructed from wood in the early Middle Ages and gradually replaced by stone from the high Middle Ages onward. Larger towns might be divided into several parishes. In these parish churches, ordinary people, along with members of the local nobility, would gather at least once a week to attend services. Although medieval parish churches survive throughout much of Europe, and although their exteriors have changed little, the interiors of these churches would have looked quite different in the Middle Ages. For one thing, they were not lit by electric light and so would have been considerably more gloomy in candlelight. For another, churches seldom housed pews as they do today: medieval people squatted on the straw-strewn floor or stood, women on the northern side of the church (the left-hand side as one looks from the back of the church toward the altar) and men on the southern side. In some places they sat on rudimentary benches, but the division by sex was maintained. Women were repeatedly warned against using the opportunity to gossip with their friends. Repeated stories and wall paintings inside churches depicted gossiping women being overshadowed by a demon who wrote down each word they said on a scroll. (Interestingly, however, when church courts came to punish people who gossiped in church, they usually ended up singling out garrulous men rather than women). In places in which the Protestant Reformation of the sixteenth century took hold, many church walls were whitewashed and today keep that same plainness in their interiors. In the Middle Ages, however, they would have been filled with bright wall paintings depicting scenes from the bible and other stories encouraging good behavior. One common scene, for instance, depicts sinners being cast into the mouth of hell, and medieval parishioners were encouraged by priests to take this as a warning.

Women played an important role within the parish, and their activities tended to mirror those performed by women in the home.[16] Women washed and mended the church linen (the altar cloths and the robes worn by priests), they baked the bread that would be used for communion, they cleaned the church, and they lodged craftspeople who came to repair the church, build additions, or paint wall paintings. They seldom held public or visible roles (although, as chapter 6 explains, there are a few English examples from the late Middle Ages in which women served as churchwardens). For the most part, women worked behind the scenes, helping to keep the parish functioning at an everyday level. One activity in which they frequently participated was fund-raising. Women joined together to raise money for specific church projects, such as the building of additional altars or chapels or the execution of large-scale repairs. In England, they sometimes raised money by holding "church-ales," in which women would gather together to brew a special batch of ale (generally with a higher alcohol content). When they sold this ale, the proceeds went to the church. By the fifteenth century, women and men in some parts of England celebrated Hocktide (the second Monday and Tuesday after Easter) with a peculiar fundraising effort: on Hock Monday, women captured and tied up the men, releasing them only after each made a donation to the church; on the following day, the roles were reversed and men tied up women. The money typically went to support smaller side-altars within the churches, particularly those dedicated to the Virgin Mary or to one of the virgin martyr saints.[17]

Women's wills are an excellent primary source for examining the ways in which they regarded the church. Married women seldom made wills, but a good number of wills survive from wealthier widows. These reflect their practical, domestic roles within the parish. Whereas men typically left gifts of money to their local parish churches, women were more likely to leave personal objects and to be quite specific about the ways in which these items might be adapted for the church's use. Sheets were to be reworked into altar cloths and brewing vats were to be used for the making of candles. Women also tended to be more specific than men in leaving objects to saints. In the Middle Ages, statues of saints were often dressed in real human clothing, so women such as Joan Mudford of Glastonbury (England), for instance, could take pleasure in knowing that the statue of St. Mary in her local church would wear her gold ring and her kerchief (head covering) and that the statue of St. Katherine would wear another of her rings.[18]

These statues clearly meant a great deal to women: when pregnant, women would seek out images of St. Margaret and ask for her special help and protection in childbirth. As chapter 5 explains, objects associated with Margaret, such as written versions of her life, were sometimes placed on a woman's stomach during labor. Some pregnant women believed that they helped ensure a safe delivery by offering the altar of St. Margaret a wax candle that measured the same in height as the woman's pregnant belly measured around. Pilgrims to Chartres (France) brought back small lead badges depicting the robe of the Virgin Mary, and it was believed that these badges could help relieve the pain of women in childbirth.[19] In the Byzantine Empire, women especially sought out images of Saint Anne, mother of the Virgin Mary, for help in conceiving and bearing healthy children.

In some places, women's devotion to the saints can be seen in the form of organizations known as religious guilds or confraternities, which carried out charitable works and might also maintain altars dedicated to particular saints. Some guilds and confraternities welcomed both male and female members, whereas others were sex-specific. Research in Italy and England has shown that women's confraternities or guilds were especially likely to be dedicated to the Virgin Mary. Women of all social statuses joined the guilds, although the guild leaders were more likely to come from wealthier families. In England, guild membership was sometimes specific to marital status, so that the maidens (unmarried women) or the wives of a particular parish might join separate guilds. These organizations provided social benefits as well as spiritual ones: they gave women an opportunity to socialize and to gain status in their communities as they supported their local churches through fund-raising.

Laywomen of all social statuses played an important role in teaching prayers and religious devotion to their children. When Joan of Arc (c. 1412–31), a peasant woman, was asked where she had first learned her prayers, she responded that she had been taught by her mother.[20] Literature depicts the role of mothers in teaching children too: in the fifteenth-century English poem, "How the Good Wife Taught Her Daughter," a poem popular among wealthier townspeople, a mother gives her daughter advice on maintaining respectability and good behavior. Among this advice are clear directions to love the church and attend regularly (even when it was raining), give tithes and offerings to the church without resentment, and pay attention during services without being distracted by gossip. Girls in Italian towns probably received similar advice from their mothers, but they were also trained in piety and motherhood in another way: they were presented with dolls representing the baby Jesus and were encouraged to clothe and care for him. Noblewomen and urban elites in the late Middle Ages, when literacy rates increased, may have modeled themselves after images of St. Anne, mother of the Virgin Mary, teaching her daughter to read. Sculptures and manuscript illustrations show the young Mary leaning against her mother's knee as she learned scripture. Boys as well as girls were taught piety at their mothers' knees. Blanche of Castile (1188–1252), mother of the French king Louis IX who became renowned as a saint, was described by chroniclers as playing a crucial role in her son's education:

> God kept him, thanks to his mother's good teachings. She taught him how to believe in God and how to love him, and she made many religious people come around him, and when he was a young boy, she made him have regard for the prayers of the Hours and hear sermons on feast days.[21]

Traditionally, women were in charge of their children's religious education until the child reached the age of seven, but some mothers clearly continued to be influential long beyond. If they were wealthier, they might commission manuscripts to instruct their sons in proper Christian behavior or provide suitable examples. In the fourteenth century, for instance, Marie de Bretagne commissioned an illustrated manuscript depicting the life of St. Eustace for her son (see chapter 5 for further discussion of this manuscript).[22]

Christianity sent lay women mixed messages about their status within the church. One example of this ambivalence can be seen in the practice by which women were excluded from the church after childbearing, but then welcomed back into the church community. The practice of excluding women after childbirth had been inherited from Jewish tradition. Post-partum women were seen as unclean and were traditionally excluded for 40 days, which meant that they missed being present at their children's baptism. Even the Virgin Mary had undergone this period of exclusion from the temple after the birth of Jesus. Once the 40 days were up, however, a ceremony known as *churching* or *purification* welcomed the woman back into the church. The woman presented herself at the church, wearing a veil, and (by the fifteenth century) carrying a long taper candle to be offered to the church. Some scholars have pointed out that women may not necessarily have viewed this practice as exclusionary or misogynist: since the churching ceremony was typically accompanied by celebration, it is possible that it served as a way to focus community joy and esteem at the birth of a child on its mother. Women often wore new clothes for their purification ceremonies, and were given gifts afterward. Moreover, during the period of 40 days when a woman was excluded from the church (and expected to stay within the house), she was often surrounded by female neighbors and was allowed the rare opportunity for rest and relaxation as she recovered from the birth. In the case of the Virgin Mary, her purification ceremony on February 2 became an important holiday in the Christian calendar. Both men and women observed this holy day, joining a procession to church early in the morning carrying long wax tapers that would be blessed by the priest. Recent mothers' exclusion from the church and their subsequent churching demonstrates how religious practice could both confine and empower women.

For those who could afford it, pilgrimage was another religious activity in which the laity could participate. By visiting relics of saints (parts of saints' bodies that had been preserved or items that they had touched or been associated with), people could earn spiritual merit and thus reduce the amount of time that they spent in purgatory after their deaths. They might also go on pilgrimage to the sites around which Jesus or saints had once lived in order to help identify with their lives. Christian women had participated in pilgrimages since the Roman era: Paula and Jerome were not unusual in traveling to Egypt and the holy land to visit groups of monks and nuns and to see the sites mentioned in the Bible. Indeed, female pilgrims sometimes made members of the church hierarchy nervous, since they feared women's vulnerability to attack and to misbehavior. St. Boniface advised the Archbishop of Canterbury in 747 to limit the numbers of English women making pilgrimages to Rome because, he claimed, they were of loose morals and were a bad influence on people of the towns that they passed through. He was fighting a losing battle: pilgrimage became even more popular during the high and late Middle Ages as the economy and the political situation improved and as the doctrine of purgatory developed. Men outnumbered women as pilgrims overall, but there were some sites of pilgrimage especially associated with women. The shrine of Godric of Finchale in England, for instance, was associated particularly with miracles involving women. In theory, lay women were supposed to secure the consent of their husbands before embarking on pilgrimages, although surviving stories of women setting out without their husbands' knowledge suggest that they sometimes disobeyed. Women might face another obstacle on arriving at the place of pilgrimage: sometimes the shrines or relics that they sought to visit were in areas of the church (or within monasteries) that women were prohibited from going. In most instances, special arrangements were made to allow women access to the holy places. This was in the church's interests as well as that of the women, since pilgrims were expected to leave large donations. Stories of a few exceptional women demonstrate that they could travel long distances, through hazardous conditions, on their pilgrimages. Some made their way through

southern France and northern Spain on the well-trodden path to the shrine
of St. James, Santiago da Compostela. Others traveled to Rome or even to
the Holy Land. Margery Kempe (c. 1373–c. 1440) of King's Lynn in England
dictated a detailed account of her eighteen-month journey to Jerusalem. Her
route took her by ship to Zierikzee (in the modern Netherlands), overland
through Constance (Germany) to Venice (Italy), where she boarded a ship for
Jaffa, the port for Jerusalem. Margery spent three weeks visiting the holy sites
around Jerusalem before returning via Rome. On another pilgrimage later in
her life, she traveled to Santiago da Compostela. Brigid of Sweden similarly
traveled to the Holy Land, to Santiago da Compostela, and to Rome. The
sights and sounds that these women experienced in an era before modern
media must have been extraordinary: Margery came from a town of about
5,000 people and Brigid from one of Europe's most northern kingdoms. Each
traveled through lands where she did not speak the language nor understand
local customs. Pilgrimages, for those who could afford them, must have been
both bewildering and exhilarating experiences.

HERETICS

The church did not approve of the spiritual activities of all Christian
women. Whereas nuns and mystics might gain reputations for great piety,
they also ran the risk of falling foul of church authorities and being branded
as heretics. Heretics were people whose religious beliefs were condemned
by church authorities: they might consider themselves to be Christian, but
the church was—for whatever reason—suspicious of their views. There was
a narrow line between extreme religiosity and heresy, and this line shifted
over time and place. Margery Kempe, the pilgrim, came perilously close to
this line at some times during her life. Kempe was in many ways a mystic
wannabe, familiar with the spiritual writings of Brigid of Sweden, Julian
of Norwich, and others. She had visions of Jesus and the Virgin Mary and
demonstrated her deep piety through great bouts of crying, some during
church services and hence annoying to her fellow church-goers. Her autobiography documents that she lectured her neighbors, fellow pilgrims,
and even monks and churchmen on appropriate spiritual behavior, and
that they did not always appreciate her reprimands. Margery's irritating
behavior was perhaps responsible for the fact that she was charged several
times with the heresy of Lollardy. Lollardy, a heresy which had emerged
in late fourteenth-century England, was particularly critical of the wealth
and corruption of the church. Margery was taken before bishops to answer
charges of heresy but was able to demonstrate that her beliefs were in line
with those of the church.

Other women were less fortunate. Marguerite Porete, the Beguine, was
burned at the stake for her alleged heresy, as was Joan of Arc. In Joan's

case, the reason was at least as much political as it was spiritual, since she had been captured and given to the English, the enemies of France in the ongoing Hundred Years War. Joan's visions of saints and reports of hearing saintly voices were received eagerly (once she had passed certain spiritual tests) by the heir to the French throne, but the English were much more suspicious and believed she had faked them. Like Marguerite, Joan was burned at the stake, the standard punishment for heretics in the late Middle Ages. Had mystics such as Angela of Foligno or Julian of Norwich found themselves caught between opposing armies in fifteenth-century France, they too may have faced the stake rather than being lauded as important spiritual figures.

Women who claimed to have received visions were especially vulnerable to charges of heresy. But so too were the rank and file members of religious movements that had been condemned by the church. Few heretical movements created concern during the early Middle Ages, but heresies became more common and more persecuted from the high Middle Ages onward. Historians used to think that women were more likely than men to be attracted to heretical movements, but recent scholarship has proven otherwise. Women certainly participated in heresies, but they did not overshadow men, either as participants or as leaders. Lollards, for instance, downplayed the role of priests and believed, much as Martin Luther and other Reformation leaders would argue a century later, that anyone could communicate directly with God without the church's intervention. In theory, this should have empowered women, who were excluded from becoming priests, but studies have shown that women in Lollard communities played much the same role as women in society at large.[23]

The same was true of women who belonged to the Cathar movement of the thirteenth and fourteenth centuries. Cathars, also known as Albigensians, believed that physical and earthly things, such as the body, were created by the devil and were inherently evil. Things of the spirit, like souls, on the other hand, were created by God. As far as Cathars were concerned, the church must be evil because it was a physical and earthly creation; indeed, they criticized it directly for being materialistic and corrupt. The church, naturally, was not impressed by these criticisms, and Cathars were persecuted. In theory, a Cathar woman could become the equal of a man by overcoming the physical constraints of her body and achieving spiritual purity (men and women who achieved such a goal were known as *perfecti*). Women were also permitted to preach according to Cathar doctrines. In practice, however, the large majority of *perfecti* were men. Women still played important roles in the Cathar movement, but these tended to be in more traditional roles, such as feeding and housing the visiting *perfecti* and helping them hide from the medieval inquisition. Women such as the fourteenth-century Alazaïs Azéma of Montaillou (France) ran messages for heretics, assisted in heretical rituals, and helped convert others to Catharism. It was Alazaïs's son Raymonde, however, who strove to become a *perfectus*.[24] Of 114 alleged Cathars interrogated by the Inquisition in Pamiers (France) between 1318 and 1325, 48 (or 42 percent) were women. Women certainly played important roles in heretical movements, but it would be wrong to see heretical communities as ones that allowed women significantly greater opportunities than they allowed men.

JEWISH WOMEN

In terms of their role in religion, Jewish women faced many of the same limitations as Christian women. Like Christian women, they were excluded from holding official religious positions, such as Rabbi, and they were not expected to read holy texts. Just as Christian women faced ambivalence on the part of the church, so too Jewish women occupied an ambivalent position within their communities. During the Middle Ages, most Jewish communities existed outside the area of the Holy Land. Most lived in the Islamic areas of Egypt, northern Africa, and Spain, but others lived in areas of Eastern and Western Europe dominated by Christians. Jewish merchant communities and trade networks between cities had been established during the Roman era and continued into the Middle Ages.

The Talmud and the Torah, the most important Jewish texts, were in some places very dismissive of women. Women were seen as a distraction to men, a temptation that took men's minds away from proper religious observance and study. Women were also excluded from the most important rituals of religious observance: they were not circumcised and hence did not bear the mark of God's covenant with the Jews, and they were not expected to recite important prayers. Women, who were not usually taught Hebrew, could not read aloud in synagogues nor serve the community as teachers or judges. Moreover, scriptures show considerable suspicion of women's bodies. Menstruating women were considered unclean, and anyone or anything coming into contact with them was unclean also.[25]

Yet at the same time that the Talmud and Torah show suspicion of women, they also depict women as valued and important. Women like Rachel, who bravely stole her father's false idols and hid them, or her sister Leah, who withstood the resentment of others and bore many sons, show that women could be strong too. The Torah and Talmud praise women in their role as mothers, especially, not only for childbearing but also for maintaining the purity of their households. Sermons written during medieval times continued to portray women positively in their roles as wives and mothers: one sermon explained that a woman was like a wall around her husband, bringing him peace, protection, and atonement for his sins. Maintaining ritual purity in the home, especially purity concerning food, was an important role for medieval Jewish women. In preparing food, Jewish women needed to take care to follow the intricate dietary laws that were an important part of religious practice. Letters show that medieval Jews looked back to Biblical women as important examples: one hoped that the new wife of a family member would be like Rachel and Leah, "who both built the house of Israel."[26] The expected role for a medieval Jewish woman was one that emphasized motherhood and work within the home.

Motherhood was expected, but glimpses from the fragmentary primary sources show us that a few women went well beyond this prescribed role. Although women were theoretically excluded from teaching, a couple of examples mention women who ran schools. Others were listed among the donors to synagogues, suggesting that they supported their religious communities even if they could not participate as religious leaders. A couple of examples even show that some Jewish women were in fact highly educated in the Torah. Some, such as Dulce of Worms (d. 1196), wife of a Rabbi, served as prayer leaders and religious teachers to other women. One of the daughters of Rabbi Shlomo ben Isaac, more commonly known as the important biblical commentator Rashi, occasionally recorded her father's dictation, an activity that would have required her to have a good knowledge of Hebrew.[27]

In the years immediately following the eleventh-century Christian attacks on Jewish communities, Jewish women were esteemed for their heroic role in protecting their children from forced conversion to Christianity. Most Christians in the early Middle Ages had accepted Jewish presence in Western Europe, but this began to change from the high Middle Ages onward. From the late eleventh century, a new wave of intolerance among Christians brought persecution to Jews, Muslims, and other minority groups. In many places, Jews were attacked or evicted from their homes. They were also subject to increasing legal restrictions that confined them to professions such as trade and money-lending. Some of the most tragic and bloody attacks took place as Christians prepared to go on crusades. When the first crusade was summoned by Pope Urban II in 1095, the crusaders attacked and slaughtered Jews living in Western Europe before proceeding to the Holy Land. In Jewish chronicles recording the tragedies, women were praised for fighting back against their attackers and for protecting their children from capture and forced conversion to Christianity. Sometimes the only way to protect their children was to kill them oneself. At Mainz (Germany), Rachel (d. 1096), wife of Rabbi Judah, asked her companions to help her kill her four children. Rachel herself sacrificed three of her four children with a knife before being killed by the crusaders. Chroniclers described her as "saintly and pious" for protecting her children from capture and conversion. Other women were given the opportunity to save themselves by accepting baptism, but refused and were killed "for the sanctification of the Divine Name."[28] Women such as Rachel, wife of Rabbi Judah, were celebrated as heroines among surviving Jewish communities in the twelfth century. As time went on, however, their role tended to be downplayed by Jewish authors. Rather than being seen as active and heroic, later writers tended to depict Jewish women martyrs as passive and focused on their sexual purity.[29]

Jewish women thus faced much of the same ambivalence as that encountered by Christian women in the Middle Ages. Excluded from the religious hierarchy, they were nonetheless praised for their efforts in producing children, maintaining purity, and protecting family members. Since lifelong virginity did not hold the same esteem in Judaism as in Christianity, few other options existed besides marriage and motherhood. Yet, just as some Christian women found ways to negotiate patriarchal constraints within their religious traditions, so too did some Jewish women.

ISLAMIC WOMEN

Christians living in Western Europe were regularly in contact with the Jews who lived among them; most knew far less, however, about Muslims. Much of Spain had been conquered by the Muslims in the eighth century but, this area aside, few Islamic women or men lived or traveled in Western Europe. Instead, they were settled mostly in North Africa and the Middle East. Islamic presence in Eastern Europe, however, was important from the high Middle Ages onward and became even more so after the city of Constantinople was captured by the Islamic Turks in 1453, signifying the end of the Byzantine Empire. The lack of contact between Christians and Muslims in the West led to some misconceptions on both parts. Christians vilified Muslims, especially during the era of the crusades, depicting them with horns growing from their heads and claiming that they were inspired by the devil. Muslims, on the other hand, deplored the ignorance of the crusaders. They may have been more justified: compared with Islamic scholarship in the early and high Middle Ages, Western scholarship was inferior in both quantity and quality. In the tough economic and political conditions that accompanied the collapse of the Roman Empire, much of the knowledge of the classical era had been forgotten in Western Europe, but it was preserved and expanded upon by Islamic scholars based in Baghdad.

Just as medieval Europeans made false assumptions about Islamic culture, so too historians of the nineteenth and early twentieth centuries sometimes assumed that the position of medieval Islamic women was one of complete seclusion and subjection. Certainly Islamic women faced some major disadvantages, just as Christian and Jewish women did. But, as in the Christian and Jewish religions, a few women found space within Islam to exercise authority and gain social esteem.

As with all religions, Islamic attitudes toward women reflected not only the beliefs of religious leaders but also cultural traditions in the places that Islam took root. The Qu'ran, the most holy book of Islam, outlaws practices such as female infanticide and marrying more than four wives in such a way that implies that these practices were common before Muhammad's time. Like Jewish and Christian texts, though, the Qu'ran is ambivalent about women's status. On the one hand, a man was still permitted to marry up to four wives (so long as he could be fair to each of them), and women were instructed to obey their husbands. On the other, the Qu'ran viewed women and men as spiritually equal, praised those who treated their daughters well, and held both Adam and Eve just as accountable for their sin in the Garden of Eden. Indeed, during the life of the prophet Muhammad and in the first generations after his death, women's status seemed to be higher than that of pre-Islamic Arabic women. Some women, such as Muhammad's first wife Khadija (555–619), were able to control their own property, and some may even have participated in public worship. But as with Christianity, these new opportunities were restricted within a few centuries, and women were expected to take a secondary role.

Some Islamic women were able to overcome the traditional restrictions on their religious status. Sayyida Nafisa (762–824), an Egyptian woman, was a descendent of Muhammad famous for her learning and for performing miracles (although she was also praised as a humble and obedient wife). Women of particularly high social status could also sometimes find ways to flout social and religious conventions. Wallādah (994–1077), a princess of Islamic Spain, refused to stay secluded within the harem or to wear the veil, and she was known to be the lover of a famous poet. Other women of means escaped the harem by undertaking the hajj (the traditional pilgrimage to Mecca expected of every devout Muslim who could afford it at least once in his or her lifetime). Although women would have been expected to stay veiled en route, they were also expected to remove their veils for hajj ceremonies. Devout women might also practice charity (another religious requirement) by paying for important buildings or donating precious objects to their mosques. Islam thus provided opportunities for women of high socioeconomic status to enjoy enhanced religious status too.

The word *ambivalence* runs through much of this chapter. On the one hand, all women, whether Christian, Jewish, or Islamic, found themselves excluded from mainstream religious practice to some degree. Whereas all three faiths recognized, to some extent, that women and men were equally capable of religious devotion, each also found ways to minimize women's religious practice, whether by keeping them from the priesthood, confining circumcision as the mark of God's covenant to men alone, or insisting on obedience to their husbands. Religion could thus serve as a tool of patriarchal societies, a way to keep women in their place. Yet on the other hand, religious practices had the potential to empower women, whether they be Christian nuns like Hildegard of Bingen, Christian mystics like Catherine of Siena, Jewish martyrs like Rachel, wife of Rabbi Judah, or Islamic holy women like Sayyida Nafisa. By gaining reputations for their piety and devotion and—in some instances—their direct communications with God, individual women could increase their own esteem within their communities. Moreover, religious settings (such as nunneries, northern sides of parish churches, or women's sections within temples or mosques) could provide opportunities for women-only space and for strengthening bonds among women. Religion during the Middle Ages was inescapable— very few medieval women or men of any faith tradition ever challenged the existence of a God—but those with the means and desire to embrace it might find opportunities for agency and autonomy that did not exist elsewhere.

NOTES

1. Romans 16:1–7; I Timothy 2:12–16; I Corinthians 14:33–36. In fact, some scholars have hypothesized that Paul did not write all the letters attributed to him and that the verse about not speaking in church is a later addition.

2. Quoted in *Sainted Women of the Dark Ages*, ed. Jo Ann McNamara and John E. Halborg (Durham: Duke University Press, 1992), 45.

3. Jane Tibbetts Schulenburg, *Forgetful of Their Sex: Female Sanctity and Society, ca. 500–1100* (Chicago: University of Chicago Press, 1998), 191–95.

4. Clarissa Atkinson, "'Precious Balsam in a Fragile Glass': The Ideology of Virginity in the Later Middle Ages," *Journal of Family History* 8 (1983), 131–43.

5. Robert Mannyng, *Robert of Brunne's Handlyng Synne*, ed. Frederick J. Furnivall, EETS, vol. 119 (London: Kegan Paul, Trench, Trübner & Co., 1901), 56–57, lines 1585–86, Bodl. 415 manuscript version; John Mirk, *Mirk's Festial: A Collection of Homilies*, ed. Theodor Erbe, EETS, Extra Series, vol. 96 (London: Kegan Paul, Trench, Trübner & Co., 1892), 96–97.

6. Schulenburg, *Forgetful of Their Sex*, 146–47.

7. Jo Ann McNamara, *Sisters in Arms: Catholic Nuns through Two Millennia* (Cambridge: Harvard University Press, 1996), 311.

8. Christopher Brooke, *The Age of the Cloister: The Story of Monastic Life in the Middle Ages* (Mahwah, N.J.: HiddenSpring, 2003), 18.

9. Penelope D. Johnson, *Equal in Monastic Profession: Religious Women in Medieval France* (Chicago: University of Chicago Press, 1991), 219–20.

10. Donald Weinstein and Rudolph M. Bell, *Saints and Society: The Two Worlds of Western Christendom, 1000–1700* (Chicago: University of Chicago Press, 1982), 220–21.

11. *Ancrene Riwle*, ed. M. D. Salu, 3rd ed. (Exeter: University of Exeter Press, 1990), 28–39.

12. Mary C. Erler, *Women, Reading, and Piety in Late Medieval England* (Cambridge: Cambridge University Press, 2002).

13. Walter Simons, *Cities of Ladies: Beguine Communities in the Medieval Low Countries, 1200–1565* (Philadelphia: University of Pennsylvania Press, 2001), 51–60; Caroline

Walker Bynum, *Holy Feast and Holy Fast: The Religious Significance of Food to Medieval Women* (Berkeley: University of California Press, 1987), 18.

14. *The Letters of St. Catherine of Siena,* vol. 1, ed. Suzanne Noffke (Binghamton: SUNY Binghamton, 1988), 217.

15. Julian of Norwich, *Revelations of Divine Love,* trans. James Walsh (New York: Harper & Row, 1961).

16. Katherine L. French, "Women in the Late Medieval English Parish," in *Gendering the Master Narrative: Women and Power in the Middle Ages,* ed. Mary C. Erler and Maryanne Kowaleski (Ithaca: Cornell University Press, 2003), 156–73.

17. French, "Women in the Late Medieval English Parish," 166–67.

18. French, "Women in the Late Medieval English Parish," 161–62.

19. Schulenberg, *Forgetful of Their Sex,* 230–31.

20. Judith M. Bennett, *A Medieval Life: Cecilia Penifader of Brigstock, c. 1295–1344* (Boston: McGraw Hill College, 1999), 44.

21. Quoted in Nicole Bériou, "The Right of Women to Give Religious Instruction in the Thirteenth Century," in *Women Prophets and Preachers through Two Millennia of Christianity,* ed. Beverly Mayne Kienzle and Pamela J. Walker (Berkeley: University of California Press, 1998), 134–45 at 134–35.

22. Judith K. Golden, "Images of Instruction, Marie de Bretagne, and the Life of St. Eustace as Illustrated in British Library Ms. Egerton 745," in *Insights and Interpretations: Studies in Celebration of the Eighty-Fifth Anniversary of the Index of Christian Art,* ed. Colum Hourihane (Princeton: Princeton University in association with Princeton University Press, 2002), 60–84.

23. Shannon McSheffrey, *Gender & Heresy: Women and Men in Lollard Communities, 1420–1530* (Philadelphia: University of Pennsylvania Press, 1995).

24. Emmanuel LeRoy Ladurie, *Montaillou: The Promised Land of Error* (New York: Vintage Books, 1979).

25. Leviticus 15:19–27.

26. Judith R. Baskin, "Jewish Women in the Middle Ages," in *Jewish Women in Historical Perspective,* ed. Baskin (Detroit: Wayne State University Press, 1991), 94–114 at 97.

27. Baskin, "Jewish Women in the Middle Ages," 104.

28. *Women's Lives in Medieval Europe: A Sourcebook,* ed. Emilie Amt (New York: Routledge, 1993), 282–83.

29. Susan Einbinder, "Jewish Women Martyrs: Changing Models of Representation," *Exemplaria: A Journal of Theory in Medieval and Renaissance Studies* 12 (2000), 105–27.

SUGGESTED READING

Baskin, Judith R. "Jewish Women in the Middle Ages," in *Jewish Women in Historical Perspective.* Ed. Judith R. Baskin. Detroit: Wayne State University Press, 1991.

Bynum, Caroline Walker. *Holy Feast and Holy Fast: The Religious Significance of Food to Medieval Women.* Berkeley: University of California Press, 1987.

French, Katherine L. "Women in the Late Medieval English Parish," in *Gendering the Master Narrative: Women and Power in the Middle Ages.* Ed. Mary C. Erler and Maryanne Kowaleski. Ithaca: Cornell University Press, 2003.

Hambly, Gavin R. G., ed. *Women in the Medieval Islamic World: Power, Patronage, and Piety.* New York: St. Martin's Press, 1998.

Johnson, Penelope D. *Equal in Monastic Profession: Religious Women in Medieval France.* Chicago: University of Chicago Press, 1991.

McNamara, Jo Ann. *Sisters in Arms: Catholic Nuns through Two Millennia.* Cambridge: Harvard University Press, 1996.

McSheffrey, Shannon. *Gender & Heresy: Women and Men in Lollard Communities, 1420–1530.* Philadelphia: University of Pennsylvania Press, 1995.

Mulder-Bakker, Anneke B. *Lives of the Anchoresses: The Rise of the Urban Recluse in Medieval Europe.* Trans. Myra Heerspink Scholz. Philadelphia: University of Pennsylvania Press, 2005.

Schulenburg, Jane Tibbetts. *Forgetful of Their Sex: Female Sanctity and Society, ca. 500–1100.* Chicago: University of Chicago Press, 1998.

Simons, Walter. *Cities of Ladies: Beguine Communities in the Medieval Low Countries, 1200–1565.* Philadelphia: University of Pennsylvania Press, 2001.

Venarde, Bruce L. *Women's Monasticism and Medieval Society: Nunneries in France and England, 890–1215.* Ithaca: Cornell University Press, 1997.

Wood, Diana, ed. *Women and Religion in Medieval England.* Oxford: Oxbow Books, 2003.

2

Women and Work

The kinds of work that women performed in medieval Europe varied enormously according to their geographic location and their social rank. Women brewed ale, wove silk, nursed babies, lent money, sold foodstuffs, sold their bodies as prostitutes, and managed wealthy households. Despite this range of occupations, women's work had one thing in common: women tended to work at lots of tasks, often simultaneously. They did not usually have the luxury of being able to spend long periods of time devoted to one task alone; instead, they had to juggle multiple occupations.

Medieval European societies were highly stratified and offered little opportunity for social mobility. That is to say, the social rank into which one was born mattered a great deal, and it was difficult to move from one social status to another. If a woman were born a peasant, chances were extremely high that she would stay a peasant all of her life. Similarly, if a woman were born into the nobility, she would likely marry another noble and be expected to uphold her family's noble status. Exceptions to these rules occurred, but they were rare indeed. Social rank affected almost everything about one's life, from the clothes that one wore to the food one ate to the work one did. This chapter is therefore organized around the kinds of work performed by women of different social classes: peasants, townswomen, and noblewomen.

PEASANT WOMEN

To understand the work of peasant women, it is necessary first to understand the status of the peasantry in general. Peasants accounted for more than 90 percent of the European population in the Middle Ages. Depending on the era and the place in which they lived, they might be divided into several categories. Some were born slaves. Medieval Europeans had inherited the tradition of slavery from the Romans, although it became much rarer during the early Middle Ages. Others were unfree peasants (known as *serfs* or *villeins*). Serfs were not permitted to leave the land on which they were born, and they were required to pay a variety of fees and dues to their manorial lords or ladies. They could not send their children to school, and they were not permitted to carry weapons. Nor were they allowed to marry anyone from another manor, since this would effectively mean that one partner or the other would have to leave their own manor and would thus be lost to their lord or lady. In addition, they were required to work on their lord or lady's land for several days each week (an obligation known as *week-work*). On the other hand, serfs had some security in that their lords or ladies rented each family a plot of land on which to work for the remaining days each week, and the peasant family derived much of its sustenance from this source. A male peasant might spend three days working on the land of his manorial lord or lady, but he was able to invest the rest of his time in growing grain for his family on the plot of land that he rented.

Free peasants enjoyed considerably more rights than serfs: they could leave the manor, find spouses from elsewhere, carry weapons, and send their children to school if they chose. Free peasants usually made their living in much the same way as serfs, by renting pieces of land from the lord or lady or hiring themselves out to work on the land of others. But to some extent they also lacked the security of serfs. In times of economic hardship, a manorial lord or lady could evict free peasants, raise rents, or refuse to employ them for wage labor, and this left free peasants more vulnerable. During favorable economic times, when labor was in demand, it was far preferable to be a free peasant. When times were bleak, however, serfs had the advantage, since their rents were fixed and they could not easily be evicted. On some occasions, free peasants gave up their freedom and took on un-free status in return for the security of serfdom. This process (known as *commending oneself* to a lord or lady) was no light undertaking, because it meant that one's descendents would thereafter be considered serfs as well.

To some extent, men's work was affected more directly than women's work by their freedom or lack thereof. Peasants, both free and unfree, usually lived together in small villages or hamlets. Male peasants who were heads of household were regarded as the lord or lady's tenants. As such, they were responsible for seeing that rents and fees were paid and that the requisite amount of labor on the lord or lady's land was carried out. Because women's labor was not seen as being as valuable as men's labor, men could not send their womenfolk along to carry out their week-work, except under particular circumstances. Women were expected to help out at certain times of the year, such as harvest-time, but they were generally exempted from the direct responsibilities of tenancy. On rare occasions, women might inherit or purchase land and thus become tenants themselves, but female tenants were often forced to hire men to carry out their week-work.

Men's work, then, usually took them to the fields. Women's work, on the other hand, was much more focused on the home and the village. While men grew grain, women worked at a wider variety of tasks during each day. They prepared food and looked after children, but they also brewed ale, tended chickens, grew vegetables, fetched water, made, washed, and mended clothing, and traveled to market to sell extra goods and buy anything that the family was lacking. In addition, they sometimes worked in the fields alongside their husbands and brothers. Archaeological evidence underscores the physical nature of peasant women's work: skeletons of medieval women found in the countryside show that their upper arms were well developed, a result of carrying heavy loads and digging vegetable gardens.[1] The multiplicity of a peasant woman's duties is emphasized in a fifteenth-century English poem in which a ploughman comes home from the fields one day to find that his dinner is not yet ready. Angry, he accuses his wife of doing little and spending her day chattering with neighbors. His wife takes offense and recounts the tasks that fill her day:

> I have more to do, if everything were known;
> When I lie in my bed, my sleep is but small,
> Yet early in the morning you will call me to get up.
>
> When I lie all night awake with our child,
> I rise in the morning and find our house chaotic.
> Then I milk the cows and turn them out in the field,
> While you sleep quite soundly, Christ protect me!
>
> Then I make butter later on in the day.
> Afterwards I make cheese—these you consider a joke—
> Then our children will weep and they must get up,
> Yet you will criticize me if any of our produce isn't there.
>
> When I have done this, yet there comes even more:
> I give our chickens food or else they will be lean;
> Our hens, our capons, and our ducks all together,
> Yet I tend to our gosling that go on the green.
>
> I bake, I brew, it will not otherwise be well,
> I beat and clean flax, so help me God,
> I heckle the tow, I winnow and mark [sheep],
> I tease wool and card it and spin it on the wheel.

Either I make a piece of linen and woolen cloth once a year,
In order to clothe ourselves and our children in together,
Or else we should go to the market and buy it very dear;
I am as busy as I may every year.

When I have done this, I look at the sun,
I prepare food for our beasts before you come home,
And food for ourselves before it is noon,
Yet I don't get a fair word when I have done.[2]

The tasks that the unappreciated Ploughman's Wife enumerates—caring for children, milking cows, making butter and cheese, feeding poultry and livestock, baking, brewing, making linen and woolen cloth, and cooking for her family—would indeed have been familiar to a peasant woman. So too would a number of other tasks that she omits (perhaps because surviving copies of the poem are incomplete): women also tended vegetable gardens; worked (where possible) for wages outside the home; washed laundry; took in lodgers; sold ale, excess breast milk, and other commodities; and completed multiple other tasks.

Although older daughters and elderly parents might help out with child-care, responsibility for the care of children ultimately fell to the mother.

A peasant woman feeds hens and chickens. Illumination from a manuscript begun prior to 1340 for Sir Geoffrey Luttrell (1276–1345). © British Library, London, UK/ © British Library Board. All Rights Reserved/The Bridgeman Art Library

Peasant villages were dirty and dangerous places, and small children needed to be protected from falling into wells or rivers as their mothers collected water or did laundry, falling into the open fires on which their mothers cooked, and getting in the way of carts or horses traveling through the village. Statistical analysis of the records of coroners, who investigated accidental deaths, has revealed that infants were more likely to die around noon (a time when their mothers were especially busy juggling multiple tasks) than in the morning or afternoon.[3] Peasant mothers breastfed their children, often until the children were two to three years old.[4] In addition to its nutritional value, breastfeeding had another practical advantage: breast-feeding mothers are less likely to conceive another child. As a result, the children of a peasant household, in which the mothers breastfed regularly, might be further spread in age than the children of a noble household, in which babies were given to wet nurses. Indeed, a peasant woman who had recently weaned her own child might find temporary employment breast-feeding a baby born into a wealthy family.

Dairy work was usually regarded as women's work, too. As the Plough-man's Wife points out, peasant wives milked cows and made butter and cheese in addition to their other duties. Manorial households also some-times employed peasant women as dairymaids. Depending on the size of the manor, dairymaids took on responsibility for the poultry and were ex-pected to perform other odd jobs as well. A thirteenth-century treatise on estate management stipulated that a dairymaid should be "modest and hon-est, faithful and hard-working, knowledgeable and experienced in the tasks of the dairy, careful and not extravagant."[5] Hiring women rather than men for these tasks represented a saving for their employers, because women could be paid at a lower rate than men: the anonymous author of a manual on agriculture advised his readers that "[i]f there is a manor in which there is no dairy then it is always advisable to have a woman there [presumably to make butter and cheese on a small scale] for much less money than a man would take."[6]

Peasant women—whether single, married, or widowed—might also work for wages at other times of the year. At harvest time, for instance, all labor was welcome. Even during these crucial seasons, however, they received lower rates of pay than their husbands and brothers. During the harvest season, men tended to perform the more prestigious and higher-paid tasks, such as mowing (cutting grain with a scythe), while women, along with boys and elderly or disabled men, were employed reaping (following the mower with a sickle and gathering grain into bundles). Female harvesters thus earned about two-thirds to three-quarters of the wages of men.[7] In the countryside around Seville (Spain), men provided the major workforce for the grain harvest in July and August, while women predominated among the olive harvesters in early winter. Grain harvesters earned, on average, about twice the wages of olive harvesters.[8] In France, women earned money during the grape harvest by picking grapes, but they earned about half as much as the men who were employed carrying the baskets of grapes away.[9] Although their income did not match men's, the money that they earned was welcomed by their households. When a woman earned a few extra pennies, her family might be able to afford an extra loaf of bread or basket of eggs. This work, however, was only available occasionally and was thus hard to build into the household budget.

The Ploughman's Wife included baking and brewing among her list of tasks, and these would indeed have seemed familiar to many peasant women, especially in northern Europe where the diet was based around bread and ale. Baking was often carried out in communal ovens, and a wife would bake several weeks' worth of bread at one time. A peasant woman might sell or loan some of these loaves to her neighbors, who would pay her back with fresh bread after doing their own baking. Because water was seldom safe for drinking, the brewing of ale was an important part of a peasant woman's duties, too. In England, a peasant household of five people might consume about 9 gallons of ale every week, yet ale could only last for a few days before it became sour and undrinkable. Moreover, ale-brewing was a time-consuming process. Neighboring women may thus have taken turns brewing ale, and excess ale beyond that needed for their own families was often lent or sold to their neighbors.[10] We know more about brewing than about many other such by-industries, because manorial courts charged a small fee each time a batch of ale was sold. Some women regularly brewed large batches of ale and used the profits generated to supplement their household incomes (see, for instance, the brewers of Middlewich mentioned in the introduction). In the English manor of Brigstock in the early fourteenth century, 38 women paid brewing fees on a fairly regular basis. Among them, these 38 women produced about two-thirds of the ale sold on the manor. In addition, 273 brewers sold ale only occasionally, accounting for about one third of the ale sold.[11] The vast majority of brewers (or *brewsters*, as female brewers were known) were married women: single women and widows brewed ale for sale more rarely.[12] Toward the end of the Middle Ages, the brewing of ale was slowly overtaken by the brewing of beer (which contained hops, tended to be more alcoholic, and lasted longer). As the industry switched from ale to beer, it also became more commercialized. Women now found themselves excluded from brewing, and a lucrative household by-industry disappeared.[13]

Just like the Ploughman's Wife, peasant women also tried to save money (and perhaps earn a little extra money) by spinning wool, preparing linen, and making their families' clothes. Although spinning wheels were common by the late Middle Ages, many women continued to rely instead on the more portable distaff and spindle, implements that held the raw fibers of wool and the spun yarn. A woman would take raw fibers from the distaff (already carded to remove major tangles) and rub them between her fingers until they formed a thread; the yarn would then be wound around the spindle. Distaffs and spindles were so closely associated with women that they were used in artistic representations to symbolize domestic virtue and female power. As a full-time occupation, spinning was one of little pay and low status. Yet women who found themselves with a spare or quiet moment—perhaps while minding sleeping babies or sitting around the fire at night—could save money for their families by taking up their distaffs and spindles. A woman who spun yarn was thus a resourceful wife, and early church writers such as Augustine and Bede used the metaphor of spinning to describe the good works that a woman was capable of performing. Images of the Virgin Mary sometimes depicted her spinning yarn, either using a distaff and spindle or a spinning wheel.[14] The yarn produced by spinners still needed to go through multiple stages before it was capable of being used for garments: sheep's wool was rough and itchy, so it needed to be softened before it could be used for clothing. Although the Ploughman's Wife describes herself as making a piece of woolen or linen cloth, most women probably relied on the services of professional weavers (usually men) to transform their yarn into fabric. The practice of knitting was known in the Middle Ages but seldom used for making sweaters or wool garments. Instead, it tended to be reserved for high-quality and expensive silk stockings, gloves, and undergarments that would have been worn only by the nobility.

The Ploughman's Wife does not mention laundry among her many tasks, but it too would have featured among her regular chores. Washing took place at local streams or ponds, or sometimes in a specially erected washhouse. According to folklore, washhouses were the site of much gossip as women enjoyed each other's company while soaping and rinsing their families' clothes.[15] Peasant families did not have the luxury of enjoying clean clothes nearly as often as people today, though mothers of infants would have had little choice but to wash out baby diapers on a regular basis. Serving as laundresses was another possibility for peasant women who hoped to earn extra money, whether from neighbors or from the local nobility.

More than that of women in the towns, the work of peasant women was determined by the seasons. During the summer, and especially during the harvest season in early fall, women spent more time outdoors tending their vegetable patches, reaping grain in the fields, and carrying food and drink to the men who mowed grain. If they lived in grape-growing regions such as parts of France, Spain and Italy, women helped produce wine, treading the grapes with their feet. They also helped to smoke and salt meat to feed their families through the winter. During winter months when fewer daylight hours limited outside work, women might spend more time engaged in spinning or sewing of family clothes. They also saw to animals penned outside or housed inside with the family for warmth. Spring brought a return to outdoor duties, as women helped to hoe and weed the newly-planted crops. In sheep-farming regions they helped with clipping wool. They also weaned the young calves and goats in order to make butter and cheese from the saved milk. Much of a woman's work—such as minding children and cooking food—was the same year-round, but the changing seasons nonetheless meant that her labor was in particular demand at certain times of the year.

The type of work that a woman performed in her home and village varied, to some extent, according to her marital status. Wives played a major role in the peasant economy, but so too did unmarried peasant women. Girls and peasant women nearing marriageable age worked at very similar tasks to their mothers, serving a kind of informal apprenticeship as they learned the techniques of brewing, spinning, and childcare. Unmarried women often earned money by hiring themselves out for a few years as servants. Particularly in northwestern Europe, women and men in their midteens might spend a few years living and working for another family. Some, as will be discussed further below, sought service in local towns and cities. Others stayed in the countryside and hired themselves out to a family member or neighbor as they sought to build sufficient assets to set up their own households. Most peasant women eventually married, but rarely a woman would stay single throughout her life. Lifelong single women found it hard to make ends meet. One such woman, Cecilia Penifader of Brigstock (England), was able to survive during the early fourteenth century by making good use of her family network. Cecilia's parents helped her acquire some property, and they left her more when they died. After their deaths, Cecilia bought more small pieces of land, often adjoining land of her brothers. In later life, Cecilia shared a house with one unmarried brother. Very likely, she and her brothers helped one another out with their tasks: her brothers may have helped with the so-called male tasks of plowing and mowing grain, while she may have helped them with so-called female tasks such as brewing or weeding. But she also probably employed male servants on an occasional basis to help her out with labor in the fields. Compared with other peasant families, Cecilia's was relatively well-to-do, and her situation was thus more fortunate than it might have been for a poorer peasant woman who remained single.[16]

The work of widows was also very similar to that of wives and single women, although—depending on their economic circumstances—it could be very hard for widows to make ends meet. In some places, such as countryside surrounding Seville (Spain), about 14 percent of households were headed by women, most of whom were widows.[17] The proportion of land holdings controlled by widows in England was remarkably similar.[18] Yet it was no easy thing for a widow to be able to support these households or work this land. Many women ceased to sell ale once widowed, for instance, because they lacked the resources to buy large quantities of supplies and equipment. Village by-laws recognized the poverty of widows, often reserving to widows the right of gleaning—that is, picking up by hand any spilled pieces of grain remaining after the harvesters had moved through. Sometimes widows were cut a little slack in manorial dues, too: at Alwalton (England) in the thirteenth century, they were excused from paying the annual fee of one penny to their lord after Christmas. Even so, their costs could be heavy. The widows of Matthew and William Miller of Alwalton were each expected to pay 4 pence in rent and to provide two laborers for three days each for carrying hay and two laborers for one day to help with the grain harvest.[19] The cost of hiring laborers to carry out these services would have been heavy. Often, such widows were forced to remarry in order to support themselves.

Work dominated a peasant woman's day, yet we know very little about what peasant women themselves thought about their work. The poem in which the Ploughman's Wife outlines her woes gives a sympathetic portrayal of how busy and harried women might have been, yet there is no evidence that it was written by a woman. Certainly when people of higher social classes thought about peasant women, they associated them closely with their work. When peasant women appeared in the margins or background of manuscript illustrations for members of the nobility, they were depicted harvesting, feeding chickens, making cheese, carrying water, or spinning wool. Only very seldom were they depicted at leisure or at worship. On the rare occasions when nobles recorded their advice to peasant women, it also tended to focus especially on their work. The fifteenth-century author Christine de Pisan, in her advice to women of different social statuses, comes across as somewhat patronizing in her words to "the simple wives of village workers." Christine recognizes that peasant women have less leisure time than noblewomen in which to fast, say prayers, or attend church, so she focuses especially on refraining from immoral work practices: peasant women must not put their animals to graze in neighbors' meadows, break down hedges, nor steal the property of others.[20] Similarly, when Anthony Fitzherbert, an English author of the early sixteenth century, addresses peasant women in his *Boke of Husbandry,* he gives advice that would probably have seemed completely self-evident to a peasant woman of his day. A peasant woman is instructed to sweep the house, set the table, milk cows, suckle calves, strain milk, get her children up and dressed, cook meals, send corn and malt to the mill, make butter and cheese, feed pigs and chickens, tend the vegetable and herb gardens, prepare flax and hemp for linens and wool for yarn, winnow grain, take excess supplies to market, and help her husband in the fields whenever she can.[21] While Fitzherbert's advice might have seemed redundant to a peasant woman who already knew to do all this and more, it nonetheless shows again that peasant women were associated closely with their work and that those who stopped to think about it were aware of the multiplicity of their chores.[22] The things on which most commentators seem to agree, therefore, are that peasant women worked hard, that they worked at a wide variety of tasks, and that their work was more domestic in focus than that of their husbands.

TOWNSWOMEN

Peasant women's work was very similar regardless of whether they were un-free or free, well-off or poor. For women living in the towns, on the other hand, the types of work available depended in large part on the status of the families to which they belonged. The very wealthiest townswomen, the wives of successful merchants, enjoyed high status and did little physical labor. Those at the lower end of the status hierarchy such as servants, however, performed just as much physical labor as their sisters in the countryside. Many of those who came to towns and worked as servants may indeed have had sisters still working in the countryside: from the high Middle Ages onward, the towns were constantly replenished by an influx of young single women. Where records or remains survive, they show that most towns had more female inhabitants than male. Analysis of skeletons from medieval York (England), for instance, shows that the city contained only 9 men for every 10 women.[23] For women, towns offered a refuge from a countryside in which land was becoming scarce and female wages were low. They also offered the hope that women might be able to rise in social status to become guildswomen or even merchants' wives and exercise more choice over their own lives. Few realized this dream, but it was powerful enough to attract female migrants in large numbers nonetheless. Townswomen worked in many different occupations, but they tended to cluster in a few trades in particular. This section will focus on women's work as slaves and domestic servants, women's work in the food and beverage industries, women's work in the textile industry, women's work as caregivers, and the situation of poor women who were unable to find legal employment.

At the bottom of the social ladder were small numbers of female slaves, known as *ancillae,* who continued to work in rich households—both rural and urban—throughout most of the Middle Ages. In fact, numbers of slaves increased during the late Middle Ages, when young women from Eastern Europe were sold to households in Western European cities, especially those in Italy. Sold around the age of 9 or 10, these women were effectively prevented from marrying by the fact that their children would be considered slaves also. If they did have children, therefore, their children could be bought or sold along with their mothers. Tasks assigned to slave girls and women tended to be the most menial work of the household: an ancilla would be responsible for tending ovens, carrying wood and water, and washing the dirtiest pots and pans. If the ancilla was particularly skilled and obedient, she might advance to work such as sewing, cooking, spinning, and weaving.[24] Hours were long: an ancilla would typically work all day for six days a week and often part of the day on Sundays.

Even in cities in which some households employed ancillae, much domestic work was carried out by servants. Many servants were drawn from the ranks of former peasant women who had migrated to towns from the countryside. Some of this migration was illegal: serfs were not permitted to leave their manors without the permission of their lords or ladies (permission which was seldom granted, since their labor was needed). Yet if a serf ran away to a town and was able to evade capture for a year and a day, he or she would be freed. Many runaway female serfs began their careers in towns by seeking work as servants, and so, too, did other new immigrants. Servants were especially important to the functioning of the household in the towns of northern and western Europe: in fourteenth-century Exeter, for instance, 37 percent of working women were servants.[25] In Italian cities, too, servants were not uncommon, although the shortage of workers after the Black Death of the mid-fourteenth century may have made it more difficult to hire workers. In late medieval Florence, most of the richer households had only one or two household servants.[26]

Service in the household of an artisan's family or a merchant's family provided secure employment, but the hours were long and the conditions often harsh. Girls often entered service in their early teens, or even younger, and remained in service until their late teens or early twenties. During this time, they might move from one employer to another. In fact, the rates of turnover were sometimes very high. In fifteenth-century Florence, when the demand for servants was considerable, many stayed only a few months before leaving—either of their own volition or as a result of being fired by their employers. In addition to much heavy carrying and menial work, a female servant was vulnerable to sexual exploitation from her master or other members of the family. Katherine Bronyng of Borstall (England), for example, was impregnated by John, son of her employers Robert Browne and his wife.[27] A servant who became pregnant reflected poorly on the master of the household, suggesting that he had poor governance over the morality of his employees. She also typically lost her job and found herself with another mouth to feed. Servants were liable to physical abuse, too: employers were occasionally charged in court with having assaulted their servants, although those charged frequently argued that they were entitled to slap or beat servants who disobeyed orders.[28] On the other hand, some servant women clearly had good working relationships with their employers and were bequeathed small items in their employers' wills. William Nunhouse, a fishmonger of York, made several bequests to his servants in his will of 1444. His servant Margaret was to receive a Prussian chest, a brass pot, a coverlet, a blanket, and a pair of sheets as long as she did not depart from his wife's service until the term of her hire was completed. Other female servants of William received sums of money. Wealthy widows who made wills were often especially generous to their servants, too: Joan Buckland of Edgcott (England) stipulated that her gowns should be divided among her women servants and that the woman who was with her at the time of her death should receive 100 shillings, a silver bowl, two spoons, and a gown.[29] Domestic service, then, could be quite tolerable or downright exploitative, and most regarded it as a way station en route to something better. Wages were low, but servant women had their food and board provided and could thus save money for their dowries.

The work that servants performed was often domestic, but they also helped in their employers' workplaces. This reflected the medieval pattern in which work and home were not nearly as strictly separated as they typically are today. A shoemaker, for instance, might have a workshop attached to the house. While he spent much of the day making shoes, perhaps aided by apprentices, his wife and servants would deal with customers, fetch materials, run errands, keep the fires tended, and bring food to the workers. If properly trained, they might also help with aspects of the production process itself—perhaps the cutting of the leather or the sewing of the shoes. Wives and servants thus worked in a wide variety of industries, moving between the home and the workshop.

In many towns and cities, guilds were incredibly important in structuring both urban trade and manufacturing, and urban social and political life. Each craftsman and merchant was required to belong to the guild appropriate to his trade. A shoemaker, then, was obliged to join the local shoemakers' guild, an apothecary joined the apothecaries' guild, while a wealthy merchant would be delighted by the power and status that accompanied compulsory membership in the merchants' guild. These guilds regulated the number of people working in any given occupation within a town: if the guild determined that the town could support only 12 shoemakers, no more than 12 would be permitted to set up shop. Guilds also set rules for their conduct of trade. They regulated prices so that no guild member could undercut another, and they inspected the work of their members for quality. To progress from apprentice to journeyman to master, one needed to secure the guild's approval. In addition to the very real economic benefits of membership, guilds also offered social and political benefits. If a guild member were to die in poverty, the guild might pay for his funeral and provide temporary (albeit meager) assistance for his widow. Guild masters had the right to wear *livery* or particular dress and badges denoting their status as part of a guild. They held feasts to celebrate important occasions and might sponsor charitable works. Guilds helped structure the political life of the town, too: for processions on holy days, men often arranged themselves according to guilds, and certain guilds were known to be especially influential when it came to acquiring local political office. In some towns, a man needed to be a member of the merchants' guild if he hoped ever to be elected to the position of city councilor or mayor. Guilds, then, provided an important part of a man's social, religious, and political identity.

So where did this leave women? In general, women were excluded from the economic, social, and political power that accompanied full guild membership. Only rarely were women able to become apprentices, and

A townswoman and her husband work together in their workshop (tempera on panel, "The Four Social Conditions: Work," by Jean Bourdichon [1457–1521]). © Bibliothèque de l'École des Beaux-Arts, Paris, France/Giraudon/The Bridgeman Art Library

often they became apprentices into trades that lacked formal guilds. Some of the best surviving data comes from Montpellier (France), in which 30 of 208 surviving apprenticeship contracts made before 1350 involve women. These women (many of whom were actually girls as young as 12) were typically apprenticed into occupations traditionally regarded as women's work—especially work with textiles—which were not regulated by guilds. They did not enter apprenticeships in the more prestigious trades such as those of money changers, merchants, or drapers.[30] In other places, women were seldom granted official apprenticeships, yet many recognized that the kind of on-the-job training they received as wives, daughters, or servants of a guildsman served as unofficial apprenticeships. Nonetheless, they were often excluded from guilds. Sometimes wives were admitted as *sisters* who paid lower admission fees and participated in only some of the guild's celebrations. In many areas, widows of guild members were allowed to take over their husbands' workshops and even train apprentices. Yet in places such as parts of Spain and Italy, widows were only permitted to carry on their husbands' workshops if they had sons who would one day take over the business.[31] Even when widows were allowed to continue workshops, their position within guilds was tenuous at best. They were not allowed to vote or hold elected positions within the guild, and the privileges that they did possess were usually terminated if they remarried. Many widows simply could not afford to continue their husbands' workshops after they died, so they either remarried and lost their guild privileges or closed the workshop and tried to find some other means of eking out a living. As a result of these various restrictions, widows only ever accounted for about 2 to 5 percent of active guild membership.[32]

As discussed below, some urban occupations were dominated by women, but these occupations seldom had guilds of their own. A few exceptions could be found in the cities of Rouen and Paris (France) and Cologne (Germany) in which women workers in the textile industries were sometimes able to band together. Even in these cities, however, women's guilds were greatly overshadowed by men's: of more than 100 Parisian guilds in the late thirteenth century, only 7 were dominated by women. Elsewhere, female-dominated trades (such as that of the London silk workers) lacked representation and identity in the form of guilds.[33] Several women's guilds were closed down from the fifteenth century onward, which has led some historians to argue for an increasingly negative view of women's work in the late Middle Ages. Other historians, however, have pointed out that only a few women ever had access to guilds anyway and that women's work throughout the Middle Ages continued to be very similar in character: low-status and poorly paid.

As in the countryside, urban women played a particular role in the preparation and distribution of food. In towns, as in the country, women brewed ale and offered it for sale. Urban brewsters were often women from households in which their labor was less desperately required by their husbands. In fourteenth-century Exeter (England), wives of merchants and men working in the metal trades were more likely to brew ale for sale.[34] Brewsters tended to come not from the very poorest groups in a town (who would have lacked capital to buy the equipment needed), nor from the very richest (who might have regarded the physical labor of brewing as undignified), but rather from those of middling status.[35] One example of such a brewster was Margery del Mulne of the small town of Middlewich (England). Margery brewed ale for sale on more than 60 occasions between 1421 and 1434, employing servants to help her. Her husband Thomas was a saltboiler who served at least one term as bailiff, suggesting that—while not among the town's elite—he was regarded as respectable. In addition, the couple owned an inn, and Margery also paid an annual licensing fee entitling her to bake bread for sale.[36] Margery's multiple trades, combined with her husband's saltboiling, enabled the couple to piece together a living. Women also controlled the brewing industry in Denmark, and some female tavern-keepers were granted exclusive rights to sell German beer in addition to Danish beer.[37] But throughout medieval Europe, the female tavern keeper seems to have had a fairly low social status. In England, such women were suspected of watering down their ale and running brothels, while in Constantinople (Byzantine Empire) they were generally regarded as disreputable.[38]

Women not only produced drink and foodstuffs, but they also played vital roles in transporting and marketing it. Towns depended on the surrounding countryside to supply much of their daily calorific needs, and women were frequently involved in connecting rural producers with urban purchasers. In particular, they worked as *hucksters* or *tranters*, petty traders who bought produce from the countryside and carried it (usually on their backs) to resell in urban markets. Such traders might visit the small peasant villages within a 5 to 10 mile radius of a town and buy excess ale, meat, vegetables, and dairy products. These would then be carried into the town and sold for a profit in the market. Hucksters were often maligned and accused of buying up the available produce before others had a chance to examine it, cheating customers with adulterated food or inaccurate measures, and extorting town-dwellers to buy their products at higher prices than they deserved. Similarly suspect were *tapsters* and *tipplers*, who resold ale that had been brewed by others. Poems, stories, and plays mock the stock character of the cheating female huckster and aleseller. Hucksters and tapsters were generally drawn from the ranks of poorer women. They needed to have a little capital in order to pay peasant women for the produce which they carried, but little else was needed in terms of equipment. In many English towns, hucksters paid an annual fee, much like brewsters, for the right to carry on their trade. Women are sometimes underrepresented in records of these fees, however, because their husbands were listed instead.

In other words, because a husband was usually responsible for his wife's debts, his name would be recorded on the court roll as responsible for the annual fee, even though it was his wife who did the actual work. For example, women were listed as responsible for between 9 and 25 percent of fees associated with food retailing in Exeter courts between 1373 and 1393, but these numbers may only represent women who were widowed or single (and thus responsible for their own debts). In places where the customs of the court scribe were different and married women's names were listed, we see a different pattern. In Middlewich in 1425, for instance, women accounted for 15 of the 16 people (94 percent) listed as common tranters and liable to pay market fees.[39] In Malmø (Denmark), the guild of fishmongers and victuallers established in 1534 consisted entirely of women, but it was not a voluntary guild in the sense of most. Rather, it was imposed by the city council as a way to try and regulate the trade in food.[40] From examples such as these, as well as the popular association in literature that women were responsible for retailing food, we can assume that this was a trade that they dominated. Working as a huckster was generally unpleasant work: it was exhausting, back-breaking, and poorly regarded. Yet it served an important role in connecting the countryside to the towns and enabled women to bring a few more pennies into the household.

While the production and retailing of food and drink employed many urban women, others made a living through the textile industry. In general, women were employed at the lower levels of textile production—carrying out such tasks as spinning and washing fleeces—while men tended to occupy the higher-status (and better-paid) parts of the process. In some Italian cities, such as Florence and Verona, women heads of household seem sometimes to have worked as weavers, although these women were widowed and presumably inherited their workshops from their husbands. Women accounted for 12 of the 269 Florentine heads of household employed as wool weavers and 8 of the 65 linen and silk weavers in 1427. Of these 20 women, 17 were widowed, one was either married or widowed, and two were of unknown marital status. Florentine widows might continue their husbands' workshops as weavers, but they were not able to play the same role in every textile-related profession: no female heads of household appeared among the 92 tailors, the 46 dyers, or the 217 wool manufacturers, merchants, and drapers who belonged to the wool guild.[41] Studies of the textile industry elsewhere show similar patterns. In fourteenth-century Shrewsbury (England), the weaving trade was dominated by men, but wives and female servants clearly helped out. While women very occasionally worked as fullers (those who increased the bulk of cloth by shrinking and beating it) or shearers (those who sheared the cloth with large shears in the final stages of its production), they did not participate in the higher status tasks of dying and tailoring.[42] Women occasionally worked as drapers in fourteenth- and fifteenth-century Denmark, but they seem to have been excluded from weaving and tailoring except under particular circumstances.[43]

Access to the textile trade often varied according to the fabric being produced. Women were, on the whole, excluded from the wool trade more than from the silk, linen, and cotton industries. In Barcelona (Spain) in the fifteenth century, women were excluded from every aspect of the wool trade except spinning. Yet they were allowed to join the confraternity of linen and cotton workers as masters, provided they passed the appropriate examinations.[44] Women dominated the silk trades in cities such as Cologne, Paris, and London, and several of the few examples of female-dominated guilds come from this industry. London silk workers did not have a guild of their own, yet in some ways they acted as if they had one. In the late fifteenth century, they were responsible for presenting several petitions to parliament to protect their monopoly on the silk trade from foreign competition. London female silk workers took on apprentices, and in a petition of 1455 they claimed to number more than 1000 (this number was almost certainly an exaggeration).[45] This quasi-guild status also seems to have existed for silk workers and other female cloth workers in eleventh-century Constantinople. Parisian silk workers, on the other hand, were organized into several separate guilds: silk spinners who used large spindles, silk spinners who used small spindles, silk ribbon makers, and more. Each guild had its own set of regulations, specifying the number of apprentices each might take on, the length of apprenticeships, and the appropriate sources from which they might buy raw silk. The silk makers of Cologne were similarly well organized and regulated, although they included men as well as women among their guild officials.[46] The silk and linen trades were—on the whole—less lucrative than the wool trade, so women's roles did not seem to threaten men's employment to the same degree. On the other hand, the wool trade was carefully guarded: the town government of Bristol (England) passed an ordinance in 1461 forbidding weavers to allow their wives, daughters, or maids to work at the loom since their labor would reduce the number of jobs available to men.[47]

In addition to the food and beverage and textile industries, women also worked as caregivers of various types. The trade of midwife was one dominated by women throughout the Middle Ages. Female friends and relatives gathered around the bedsides of women in childbirth, but particular villagers or townswomen were known as especially skilled in coaxing the baby to emerge. For most of the Middle Ages, it was accepted that midwives' training was unofficial and that women learned informally from one another. By the late Middle Ages, however, some cities began to regulate the activities of midwives. Midwives in some French and German towns were hired by the municipality and care was taken to ensure that they were of good character and morals. Fifteenth-century midwives in Lille (France) were required to pass an examination by a doctor, and the women whose babies they had delivered were asked to report on their work. By the early sixteenth century, regulations had become quite elaborate: the 1522 midwives' ordinance from the German city of Nuremberg included clauses requiring an oath from midwives to perform their duties conscientiously, to refrain from hurrying or delaying births, to choose wisely in selecting apprentices, and to refrain from drinking too much wine or charging excessive fees.[48]

Women played an important role in the next part of a baby's life, too: they served as wet nurses, either for women who were unable to breastfeed or for members of the elite who preferred to send their children out for breastfeeding. In Florence, for example, middle class families in the late Middle Ages commonly sent their babies out to nurse. Peasant women and poorer townswomen who weaned their babies early or whose babies died very young could thus make money by taking care of a baby belonging to a richer family. If they moved temporarily into the household of the baby's family, they might make a particularly good wage, higher than that of any other servants. If they stayed in their own houses, their rate of remuneration was usually lower, but still worthwhile. The wife of Piero Puro of Florence breastfed at least six children (on separate occasions) for terms that ranged between a few days and 23 months. In some cases, she had to send out her own children for breastfeeding elsewhere in order to take on other commissions. Weaning began at about 19 months, and children were returned to their families of origin about 6 weeks later. Like midwives, the morality of wet nurses was supposed to be beyond reproach: a wet nurse who became pregnant was thought to produce perverted and weaker milk, less nutritious for the baby.[49] Towns, as well as individual families, hired wet nurses. Foundlings and orphans needed feeding as much as babies of the rich, so municipal authorities boarded the children with wet nurses. The town of Montpellier (France), hired an average of 26 nurses annually by the 1490s. Most nurses were married women, wives of craftsmen and agricultural workers. Breastfeeding foundlings in Montpellier was less lucrative than nursing the babies of the rich in Florence, however; nurses' wages were fairly low compared with other occupations open to women during this time.[50]

Women played a smaller role among the hospital staffs and medical faculties of universities. Although a few examples of female physicians and medical professionals survive, these are very rare. For instance, eight female doctors are thought to have been working in Paris in 1292, yet these women would not have been trained at the universities, which were restricted to men only. The University of Paris argued that all doctors should be subject to certification, and unlicensed women physicians were prosecuted during the fourteenth century.[51] Even so, women doctors continued to practice unofficially. By the early modern period, women who practiced medicine, wet-nursing, or midwifery had become increasingly suspect in the eyes of both church and civil authorities. These women found themselves especially vulnerable to charges of witchcraft in the centuries that followed.

Besides jobs in the food and beverage, textile, and caregiving industries, women worked in a variety of other occupations, too. In both Italy and Spain, for instance, women played important roles in the emerging print and publishing industries after the first printing press was invented in the mid-fifteenth century. Widows and daughters of printers continued the pioneering printshops that produced Europe's first printed books. Caterina de Silvestro, widow of Sigismondo Mayr of Naples, not only continued printing after his death in 1517 but added italic type and ornamental letters. Initially, the works she printed identified her as Mayr's widow, but within a few years she printed books under her own name with no mention of him.[52] Women also served as money lenders in some places: they constituted about 16 percent of those lending money in Ghent (Low Countries), almost one-quarter of those lending money in twelfth-thirteenth century Genoa (Italy), and perhaps as many as one-third of all creditors in thirteenth-century France. Jewish women were especially important in the money-lending industry, since Christians were (in theory, at least) prevented from charging interest on loans. Richer widows were able to invest money from their dowries or inheritances in trade and commerce, lending particularly to family members and friends. Although women did not typically lend money with the same frequency as men, and while the sums they lent were generally smaller, their participation as creditors was nonetheless important in stimulating the medieval economy.[53]

In many towns, the participation of married women in the economy was limited by the expectation that wives' legal status was subsumed into that of their husbands. This meant that a husband was responsible for any debts that a woman might incur and that he—rather than she—must use the courts to pursue any debts owed to her. In some places, however, women were able to declare themselves financially independent of their husbands and take on the status of *femme sole*. Although some women traders on the continent were able to achieve a degree of financial independence from their husbands, the *femme sole* convention was best known in England, and especially in the city of London. Women who adopted the status of *femmes soles* were allowed to take on their own apprentices and were not responsible for their husbands' debts. On the other hand, they were not permitted to receive assistance from their husbands, whether financial or otherwise. In an era when the work of couples was very much intermingled, this may have seemed too restricting for some women. *Femmes soles* were also supposed to register as such and to pay a fee, again discouraging some women from declaring *femme sole* status.[54]

Women thus played multiple roles in the workplace of medieval towns. But what happened to women who were not able to find regular and stable employment? Towns contained few safety nets for such women. Charitable institutions such as hospitals provided assistance to small numbers of the poor, but they were generally inadequate to address more than a fraction of the need. Research on Paris has shown that hospitals and hospices provided between about 1,000 and 12,000 places, but as many as 100,000 Parisians found themselves desperately poor at some point in their lifetimes. Many female immigrants to towns found their first few weeks particularly difficult; others found themselves in crisis when afflicted with a sudden illness, injury, or pregnancy, and unable to work. Such women often relied on support from friends and family members who accompanied them or had preceded them in their trek to the towns. Nicole of Rubercy, for example, moved to Paris from the region of Normandy and found work as a laundress. When, in 1272, she suffered what seems to have been a stroke, she was cared for by her friends, one a widow who lived in the same hostel and another who owned the yard in which Nicole hung her laundry. These two women helped feed and dress Nicole, and they took her to the tomb of St. Louis at St.-Denis, about five miles outside Paris. Without the help of these friends, Nicole would almost certainly have died. Nicole probably met her friends in Paris, but other women migrated in small groups who continued to provide mutual support for one another. Amelot of Chaumont traveled from her home village to St.-Denis in 1277 along with two other women. When one of Amelot's legs became paralyzed, a few days after her arrival, her travel companions and new acquaintances helped carry her on a stretcher to the saint's tomb in search of a cure. Informal charity and female networks provided an important safety net for both Nicole and Amelot.[55]

Some women, however, were less fortunate than Nicole and Amelot. For women in such desperate straits, the options were few. Pickpocketing and petty thievery might provide enough to survive for a day or two, but chances were that one would be caught fairly soon. A more common strategy, therefore, was to turn to prostitution as a means to survive. In many European cities and towns, prostitutes numbered between about 3 and 8 percent of the population. Recent immigrants made up a substantial proportion of this number. Many women did not practice prostitution on a full-time or year-round basis but rather engaged in it when money was especially scarce: compared to other occupations open to women without capital, prostitution was relatively well paid. In Exeter, for instance, 9 percent of the 160 female servants identified in court records were also charged as prostitutes.[56] Laundresses and alesellers were also associated with prostitution in the popular imagination (for further discussion of prostitution and medieval attitudes toward it, see chapter 4).

Despite the many dangers of urban life, young women nevertheless migrated to towns in large numbers, especially during the late Middle Ages. Towns offered the hope for greater personal freedom, away from the close-knit villages of the medieval countryside. They also offered the hope for a young woman that she might rise in social status, either through a fortunate marriage or through her own hard work. The reality was often very different, but the hope of social advancement was sufficient to overcome concerns about poverty and drudgery. Late medieval towns have sometimes been described as the site of a golden age for women, a place in which a woman had far more freedom and choices than before. This characterization is surely an exaggeration, yet it does underscore one important point: women in towns worked in a much broader range of occupations than they did in the countryside. While an individual woman might not have had much control over her own fate or the opportunities open to her, women as a group found themselves dispersed throughout urban society: some were prostitutes or servants, while others worked in their husbands' craft workshops or carried on their husbands' businesses once widowed. Some supported themselves as wet nurses, while others ran their own businesses. By contrast with their sisters in the countryside, the range of possibilities open to townswomen was much more varied. Yet this variation did not necessarily mean that a poor migrant girl had any better chance of social and economic security than one who continued the life of a peasant.

NOBLEWOMEN

The lives of noblewomen were certainly more comfortable than those of their poorer counterparts among the peasantry and townswomen, but they were no less busy. Noblewomen are often imagined as leading lives of leisure, yet historians have uncovered evidence that many worked long hours. Their primary task was that of running and maintaining the household, often in the absence of their husbands. A noblewoman had to hire, fire, and supervise staff, order and keep track of provisions needed for feeding a large household, ensure that her staff and family were properly clothed, and supervise children from families of slightly lesser noble status sent to her household for training. In addition, a noblewoman needed to help maintain her family's social status through such practices as arranging respectable marriages for her children, visiting and receiving visits from other women of comparable status, and charitable donations to the poor and to religious houses. Much like the lives of peasant women and townswomen, therefore, the lives of noblewomen were always busy and often chaotic.

The first responsibility of a noblewoman was to oversee the running of the household on a day-to-day level. On her belt, the lady of the noble household often carried a set of keys that gave her access to storehouses, the treasury, linen closets, the larders, and the spice chest. In addition to their very practical use, these represented her authority and responsibility, since she was charged with ensuring that everyone within her home—staff and visitors alike—was well-fed and housed. Excerpts from the surviving account records of Eleanor, Countess of Leicester (England), from 1265 give clues as to what was involved in running a household: Eleanor had to arrange for stabling of new foals, purchase, repair and greasing of carts, purchase of wine, shoes, and clothing, medical care for members of her household, and hiring of messengers to take messages to and from her husband.[57] Noblewomen's responsibilities were intensified when their husbands were away, as was very often the case in the Middle Ages. Due to their husbands' participation in warfare and the risks involved in travel, noblewomen also ran a high risk of becoming widows, often while their children were still young. In their husbands' absences, women served for all intents and purposes as lords of their manors. Aided by their bailiffs and other manorial officials, they were responsible for overseeing the collection of rent, dealing with any problems raised by tenants, overseeing the employment of agricultural workers, and even—on occasion—defending their lands from attack. Books that advised women on how best to carry out their role thus assumed that any noblewoman knew all aspects of estate management, not just those concerning the interior of the household and its provisioning.

Several surviving advice manuals for noblewomen demonstrate the breadth of expertise required. Robert de Grosseteste's thirteenth-century manual was written for Countess Margaret of Lincoln (England), the widow of a friend, soon after her husband died. Grosseteste sets out 28 rules for effective estate management, covering everything from the ways in which she should give instructions to her bailiff and manage the rest of her staff to the best fairs at which to purchase household items. Grosseteste's eighteenth rule, for instance, instructs noblewomen on how to handle staff whose homes are beyond the household walls:

> As little as possible give leave to those who keep office in your house to go to their own homes, and when you give leave, give them a short time to return to you, if they wish to serve you; and if any of them speak back or grumble, tell them that you will be lord or lady, and that you will that all serve your will and pleasure, and whoever will not do so send away, and get others who will serve your pleasure—of whom you will find enough.[58]

Christine de Pisan's advice, compiled more than 150 years later, is similarly concrete. Like Grosseteste, de Pisan insists that noblewomen should have an intimate knowledge of the estate, what it can be expected to yield, and the customs and rights of those living on the land. As she instructs her readers repeatedly, "the lady must be knowledgeable enough to protect her interests so that she cannot be deceived." She must understand not only the physical conditions of estate management—the need for fertilization of the soil, good care of sheep, and appropriate seasons for particular kinds of work—but must also appreciate the psychology of her workers. Workers, Christine argues, are inclined to laziness and are unlikely to work unless they know the lady is watching. For this reason, the lady of the household should get up early and watch from the window until she sees her workers head out to the fields. She should walk through the fields during the day and supervise harvesters to ensure that they do not pilfer grain.[59]

Where we can find examples of the lives of real noblewomen, it is clear that many performed all these duties and more. Doña Ana de Almonte, for instance, a Spanish noblewoman of the early sixteenth century, ran her husband's estate during his many absences. She bought and sold land, mortgaged property to cover loans, hired workers, and marketed the olive oil they produced.[60] Medieval noblewomen often provided hospitality to visitors, too. The fifteenth-century household accounts of Dame Alice de Bryene, an English woman of the lesser nobility, show that she frequently housed visitors along with their servants. On New Year's Day 1413, her household provided dinner for 160 people. Between them, these guests ate 314 white and 40 black loaves of bread, 2 pigs, 2 swans, 12 geese, 2 joints of mutton, 24 capons, 17 rabbits, plus various supplies of beef, veal, piglets, and milk.[61]

In the absence of men, noblewomen sometimes found themselves faced with defending their estates in a very literal sense. Christine de Pisan instructed noblewomen that they ought to "know the laws of arms and all things pertaining to warfare, ever prepared to command [their] men if there is need of it." This included, Christine explained, both methods of defense and assault. A noblewoman should also have a good estimation of the strength of her forces so that she can know how long she can hold out before reinforcements arrive.[62] Women such as Margaret Paston, a member of the English gentry (lesser nobility), seemed to follow Christine's advice. Margaret calmly sent a message to her husband in 1448 that she needed crossbows and poleaxes (in addition to almonds, sugar, and cloth for children's gowns) to defend herself against Lord Moleyns, a threatening neighbor.[63] Her fears were well-founded, for two years later Moleyns sent a well-equipped army of more than 1,000 men to capture and ransack her house. Margaret and her household were evicted, shaken but unhurt. A few women, such as the Anglo-Saxon queen Æthelflæd in the tenth century, discussed further in chapter 6, developed great reputations as warriors. Æthelflæd ruled the kingdom of Mercia after the death

A noblewoman defends her castle in this fourteenth-century manuscript written in Italy and illuminated in England. © British Library, London, UK/ © British Library Board. All Rights Reserved/The Bridgeman Art Library

of her husband and led her troops successfully against Viking invaders on multiple occasions.

Noblewomen were expected to take on the responsibilities of men when needed, but they also faced considerable pressure to carry out so-called women's work in the form of producing heirs. Those who were fortunate enough to be fertile would have spent a good proportion of their adult lives pregnant. Eleanor of Aquitaine, for example, bore 10 children, plus at least 1 still-born child, over the course of 22 years. Pregnancy was a risky business: in the seventeenth century, more than 10 percent of noblewomen died in childbirth, and it is likely that the numbers were higher in the Middle Ages. Things were worse, though, for noblewomen who were unable to produce children. Unless their husbands were incapable of performing sexually, it was assumed that infertility was a woman's fault, and infertile wives were sometimes treated quite badly. Alfonso X of Castile (Spain) sent for another bride when his first wife, Violante of Aragon, whom he had married when she was aged 10, failed to conceive for several years. When the second fiancé arrived in Spain, however, she found that Violante was finally pregnant. Alfonso scrapped his plans to annul his first marriage and married off the second fiancé to one of his brothers. Violante, on the other hand, went on to have 12 children.[64] For queens like Violante, pressure to produce sons was particularly intense, since everyone feared political instability if a king died without a legitimate heir. For example, after the only legitimate son of Henry I of England was killed in a shipwreck in 1120, Henry named his daughter Matilda as his heir. When he died 15 years later, however, his nobles chose Matilda's cousin, Stephen of Blois, to become their king instead. This prompted a bloody civil war between Stephen and Matilda which disrupted England for almost 20 years. Far more fortunate, then, was the queen or noblewoman who could give birth to sons (minimally, "an heir and a spare").

Noblewomen did not usually breastfeed their babies, yet their children continued to be very much their responsibility. In the early years of children's lives, mothers did little hands-on childcare but remained responsible for their moral education. A mother would thus lead her children in prayers and teach them basic manners. After boys reached about the age of seven, their more formal education often began, and they might be instructed by tutors or sent to another noble household to learn appropriate behavior and military training. Responsibility for girls usually remained with their mothers, although they too were sometimes sent to another household for practical training. Although noblewomen did not spend as much time with their children as did peasant women or townswomen, their responsibilities to their children continued until their children's adulthood (and often beyond). If they were widowed before the children were of age, mothers needed to protect their children and their children's inheritances. Some women, such as Countess Ermessend of Barcelona (Spain), were able to rule over large territories as guardians for their sons.[65] Blanche of Navarre, Countess of Champagne (France), was in a similar situation. Pregnant when her husband Count Theobald III died, Blanche ruled the county of Champagne as regent from 1201–2 until their son Theobald IV came of age. In order to protect her son's rights, Blanche was forced to negotiate with both the Pope and the King of France.[66] Other women found their rights (and those of their children) threatened by their husbands' families and even by the king.

Noble mothers, both married and widowed, also played a large role in finding suitable marriage partners for their children. In doing so, they helped build alliances and promote the political and social interests of their families. Children themselves generally had little say in their own marriages, even though consent was theoretically required, and mothers could wield a great deal of influence over a child reluctant to marry. When her daughter Elizabeth was unwilling to marry a widower more than twice her age, Agnes Paston saw to it that she was "[for] the most part . . . beaten once in the week or twice, sometimes twice on o[ne] day, and her head broken in two or three places."[67] Elizabeth finally yielded to the pressure and agreed to marry her mother's choice, but for some reason the marriage did not go through. Distasteful as this kind of coercion might seem today, noblewomen who put pressure on their children to secure politically advantageous marriages were nonetheless carrying out their prescribed roles as guardians of their families' interests.

In addition to responsibilities to their families, noblewomen also played important roles with regard to the communities around them. Part of this responsibility was financial. Noblewomen gave alms and made charitable bequests to their local parish churches, monasteries and nunneries, and often the local poor. Elizabeth de Burgh of England, for instance, distributed money among the poor on the anniversary of her third husband's death. She also distributed money on Maundy Thursday, the Thursday before Easter, a traditional date for giving money to the poor. Other noblewomen made sizable donations to their parish churches, to religious guilds, to hospitals, and to houses of friars, monks, and nuns.[68] Byzantine noblewomen were especially prominent in founding and rebuilding monasteries and nunneries. Of 22 monasteries and nunneries in Constantinople restored between 1282 and 1328, women served as patrons for 9. In addition, they founded 4 of the 10 new religious houses during this era. One example of a female patron is that of Theodora Raoulaina, niece of one of the Byzantine Emperors. During her widowhood, Theodora restored St. Andrew at Krisei, a monastic institution dating from at least as far back as the sixth century, which had been much damaged during invasions. Between 1282 and 1289, she restored the former monastery as a nunnery, enlarged its church, and arranged for it to receive temporarily the bones of the patriarch Arsenios. Theodora later spent 15 years of her life at Krisei as a nun.[69] Countess Adela of Blois (c. 1067–1137) similarly retired to a nunnery during her widowhood, but she also served as patron to around 40 religious houses, both of monks and nuns. Surviving documents written by monks in the institutions she supported pay testament to her generosity and power.[70]

Support of communities did not always mean financial support, however; some noblewomen were in a position to serve as diplomats and intercessors in matters that went well beyond their own immediate concerns. Queens might intercede with their husbands on behalf of petitioners, as Queen Philippa of England was said to have done for the six burghers of Calais who offered to give up their lives in 1347 in order to free the rest of their townspeople (see chapter 6). Countess Matilda of Tuscany also served as an intermediary in the ongoing struggle between various popes and Holy Roman Emperors in the eleventh century. Matilda, an heiress, actively supported the popes, and when the Investiture Crisis (a particularly intense conflict between Pope Gregory VII and Emperor Henry IV) erupted in the 1070s, she allowed Pope Gregory to come to her castle at Canossa. Matilda thus ended up hosting one of the most dramatic events in medieval history in which Henry IV, excommunicated by the pope, was forced to come and beg for forgiveness and readmission into the church. When Pope Urban II asked her, at the age of 43, to marry one of the contenders to the German throne, Matilda did so, despite the fact that it immediately embroiled her in warfare.[71] Few medieval women had as much power as Matilda of Tuscany or Queen Philippa of England, yet their stories were replicated on a smaller scale by noblewomen who pleaded with their husbands on behalf of poor tenants and with their husbands' enemies in the hope of releasing their husbands from capture or gaining more favorable political terms.

The work of noblewomen was in many ways less visible than that of peasant women or townswomen in that they did not produce much that could be seen or touched. Even though her husband might claim that her work was minimal, a peasant woman could point to her ale, her spinning, the meals she cooked, and the wages she made as tangible results of her labors. A noblewoman, on the other hand, was primarily a manager. She managed the household, managed the estate in her husband's absence, managed the lives of her children (and, on occasion, her husband), and managed the relationship between her family and its community.

No matter what their social status, therefore, women's role as workers in medieval Europe was characterized by its busyness. Women seldom had the luxury to work at one task for long periods. Instead, they found themselves juggling multiple demands and patching together incomes from multiple sources. Status certainly played a large role in determining what types of work a medieval woman would be expected to perform and how pleasant or unpleasant her tasks might be, but it made little difference to the overall, hectic character of a woman's day.

NOTES

1. Simon Mays, "Wharram Percy: The Skeletons," *Current Archaeology* 193 (Aug. 2004): 45–49.

2. *Women in England, c. 1275–1525*, ed. and trans. P.J.P. Goldberg (Manchester: Manchester University Press, 1995), 169–70. I have edited this text further.

3. Barbara A. Hanawalt, *The Ties that Bound: Peasant Families in Medieval England* (New York: Oxford University Press, 1986), 175–76.

4. Hanawalt, *The Ties that Bound*, 178–79.

5. *Women's Lives in Medieval Europe: A Sourcebook*, ed. Emilie Amt (New York: Routledge, 1993), 182.

6. *Husbandry* ch. 19 in *Walter of Henley and other Treatises on Estate Management and Accounting*, ed. Dorothea Oschinsky (Oxford, 1971), 427. This text is often attributed to Walter of Henley.

7. Sandy Bardsley, "Women's Work Reconsidered: Gender and Wage Differentiation in Late Medieval England." *Past and Present* 165 (November 1999), 3–29.

8. Mercedes Borrero Fernández, "Peasant and Aristocratic Women: Their Role in the Rural Economy of Seville at the End of the Middle Ages," in *Women at Work in Spain: From the Middle Ages to Early Modern Times*, ed. Marilyn Stone and Carmen Benito-Vessels (New York: Peter Lang, 1998), 11–31, at 15.

9. E. Perroy, "Wage Labour in France in the Later Middle Ages," *Economic History Review* 2nd ser, 8 (1955–6).

10. Judith M. Bennett, *Ale, Beer, and Brewsters: Women's Work in a Changing World, 1300–1600* (New York: Oxford University Press, 1996), 19.

11. Bennett, *Ale, Beer, and Brewsters*, 19.

12. Bennett, *Ale, Beer, and Brewsters*, 27.

13. Bennett, *Ale, Beer, and Brewsters*, 77–97.

14. Frances M. Biscoglio, "'Unspun Heroes': Iconography of the Spinning Woman in the Middle Ages," *Journal of Medieval and Renaissance Studies* 25, 2 (Spring 1995), 159–76 at 167.

15. Henrietta Leyser, *Medieval Women: A Social History of Women in England 450–1500* (London: Phoenix Press, 1995), 152.

16. Judith M. Bennett, *A Medieval Life: Cecilia Penifader of Brigstock, c. 1295–1344* (Boston: McGraw Hill College, 1999), esp. 79–82, 91–93.

17. Fernández, "Peasant and Aristocratic Women," 13.

18. Judith M. Bennett, *Women in the Medieval English Countryside: Gender and Household in Brigstock before the Plague* (New York: Oxford University Press, 1987), 279, n. 10.

19. *Women's Lives in Medieval Europe*, ed. Amt, 183.

20. Christine de Pisan, *A Medieval Woman's Mirror of Honor: The Treasury of the City of Ladies*, trans. Charity Cannon Willard, ed. Madeleine Pelner Cosman (New York: Persea, 1989), 219–21.

21. *Women in England*, ed. Goldberg, 167–68.

22. Madonna J. Hettinger, "*So Strategize:* The Demands in the Day of the Peasant Woman in Medieval Europe," in *Women in Medieval Western European Culture*, ed. Linda Mitchell (New York: Garland, 1999), 47–64.

23. Mays, "Wharram Percy: The Skeletons," 49.

24. Susan Mosher Stuard, "Ancillary Evidence for the Decline of Medieval Slavery," *Past and Present* 149 (November 1995), 3–28; Susan Mosher Stuard, "Single by Law and Custom," in *Singlewomen in the European Past, 1250–1800*, ed. Judith M. Bennett and Amy M. Froide (Philadelphia: University of Pennsylvania Press, 1999), 106–26.

25. Maryanne Kowaleski, "Women's Work in a Market Town: Exeter in the Late Four-teenth Century," in *Women and Work in Preindustrial Europe*, ed. Barbara A. Hanawalt (Bloomington: Indiana University Press, 1986), 145–64 at 148.

26. Christiane Klapisch-Zuber, "Women Servants in Florence during the Fourteenth and Fifteenth Centuries," in *Women and Work in Preindustrial Europe*, ed. Hanawalt, 56–80 at 61.

27. *Women in England*, 95–96.

28. *Women in England*, 94–95.

29. *Women in England*, 94.

30. Kathryn L. Reyerson, "Women in Business in Medieval Montpellier," in *Women and Work in Preindustrial Europe*, ed. Hanawalt, 117–44 at 120–21.

31. Jennifer Ward, *Women in Medieval Europe 1200–1500* (Harlow, U.K.: Longman, 2002), 85–86.

32. Maryanne Kowaleski and Judith M. Bennett, "Crafts, Gilds, and Women in the Middle Ages: Fifty Years after Marian K. Dale," in *Sisters and Workers in the Middle Ages*, ed. Judith M. Bennett et al. (Chicago: University of Chicago Press, 1989), 11–39.

33. Kowaleski and Bennett, "Crafts, Gilds, and Women in the Middle Ages."

34. Maryanne Kowaleski, *Local Markets and Regional Trade in Medieval Exeter* (New York: Cambridge University Press, 1995), 133–36.

35. Bennett, *Ale, Beer, and Brewsters*, 31–32.

36. The National Archives: Public Record Office, London, SC 2 156/1–7.

37. Grethe Jacobsen, "Women's Work and Women's Role: Ideology and Reality in Danish Urban Society, 1300–1550," *Scandinavian Economic History Review* 31:1 (1983), 3–20, at 17.

38. Bennett, *Ale, Beer, and Brewsters*, 122–44; Angeliki E. Laiou, "Women in the Marketplace of Constantinople, 10th–14th Centuries," in *Byzantine Constantinople: Monuments, Topography and Everyday Life*, ed. Nevra Necipoğlu (Leiden, The Netherlands: Brill, 2001), 261–73 at 263.

39. Kowaleski, "Women's Work in a Market Town," 148–49; The National Archives: Public Record Office, London, SC2 156/5.

40. Jacobsen, "Women's Work and Women's Role," 11.

41. David Herlihy and Christiane Klapisch-Zuber, Census and Property Survey of Florentine Domains in the Province of Tuscany, 1427–1480. Machine readable data file. Online Catasto of 1427 Version 1.2. Online Florentine Renaissance Resources: Brown University, Providence, RI, 1999.

42. Diane Hutton, "Women in Fourteenth Century Shrewsbury," in *Women and Work in Pre-Industrial England*, ed. Lindsey Charles and Lorna Duffin (London: Croon Helm, 1985), 83–99.

43. Jacobsen, "Women's Work and Women's Role," 12–13.

44. David Herlihy, *Opera Mulebria: Women and Work in Medieval Europe* (Philadelphia: Temple University Press, 1990), 169.

45. Marian K. Dale, "The London Silkwomen of the Fifteenth Century," reprinted in *Sisters and Workers in the Middle Ages*, ed. Judith M. Bennett et al. (Chicago: University of Chicago Press, 1989), 26–38 at 27.

46. Laiou, "Women in the Marketplace of Constantinople," 262; Ward, *Women in Medieval Europe*, 88–90.

47. Herlihy, *Opera Mulebria*, 178.

48. Ward, *Women in Medieval Europe*, 56–57, 98–99. A translation of the ordinance may be found in *Ages of Woman, Ages of Man: Sources in European Social History, 1400–1750*, eds. Monica Chojnacka and Merry E. Wiesner-Hanks (London: Longman, 2002), 8–10.

49. Christiane Klapisch-Zuber, *Women, Family, and Ritual in Renaissance Italy* (Chicago: University of Chicago Press, 1985), 132–64.

50. Leah L. Otis, "Municipal Wetnurses in Fifteenth Century Montpellier," in *Women and Work in Preindustrial Europe*, 83–93.

51. Herlihy, *Opera Mulebria*, 113, 146–47.

52. Deborah Parker, "Women in the Book Trade in Italy, 1475–1620," *Renaissance Quarterly* 49:3 (1996), 509–41, at 525, 527.

53. Mark Angelos, "Urban Women, Investment, and the Commercial Revolution of the Middle Ages," in *Women in Medieval Western European Culture*.

54. Marjorie K. McIntosh, "The Benefits and Drawbacks of *Femme Sole* Status in England, 1300–1630," *Journal of British Studies* 44 (2005), 410–38.

55. Sharon Farmer, "'It is not good that [wo]man should be alone': Elite Responses to Singlewomen in High Medieval Paris," in *Singlewomen in the European Past*, 82–105.

56. Kowaleski, "Women's Work in a Market Town."

57. Bonnie S. Anderson and Judith P. Zinsser, *A History of Their Own: Women in Europe from Prehistory to the Present*, rev. ed. (New York: Oxford University Press, 2000), 289.

58. "The Rules of Saint Robert Grosseteste," Andy Staples, 2002. Available online at http://www.uwm.edu/~carlin/doc.grossetesterules.htm

59. Christine de Pisan, *Treasury of the City of Ladies*, 171–73.

60. Fernández, "Peasant and Aristocratic Women," 24.

61. *Women's Lives in Medieval Europe*, ed. Amt, 166–68.

62. Christine de Pisan, *Treasury of the City of Ladies*, 169.

63. *The Paston Letters: A Selection in Modern Spelling*, ed. Norman Davis (Oxford: Oxford University Press, 1963), 13–14.

64. Janet L. Nelson, "Medieval Queenship," in *Women in Medieval Western European Culture*, 193.

65. Amy Livingstone, "Powerful Allies and Dangerous Adversaries: Noblewomen in Medieval Society," in *Women in Medieval Western European Culture*, 20.

66. Ward, *Women in Medieval Europe*, 121; Christine Owens, "Noblewomen and Political Activity," in *Women in Medieval Western European Culture*, 215.

67. *Paston Letters*, 24.

68. Jennifer C. Ward, "English Noblewomen and the Local Community in the Later Middle Ages," in *Medieval Women in their Communities*, ed. Diane Watt (Toronto: University of Toronto Press, 1997), 186–203.

69. Alice-Mary Talbot, "Building Activity in Constantinople Under Andronikos II: The Role of Women Patrons in the Construction and Restoration of Monasteries," in *Byzantine Constantinople*, ed. Necipoğlu, 329–43.

70. Kimberly A. LoPrete, "The Gender of Lordly Women: The Case of Adela of Blois," in *Studies on Medieval and Early Modern Women: Pawns or Players?* eds. Christine Meek and Catherine Lawless (Dublin: Four Courts Press, 2003), 90–110.

71. Patricia Skinner, *Women in Medieval Italian Society 500–1200* (Harlow, U.K.: Longman, 2001), 136–38.

SUGGESTED READING

Bennett, Judith M. *Ale, Beer, and Brewsters: Women's Work in a Changing World, 1300–1600.* New York: Oxford University Press, 1996.

Bennett, Judith M., et al. eds. *Sisters and Workers in the Middle Ages.* Chicago: University of Chicago Press, 1989.

Bennett, Judith M. *Women in the Medieval English Countryside: Gender and Household in Brigstock before the Plague.* New York: Oxford University Press, 1987.

Charles, Lindsey and Lorna Duffin, eds. *Women and Work in Pre-Industrial England.* Dover, N.H.: Croon Helm, 1989.

Goldberg, P.J.P. *Women, Work, and Life Cycle in a Medieval Economy: Women in York and Yorkshire c.1300–1520.* New York: Oxford University Press, 1992.

Hanawalt, Barbara A., ed. *Women and Work in Preindustrial Europe.* Bloomington: Indiana University Press, 1986.

Herlihy, David. *Opera Mulebria: Women and Work in Medieval Europe.* Philadelphia: Temple University Press, 1990.

Mitchell, Linda E., ed. *Women in Medieval Western European Culture.* New York: Garland, 1999.

Stone, Marilyn and Carmen Benito-Vessels, eds. *Women at Work in Spain: From the Middle Ages to Early Modern Times.* New York: Peter Lang, 1998.

Ward, Jennifer C. *English Noblewomen in the Later Middle Ages.* New York: Longman, 1992.

3

⸺⸙⸺

Women and the Family

When medieval commentators divided men into separate groups, they usually classified them according to their social status. Advice literature, for instance, might be addressed to nobles, townsmen, and peasants. But when commentators discussed women, they sorted them instead according to their marital status: typically virgin, wife, or widow. Marital status was one of the most salient parts of a woman's identity. This chapter examines six familial roles of women: girl, adolescent maiden, lifelong single woman, married woman, mother, and widow. Each of these stages offered both advantages and limitations for women.

GIRLS

Historians' views of medieval children—both male and female—have changed considerably since the middle of the twentieth century. In 1960, the French historian Philippe Ariès published a highly influential book entitled *Centuries of Childhood: A Social History of Family Life.* Ariès argued that childhood as a concept did not actually emerge until the early modern era and that medieval people did not see children as a separate category. Rather, he argued, they were seen as miniature adults. He also argued that medieval children encountered little love and affection from their parents, due in large part to high infant mortality rates which made parents cautious about investing too much love in a baby who might not survive infancy. Ariès's study was highly influential—it is still cited in sociology and psychology texts, for instance—but it was based on very partial evidence. Ariès looked particularly, for instance, at paintings of family groups in which children were often painted as smaller versions of their parents. More recent historians, examining a wider array of sources, have largely debunked Ariès's theory. Dhuoda's manual, for instance, discussed in chapter 5, demonstrates a mother's deep and genuine concern for both her older son, William, and her younger son, taken away from her before he was even named. Coroners' rolls record mothers who died from smoke inhalation while searching for their children in fires, quite in contrast to the callous parents suggested by Ariès. Toys for children found in archaeological digs and illustrated in manuscripts show that adults invested time creating playthings for their children. And theoretical discussions of the so-called ages of man acknowledged the role of childhood as they divided human life into separate stages, including infancy (from birth until age seven), childhood (from age 7 to 12 or 14), and adolescence (from 12 or 14 until marriage or, in some cases, until age 21). The specific ages relating to each stage sometimes varied according to context, yet the very fact that the categories existed helps to discredit Ariès's thesis. Examination of a broader array of evidence thus suggests that medieval children were indeed loved, nurtured, and seen as separate from adults.

While medieval children, on the whole, were welcomed and loved, there was often a difference between the treatment of male and female children, even from babyhood. The nursery rhyme that claims girls to be made from "sugar and spice and all things nice" (in contrast to boys, made from "frogs and snails and puppy dogs' tails") comes from a later era. However, medieval people, like their descendents, viewed boys and girls as inherently different, made from different substances. Some medieval scholars, in fact, regarded girls as the result of weaker or damaged sperm, while boys resulted from sperm produced by men at their most virile. Even in infancy, distinctions were drawn between babies on the basis of their sex. At baptism, boys were placed on the right side of the priest (the side considered more holy and important) while girls were placed on his left. The system of primogeniture, under which the oldest son inherited his father's land (and, in the case of the nobility, often his title too), meant that boys were often welcomed more warmly than girls. Among the peasantry, girls were likely to bring less money into the household and would almost certainly leave the family home once they married. Among the nobility, they represented a future cost in the form of a dowry. Female babies were thus more likely than males to be abandoned and their infant mortality rates were sometimes higher, suggesting that boys were given greater care. Girls constituted about 57 percent of foundling babies admitted to the Florentine hospital of Santa Maria degli Innocenti in the fifteenth century, for instance. They also constituted 79 percent of Innocenti babies dying from intestinal diseases and 61 percent of those dying of malnutrition or starvation.[1] Indeed, the sex ratio among children in fifteenth-century Italy shows a predominance of boys: in some places, boys of a particular age outnumbered girls of the same age by as much as two to one.[2] Girls were similarly underrepresented among ninth-century French peasants and among fourteenth- and fifteenth-century Londoners.[3] Perhaps the Florentines, Londoners, and French peasants were following similar advice to that contained in a late medieval Icelandic saga: "If you bear a girl, you must expose it [leave it outside to die]; but if the child is a boy, you shall rear him."[4] Or perhaps girls were not, in general, given the same degree of care as boys. In both Italy and England, girls were typically breastfed for a shorter period and hence often had difficulty digesting solid foods. Even when richer townspeople employed private wet nurses, boys were favored: Florentine boys were more likely to be wetnursed at home (a more expensive practice) than sent to the countryside and were nursed, on average, a month and a half longer than their sisters.[5] Attitudes toward female babies were not always negative, by any means: girls helped their mothers around the house, and their marriages could cement alliances between families. Indeed, too many boys, each requiring some means of livelihood without detracting from that of their older brothers, could prove a problem in terms of family strategy too. Some families, then, may have been glad to learn that their new arrivals were girls rather than boys. In general, however, the reverse was true: girls entered a world in which their sex automatically cast them as inferior and less wanted.

Differences between the treatment of boys and girls continued beyond babyhood. Even by as young as two or three, the day-to-day activities of girls differed from those of boys. One of our best primary sources for insights into how children (especially peasant children) spent their day comes from the coroners' rolls that record accidental deaths. These show that girls were most likely to be killed in accidents around the house, helping their mothers prepare food, do laundry, or draw water. In 1271, for instance, three-year-old Annora, daughter of Agnes Oter, followed her mother outside their house in Edworth, England, while her mother was looking for firewood. Annora fell into a ditch and drowned.[6] Little boys, on the other hand, were more likely to be killed watching their fathers work in the fields, chop wood, or carry out other heavy tasks. As children grew, these differences became even more marked. Boys aged 6 to 12 often worked outside the home, either helping their fathers or bringing in some extra income. They met with accidental deaths through fishing, herding animals, and running errands. Girls of this age, on the other hand, continued to work mostly within the context of the household, minding younger children, fetching water, and helping with cooking and laundry.[7]

While peasant children were trained to help their parents from an early age, children of the nobility typically began a more formal training around the age of seven. Whereas mothers were previously responsible for the moral education of both boys and girls, fathers often oversaw a boy's education from the age of seven onward. Girls remained, however, under the tutelage of their mothers. From this point onward, the ways in which boys and girls were treated began to differ more markedly. Boys were more likely than girls to be beaten as part of the educational process. Tutors and schoolmasters were often depicted with rods or birches, whipping unfortunate schoolboys who neglected to learn their lessons. Corporal punishment was certainly inflicted on girls from time to time, too, but not in the same routine way. The substance of education varied according to sex, too. Boys were far more likely to be taught skills of basic literacy, along with physical training in the arts of warfare. Girls, on the other hand, received a more practical education in how to run a noble household. They were taught to order provisions, supervise servants, receive guests hospitably, and perhaps embroider or sew.

Even at the level of the nobility, however, girls were less likely than their brothers to receive a formal education. By the later Middle Ages, many girls were taught basic skills of reading, addition, and subtraction in order to help them oversee the household accounts. As chapter 5 discusses, images of St. Anne teaching the Virgin Mary to read often served as a model for noblewomen instructing their daughters. Girls were less often taught how to write, however: whereas reading and writing are usually taught simultaneously today, they were taught as separate skills in the Middle Ages. Letter writers such as Margaret Paston often dictated their messages to scribes rather than relying on their own handwriting. Moreover, girls were most often taught to read only the vernacular languages, while the more formal Latin was reserved for boys. The education given to noble girls was thus different from that of many boys, but it was sufficient for the roles expected of them as they grew into adulthood.

Girls sent at a young age to board in nunneries were more likely to pick up some rudimentary Latin, but these were the exception to the rule: even most nuns were regarded as illiterate, which in the medieval sense meant that they were unable to read or write Latin. When a cleric translated some of the records of Godstow Abbey (England) into English in the mid-fifteenth century, he explained that he did so because "women of religion . . . [were] excused of great understanding" in reading books written in Latin since it was not their mother tongue. Since these nuns did not have "truly learned men" always available to interpret for them, their records thus needed to be translated.[8] Some of the powerful abbesses of the early Middle Ages, discussed in chapter 1, both read and wrote in Latin and encouraged their charges to do the same. Members of the royal family in the Holy Roman Empire, for instance, founded and headed the nunneries of Gandersheim, Quedlinburg, and Gernrode. In the ninth to eleventh centuries, girls educated at such nunneries could gain an impressive education. The works of

Hroswita, product of the nunnery at Gandersheim, show that she expected her audience not only to understand the Latin in which she wrote her plays but also to appreciate her discourses on arithmetic, musical harmony, and other more advanced subjects.[9] As the power of abbesses waned, however, less emphasis was placed on education.

Whereas formal education was often thought unnecessary for girls, moral education was important for all. By the late Middle Ages, especially, vernacular religious and didactic texts abounded, and many of these would have been read aloud in noble households or transformed into sermons in church. While some of these texts were addressed to both men and women, others focused on behavioral expectations for one sex or the other. In the late fourteenth century, for instance, the French knight Geoffrey de la Tour Landry compiled a book for his daughters in which he retold moral stories from the Bible, sermons, chronicles, and other sources intended for their edification. The *Book of the Knight of the Tower* became popular throughout both France and England in the late Middle Ages. Other household reading included excerpts from *commonplace books*, books into which people copied a variety of texts that interested them. The Digby Manuscript of the late thirteenth century, for instance, included prayers, short accounts of saints' lives, fables, moral stories, and poems. Similar collections also included proverbs and nursery rhymes. Poems and advice texts from commonplace books might be aimed specifically at girls and women, too. The English poem "How the Good Wife Taught Her Daughter," for instance, found its way into such commonplace books and may have been read aloud in households of the gentry or—as one scholar has argued—of the aspiring urban bourgeoisie.[10] It instructs women in such practical matters as managing their servants, along with moral injunctions to give tithes to the church and honor their husbands. Very similar messages were sent by the German poem "Good Conduct for a Young Lady," in which a mother-narrator tells her daughter to be subservient to her husband, avoid gossip, speak kindly and softly, manage her servants with care, attend church regularly, and more.[11] And, as chapter 5 discusses, Christine de Pisan's conduct books for women provide an exhaustive survey of appropriate female behavior in multiple contexts. Poems aimed at boys and men, on the other hand, tended to focus more on proper manners in public and honorable behavior around other men. In fact, as some scholars have noted, the very way in which conduct literature was written differed according to its primary audience. Authors writing conduct manuals for girls provided more concrete tangible examples and fewer abstract ideas. They also assumed that girls would absorb the messages through listening to works read aloud rather than reading them individually. Thus many conduct-related poems for girls included refrains and catchy summaries, compared with poems for boys. Moral education thus differed both in format and in message.[12]

Despite Ariès's claims, scholarship on medieval children, both boys and girls, demonstrates that considerable care went into their upbringing. Indeed, the close attention paid to crafting messages for girls about how to behave properly and uphold family honor shows that childrearing was taken seriously. Girls were certainly taught from a young age that their role in society was inferior to that of their brothers, but they were not—on the whole—neglected. Instead they learned that good behavior was important and that poor behavior had the potential to shame not only themselves but their families as a whole.

MAIDENS

Messages about family honor and shame were reinforced as girls grew into young women. Medieval people referred to this stage of life as maidenhood, a time of potential perfection yet also vulnerability. Virgins appeared as idealized characters in literature, echoing the perfection of the Virgin Mary. Yet their post-pubertal status also suggested the potential for sexual activity, and strong messages were sent to girls by families and church alike about the evils of sexual dalliance. How seriously these messages were taken depended in part on the social status of the maidens and the extent of personal freedom they exercised. Young peasant women who migrated to towns, for instance, away from the oversight of family and friends, were more likely to end up pregnant than their sisters in the countryside.

For young women of all social statuses, entry into maidenhood often meant a shift out of the family home. Women of peasant status frequently took the position of servants in the households of other peasant families or in nearby towns. Rarely they might enter craft apprenticeships, although the vast majority of apprentices were boys. Among the nobility, girls were often sent to other noble households as a kind of apprenticeship for noble marriage, just as boys were sent to other households for knightly training. There, along with other girls their own age, they would refine their skills of embroidery and courtly behavior and serve as ladies-in-waiting to the lady of the household. Such positions were not always welcomed by girls: in the early sixteenth century, Dorothy Plumpton was sent as a teenager to the household of Lady Darcy at Birkin, about 25 miles from her father's house. She found herself terribly homesick, however, and wrote her unsympathetic father repeated letters begging him to let her come home.[13] Along with this movement outside the family household—whether willing or unwilling—often came a degree of financial and even legal independence. Young women of richer peasant families could begin to accumulate small pieces of property, often the gifts of their parents. Cecilia Penifader of Brigstock (c. 1295–1344), for instance, first acquired small plots of land from the age of about 20. Responsibilities accompanied this new property: since

Cecilia became a tenant of the local lord, she was required to attend regular court sessions.[14]

Once they hit puberty, young women and men of the nobility were likely to find themselves confined largely to separate spaces. For example, whereas the children of the fourteenth-century English prince John of Gaunt shared a bedroom until his eldest daughter reached puberty, they slept separately thereafter.[15] Wealthy households had rooms set aside for women, separate from those for men, and medieval romances attest to the lengths to which young men and women had to go in order to meet illicitly. Among peasants and poorer townspeople, separation of the sexes was less possible because of space constraints. Even so, a daughter of peasants or artisans might find that she was guarded more closely by her parents as she approached puberty.

In England, a young woman might be encouraged to join a maidens' guild, a group of young women who gathered together to raise money for candles in their local church or perform other works of devotion. Maidens' guilds, often dedicated to the Virgin Mary, were generally run by the young women themselves. As chapter 1 explains, women participating in maidens' guilds (or the corresponding wives' guilds) benefited not only from the opportunity to socialize with one another but also from the chance to enhance their own status by supporting the local church. In the English parish of Morebath, for instance, the maidens' guild (along with the young men's guild) raised money to replace a stolen chalice. The names of contributors were recorded, indicating that they were probably read aloud in church. Maidens' guilds also participated in feast days and celebrations: in the parish of St. Martin's in Leicester, they formed part of the Whitsunday procession, and in the parish of St. Mary at Hill in London, they observed St. Barnabas Day by selling garlands of roses. Maidens were especially prominent in May Day celebrations and Hocktide festivals (discussed in chapter 1). Although parish officials seem to have kept a close eye on the activities of maidens' guilds, they nonetheless provided an opportunity for peer socialization, fun, and a degree of autonomy.[16]

Advice literature reflects an overwhelming concern that maidens protect their virginity and behave devoutly. As chapter 1 explains, the term *virginity* was often interpreted more broadly to mean not only sexual chastity but also a more general purity. *True virginity*, according to commentators like the fifteenth-century moralizer John Mirk, involved restraint in speech as well as sexual behavior. As he explained in one sermon,

[A] maiden is of little worth who cannot suffer any oppression nor any diseases, without complaining; and is a clatterer, a jangler [gossip], a flyter [one who argues], a curser, a swearer, and a scold of her mouth. This does not defend maidenhood, but rather casts it down. Therefore a maiden must be of few words, and look that she speak with honesty and respect to her person, for it is an old English saw: "A maiden should be seen, but not heard."[17]

Other authors agreed: to be a true and proper maiden, one must not only refrain from sex but also be well-behaved and quiet. Christine de Pisan advised young unmarried women to use "good, simple, and devout" language, wear modest clothes, and keep their eyes lowered.[18]

At what age did maidens cease to be regarded as children and become viewed as adults? No easy answer exists. For boys, adulthood might be marked by the ability to swear a binding oath at the age of 12 or 14, entry into the frankpledge (a system in which adult English men were required to answer for one another's crimes) at the age of 12, or the ability to serve on a jury at the age of 15.[19] For girls, the age of majority was even less clear, although it was typically a few years younger than that of boys. Some jurisdictions, for instance, said that boys were of sufficient age to inherit property once they reached 21, while girls could inherit at 16. Other jurisdictions set the age of inheritance for boys at 14 and girls at 12. Ages of marriage presumed an earlier maturity for girls, too, and marriage may sometimes have served as a rite of passage into adulthood. In several European languages, the word for *wife* also meant adult woman: as in the German *frau,* the Spanish *mujer,* and the French *femme.*[20] Ages of consent to marry varied according to time and place, but most agreed that girls were able to marry from the age of 12, while boys could marry once they reached the age of 14. Since, in order to be legally married, a couple needed not only to exchange marriage vows but also to consummate the marriage by sexual intercourse, few noble marriages were binding until the woman was closer to 15. But there were exceptions: Margaret Beaufort, for instance, mother of the English king Henry VII, was married at the age of 12 and gave birth to the future king in 1455 at the age of 13. The tenth-century Godila, wife of Margrave Liuthar of the Northmarch, bore her son Werner at the same age. Margaret and Godila were unusual, however, since the age of menarche (first appearance of the menstrual period) was a little later in the Middle Ages than it is today. Most 12-year-old girls in the Middle Ages would not yet have reached physical maturity.

Marriages at such early ages were confined almost entirely to members of the nobility who used marriage as a means of forging or securing political alliances, and even most nobles delayed consummation until the woman was 15 or older. Many elite families seem to have treated young brides as more like older children than as adults: they were sometimes expected to live apart from their husbands for a few years and were provided with tutors or other caregivers.[21] Among peasants and townspeople, both men and women were typically older at marriage, so marriage may have served as more of a genuine coming-of-age marker. In the southern Mediterranean, women were usually married in their late teens to men who were a decade or more older than themselves, but even wives in their late teens were not always thought of as fully mature. In northern and western Europe, couples were typically closer in age, both being in their late teens to mid-twenties. Some research has suggested that women living in towns tended to delay marriage longer than those in the countryside, but more work needs to be done to establish the ubiquity of this pattern.[22] Marriage thus *could* serve as a marker of true adulthood, especially among the peasantry, but it did not necessarily do so. No single event marked coming of age for medieval women: rather, entry into adulthood was probably a more gradual transition.

Maidenhood was in many ways regarded as a perfect age for a woman, a stage of her life between the onset of physical maturity and the resumption of adult responsibilities (most particularly marriage and motherhood). A woman who was physically capable of sexual intercourse yet managed to keep her lust in check was seen as especially desirable. Depictions of women in poems such as the fourteenth-century *Pearl Maiden,* in narratives such as lives of virgin martyrs, or in visual representations such as manuscript illustrations of the Virgin Mary, focus on their youth. While the so-called perfect age of men was thought to be 33, the age of Jesus at the time of his death, social convention regarded the early to late teens as the correspondingly perfect age for a woman.[23]

LIFELONG SINGLE WOMEN

Some women—usually between 10 and 20 percent—remained single throughout their lives. These lifelong single women (as opposed to the life-cycle single women who would eventually marry) increased in number in the late Middle Ages and early modern era.[24] Although the proportions of single women to married women varied considerably over time and place, women were less likely to marry if they lived in northern or western Europe rather than the Mediterranean, and in towns rather than the countryside. The reasons behind this demographic trend are uncertain: some historians have hypothesized that women were more likely to stay single if they had an abundance of work options available, while others emphasize imbalanced sex ratios in late medieval towns resulting from female migration. The fourteenth-century Black Death, which killed over one-third of Europe's population, may have encouraged women to get married and have children, but it might also have had the opposite effect: fewer available workers meant a broader range of job opportunities for women, and a greater likelihood that women could support themselves independently without the support of a husband. While the underlying causes of the late medieval and early modern increase in single women are uncertain, they had an important impact on the overall population. In northern and western Europe, the population took almost two centuries to recover from the Black Death, and some demographers have suggested that much of this delay may have resulted from the increased number of women who remained unmarried. If a significant number of women never married, fewer children were born (some, of course, had illegitimate children, but these were generally fewer in number than the children produced in a marriage). Single women were usually poor and often marginal, yet their presence could have a dramatic impact on the population as a whole.

Regional variations in the proportions of lifelong single women can be seen by comparing data from Italy with that from northern Europe. In Italy, as in other southern Mediterranean countries, women married at a younger age and a smaller proportion stayed single throughout their lives. Among lay women aged 15 to 30 in the city of Prato in 1372, for instance, only 1.5 percent had never married. The proportions of single women increased slightly by the early fifteenth century: by 1427, women who had reached the age of 50 without marrying accounted for 5.4 percent of women in Prato, 3.8 percent of women in Florence, and 1.7 percent of women in rural areas of Tuscany (this data excludes nuns from the numbers of single women, since nuns tended to come primarily from the ranks of the elite and since they saw themselves as married to Christ). The Italian data, drawn from detailed tax records, is remarkably comprehensive; data for places elsewhere tends to be spottier and less reliable. As many as 31 percent of women may have been single, for instance, in the German city of Freiburg in 1447. Similarly, single women may have numbered as many as 41 percent of women in the French city of Reims in 1422 and 49 percent of women in the Swiss city of Zurich in 1467 (although some of these may have been widows rather than women who had never married). The figures for Freiburg, Reims, and Zurich include some women who were life-cycle rather than lifelong single women—that is to say, some of the women included in these counts would eventually marry—but chances are that the numbers remaining single were higher than those in Italy. In England, too, the proportions of single women are high: about 30 percent of women listed in the poll tax rolls from 1377 were single. This tax recorded the names of everyone aged 14 and older, so many of these women would have gone on to marry. Even so, the 30 percent of English women unmarried by the age of 14 is considerably higher than the 1.5 percent of women from Prato unmarried by 15 and probably reflects not only a higher age of marriage in England but also a larger number of women who never married.[25]

Imprecise statistics on lifelong single women reflect the fact that they were often regarded as invisible in medieval society. Single women were generally relegated to the most marginal occupations, such as prostitute, servant, or menial worker, and were very seldom mentioned in medieval sources. Tax records, usually one of the best primary sources for assessing demographic patterns, often omitted single women because their incomes were below the lowest threshold for paying tax. The records of charitable institutions sometimes make mention of single women, although they were more likely to help widows than women who had never married. Glimpses of single women can occasionally be seen in sources such as miracle stories associated with saints. Amelot of Chaumont, as mentioned in chapter 2, was a single woman who became paralyzed after moving from her hometown to St.-Denis (near Paris) in 1277. The miracle story tells of how her visit to the tomb of King Louis IX led to her miraculous cure, and it was recorded as part of the canonization proceedings that would make Louis a saint. For modern historians, however, the story is also interesting for what it reveals of Amelot's life: she traveled to the city along with two other young single women, and she relied on her companions and other single women to support her when she was disabled and transport her to the king's tomb. Had she not been paralyzed and miraculously cured, Amelot would have remained invisible to historians.[26] Probably there were many more Amelots in medieval Paris, London, Zurich, and elsewhere whose names were never recorded.

The reasons that some women remained single are also hard to gauge. Migrants to medieval towns and cities, like Amelot of Chaumont, encountered an imbalanced sex ratio and had fewer potential husbands among whom to choose. Others may have found that physical disabilities or poverty made it harder to gain a husband. Others still remained single by choice, whether because they strove to preserve their virginity for religious reasons or because their primary attachment was to women rather than men. Very little is known about medieval lesbians, and most commentators were more concerned about male homosexuality than female. Nonetheless, passing references in court cases, rules for convents, and penitentials (lists of sins with appropriate penances) show that lesbianism was not unknown. Hildegard of Bingen (1098–1179), for instance, condemned any "woman who takes up devilish ways and plays a male role coupling with another woman," while a ninth-century penitential prescribed three years of penance for "a woman who joins herself to another woman after the manner of fornication."[27] Whether or not they had sexual relationships, single women often cohabited. The phenomenon of so-called spinster clustering, in which several single women shared a house or, if especially poor, a room, helped them to survive in the constrained circumstances of a medieval town.

Lifelong single women were often among the poorest in medieval societies. As women, they earned lower wages than men, typically received smaller inheritance portions than their brothers, and had fewer opportunities to receive training that would help them gain better-paid jobs. Yet although contemporaries saw them as marginal and seldom mentioned them in surviving sources, their demographic impact could be considerable. Whether they remained unmarried by choice or as a result of circumstances, women who stayed unmarried had no children or fewer children than their married sisters, and over several centuries they could lower the birthrate, and hence the population, significantly. More research needs to be done to show why this happened particularly in countries in the north and west of Europe, such as England and Germany, while women in Mediterranean countries, such as Italy, very seldom stayed single.

MARRIED WOMEN

While a minority of women would indeed remain single throughout their lives, most married at least once. Since the average life expectancy was higher for a woman than for a man, in fact, many women married several times. The fictional Wife of Bath from Chaucer's *Canterbury Tales*, widowed five times and on the lookout for her sixth husband, was a caricature of this situation, yet many women did marry twice and some three times or more. Marriage was normative and expected at all social levels.

The legal aspects of marriage—the requirements for a legal marriage, the ability of women to choose their own marriage partners, and the provision of dowries and dowers—are discussed in chapter 4. How, though, might a woman's life change once she was married? While she yielded to her husband the right to control her own property, she simultaneously gained a degree of social esteem. Wives lacked legal authority, but they often gained moral and social authority. Thus theologians such as Thomas Chobham assumed that wives could influence the behavior of their husbands if they spoke to them gently, alluringly, and in the context of the bedchamber. Thomas seemed to think that women could take advantage of their husbands' lust to extract promises of devout conduct.[28] Similarly, Christine de Pisan urged wives of artisans and laborers to influence their husbands for the better. She advised artisans' wives to ensure that husbands' income exceeded their expenses and suggested that they warn their husbands against taking on commissions that could end up losing them money.[29] Laborers' wives were told to "encourage their husbands to prudence" in dealing honestly with their manorial lords.[30] Although married women were legally subject to their husbands, therefore, their relationships clearly involved some give and take.

To what extent was love important in a medieval marriage? This is difficult to measure from surviving sources. Certainly examples abound of husbands and wives who express love toward their partners and distress on their deaths. The Byzantine Emperor Justinian, for instance, was reputed to have sunk into depression after the death of his wife Theodora in the sixth century. Similarly, King Edward I of England was so distraught at the death of his wife Eleanor of Castile in the late thirteenth century that he built three tombs for her, one each for her entrails, heart, and body. He also ordered a cross to be erected at each place her body rested overnight on its journey from Harby (near Lincoln), where she died, to London. Margery Brews Paston (d. c. 1495) also expressed love for her husband, John Paston III. Prior to their marriage she told him in her letters that "my heart bids me ever more to love you truly over all earthly things," and during their marriage she addressed him as "my own sweet heart."[31] Some historians have tried to measure levels of affection between spouses by examining the language they use in their wills. A husband who refers to his wife as "most dear," for instance, might be supposed to love her greatly. The problem with this assumption is that wills were typically dictated to clerics or notaries and often followed the same format. A husband might tell the notary "my wife gets everything," for instance, and the notary might record, "I leave my property to my dearest wife." The language of affection thus becomes one of convention rather than sincere feeling. Historians have also measured changes in the numbers of husbands and wives choosing to be buried together, but again these changes might be affected by shifting social norms. A widow who entered a convent and chose to be buried there was not necessarily insulting her late husband. A third measure for examining marital affection is equally flawed: some historians have traced the numbers of husbands whose wills reduce the amount of money given to their widows if they remarry. A husband making such a stipulation may, in fact, be seeking to ensure that his love for his wife is matched by her lifelong loyalty. However, he might also be trying to protect the inheritance of their children (a widow who remarried and had more children could dilute the inheritance to the first husband's children by requiring that the property be split among more heirs).[32] One cannot, therefore, assume that medieval people necessarily experienced love in the same way as people today, but nor can we assume that they did not. Some medieval commentators regarded marital love as unimportant; others assumed that it arose after the couple was already married. Very few imagined that people fell in love before getting married.

The relationships between husbands and wives were probably affected somewhat by differences in their ages. Whereas wives and husbands in northwestern Europe were typically of a similar age, men in Mediterranean regions were often a decade or more older than their wives. Records from fifteenth-century Florence, for example, show that men were, on average, 13 years older than their wives. Similar patterns have been found in southeastern France and in Ragusa (now Dubrovnik, in modern Croatia).[33] Such gaps sometimes resulted in men treating their wives more like younger sisters or daughters than partners. The anonymous fourteenth-century author known as the Ménagier (or householder) of Paris reflects something of this tone in the manual he wrote for his wife:

> Dear Sister, At the age of fifteen years, in the week that you and I were wed, you asked me to be indulgent to your youth and to your small and ignorant service, until you had seen and learned more; to this end you promised that you would give me all heed and would be very careful and diligent to keep my love; you spoke full wisely, and, I am sure, with wisdom other than your own, beseeching me humbly in our bed, I remember, for the love of God, not to correct you harshly before strangers or before our own people, but rather each night, or from day to day, in our chamber, to remind you of unseemly or foolish things done in the day or days past, and chastise you, if it pleased me, and then you would strive to amend yourself according to my teaching and correction, and to serve my will in all things, as you said.[34]

The Ménagier goes on to outline how his young wife should live a devout life; how to run his household, oversee servants, order provisions; and how to amuse herself with appropriate games and pastimes. The way in which he addresses his wife reflects the fact that their relationship is not one between equals but rather that of a middle-aged man instructing a wife barely out of childhood. When an older man married a younger woman, as was the case with the Ménagier and his wife, social norms that posited men as authority figures could remain intact.

Relationships between spouses of similar ages may have been closer to a partnership than relationships in which the man was older. Letters from English wives to their husbands reflect, on the whole, a more confident tone as they send advice and request provisions. Wives such as Margery Kempe, who dictated her autobiography in the early fifteenth century, show that wives could strike deals with their husbands to get what they wanted. Margery wished to become celibate, and she bargained that she would pay her husband's debts (from money left to her by her father) if he agreed to a chaste marriage. On the other hand, Margery's ability to exercise power within her marriage should not be overemphasized: she had already had 14 children when this agreement was forged. While women of similar ages to their spouses may indeed have had a little more power than women who were much younger than their husbands, they still lagged far behind any ideal of equality. Medieval law, religion, and custom all sent the message that the husband was to rule over his wife and, as chapter 4 explains, most jurisdictions turned a blind eye to wife-beating except in the most egregious cases.

When a couple disrupted this social expectation that the man be the authority figure, they could find themselves subject to rituals of public humiliation. If an older woman married a younger man, or if a husband was reputed to be henpecked by a nagging wife or cuckolded by an adulterous wife, the couple faced considerable ridicule. Such couples could be visited (usually at night) by noisy villagers banging pot lids, singing rude songs, and generally making noise. In France, these rituals of shaming were known as *charivari;* in Italy, they were *scampanate* and *mattinata;* in Germany, *harberfeld-treiben, theirjagen,* and *katzenmusik,* and in England, *rough music, Skimmingtons,* or *the riding of the stang.* The precise format of these rituals varied over time and place. Often they involved a processional element, forcing a henpecked or cuckolded husband to ride a donkey or a horse or to pretend to ride on a pole or cart. Ridiculed husbands were frequently forced to ride facing backwards, symbolizing the notion that they were turning the expected gender order upside down through their passive behavior. The ritual might end with villagers throwing dung or rotten fruit at the aberrant couple or dunking them in water. Images from woodcarvings, woodcuts, and engravings celebrate such scenes of public humiliation. They also appear in plays, some of which cast Joseph as the cuckolded husband after Mary becomes pregnant with Jesus.[35] The expected and normal relationship was thus one in which husbands exercised authority over their wives, and couples whose relationships threatened this norm could face public censure.

Marriage was certainly an important legal institution, as discussed in chapter 4, but for many people the social convention of marriage mattered more than its legal status. Some, indeed, never became officially married but rather lived as husband and wife without the official blessing of the church or the law. Certainly the church strove to outlaw informal marriages and concubinage, especially between priests and their so-called wives, but it was never completely successful. Church lawyers generally agreed, in fact, that children of an informal marriage could usually be legitimized, as long as their fathers were members of the laity rather than priests. People who lacked significant property might therefore set up a household together without going through the ceremonies (and expenses) of a formal marriage. William, an Englishman living in Bologna in the late thirteenth century, for example, referred to his concubine Zoana as his wife and, even though he had not officially married her, had agreed not to marry anyone else. (Unfortunately he also considered that he had the husbandly prerogative to beat her.)[36] Such informal arrangements were less common among the nobility, although many noblemen had concubines in addition to their wives. Because marriages could serve as important diplomatic devices, and because heirs might inherit a significant amount of property, legitimacy was important. Family members tended to be involved in marriage preparations from the beginning, sending ambassadors to negotiate for good matches. Charles VI of France, for instance, when attempting to marry his daughter Katherine to Henry V of England in the early fifteenth century, tried to impress his English counterpart by sending 350 knights to the negotiations. Such delegations were often followed by meetings between the parents of the future spouses at which the details of marriage alliances might be hammered out. Especially among the upper ranks of the nobility, lavish feasts and gifts accompanied such meetings. Meetings between the future husband and wife were not necessarily essential to this process, and some young spouses did not meet until celebrations for the marriage itself were underway.[37] The process of making a marriage, along with its legal and social legitimacy, was thus more important among the top ranks of society.

Social class also correlated with the freedom to choose one's marital partner. Nobles typically had the least freedom of choice, since family members exerted strong pressure to make marriages that would benefit family status. Although the notion of a love match was not unknown, it tended to be frowned upon. For one thing, a child might marry someone who would hinder rather than help the family's status. Such was the case when the fifteenth-century Margery Paston mortified her socially aspirant family by marrying the Pastons' bailiff. For another, a love match implied intimacy between the couple and, with it, the risk that improper behavior had occurred. Although church law did recognize individuals' rights to consent to marry, familial pressure could make life very difficult for nobles who chose to exercise this right against the will of their families. Peasants and poorer townspeople typically faced fewer pressures from family members and enjoyed greater freedom to choose marital partners. In practice, however, many consulted with their parents and guardians before selecting a spouse.

Pressure from families and from society at large played an important role in determining the choice of partner and the appropriate ceremonies of marriage, and this pressure continued after a couple was married. No matter what their social class, couples were expected to stay married and produce children, since medieval church law did not, theoretically, allow for separation or divorce. Indeed, husbands and wives who lived separately were instructed by church courts to live together once more, even in situations of domestic violence (as chapter 4 explains, domestic violence was typically overlooked by medieval courts, unless the severity of the violence was considered excessive rather than reasonable). Yet some couples did break with the expected pattern by living apart or by engaging in chaste marriages (meaning that they did not have sexual relations with one another). It is unclear how often couples granted themselves unofficial divorces by choosing to live apart. Wills and maintenance agreements of fourteenth-century Venetian nobles, for instance, reveal a number of cases in which husbands and wives were living separately. In some situations, this separation resulted from violence or adultery and was accompanied by great bitterness; in others, the separation seems to have been relatively amicable.[38]

Chaste marriages were more complicated: officially, the church recognized separations only when both the husband and the wife agreed to abstain from sex in order to live religious lives. Such arrangements were present in Christianity almost from its very beginnings. As the position of priest was professionalized and became more important in the Christian church, the clergy were increasingly urged to refrain from marriage. Those who had married were instructed by various church authorities to abstain from sexual relations (although the many references to priests' children make it clear that this instruction was not often heeded). Married priests and their wives did not usually choose celibacy; rather, it was imposed on them. But other couples seem to have chosen this path voluntarily, either from the beginnings of their marriage or after having had children. During the last centuries of the Roman Empire, with its wavering population levels, young people faced pressure to marry from their families, from society at large, and even from the state, which penalized those who avoided marriage. Young Christians, heeding the advice of patristic authors such as Jerome and Augustine that virgins were more valuable in the eyes of God, thus sometimes entered into spiritual marriages in which both agreed in advance not to engage in sexual intercourse. Saints' lives and other biographies of religious people attest to multiple instances in which a young man or woman, forced into marriage, persuades his or her new spouse to remain chaste and to take a vow of celibacy. Such was the case for St. Cecilia, St. Æthelthryth, and Marie d'Oignies (one of the founders of the Beguines).[39] Others waited until later in life to vow celibacy, as evidenced above by Margery Kempe whose husband agreed to celibacy only after the births of their 14 children.

From the perspective of the church, celibate marriages might have been admirable. From the perspective of family members eager for heirs, however, they might have been alarming. Indeed, as far as family members were concerned, infertility might sometimes have been mistaken for celibacy and vice versa. Infertile couples often faced considerable pressure, while governments such as those of Florence provided tax incentives for large families (200 florins of tax exemption per child in 1427).[40] Guibert of Nogent, a monk who recorded his autobiography in the eleventh to twelfth centuries, explained the plight of his parents in the early years of their marriage. According to Guibert, his parents married very young and were initially incapable of consummating their marriage. Guibert attributed their inability to "magical arts" performed by his father's stepmother, who had wanted Guibert's father to marry one of her nieces. When, after three years, the couple had produced no children, the family of Guibert's father pressured him to divorce his wife (annulment would have been possible in this instance since the marriage had not been consummated and was thus not considered to be a true marriage). Guibert's father resisted, so the family turned their efforts to Guibert's mother:

[T]hey began to hound the girl herself, far away as she was from her kinsfolk and harassed by the violence of strangers, into voluntary flight out of sheer exhaustion under their insults, and without waiting for divorce. Meanwhile she endured all this, bearing with calmness the abuse that was aimed at her, and, if out of this rose any strife, pretending ignorance of it. Besides certain rich men perceiving that she was not in fact a wife, began to assail the heart of the young girl; but Thou, O Lord, the builder of inward chastity, didst inspire her with purity stronger than her nature or her youth.

Guibert's mother, having resisted the insults of his father's family and the advances of rich men, was vindicated when "that bewitchment was brought to naught" through the help of an old woman who knew about witchcraft. The couple was then able to have sex, and Guibert and his siblings were duly conceived.[41] Other couples were less fortunate in finding ways to lift the burden of infertility, and in most cases it was considered that fault lay with the woman rather than the man. Just as most women were expected to marry and become wives, most wives were expected to have children and become mothers.

MOTHERS

Motherhood was expected for most women, yet the experience of motherhood varied somewhat according to when and where a woman lived and the social class she occupied. For instance, the number of children a woman might expect during her lifetime could vary significantly. In addition, the extent of her involvement in the lives of her children was highly variable. Peasant mothers breastfed their children and cared for each child directly, although they might, if fortunate, receive help from other family members. Noblewomen, on the other hand, might have seen little of their children on a day-to-day basis, and their involvement in their children's lives might take the form of oversight rather than direct care.

Female fertility levels certainly varied. Prior to the year 1000, the diet of most women contained little iron: because the general standard of living was low, most families could afford to eat little meat and instead subsisted on vegetables and grains. The medieval agrarian revolution which began around the tenth century resulted in increased grain yields, which in turn allowed for the raising of more animals and a diet richer in iron. Female fertility levels thus increased and the number of children per fertile marriage rose significantly during the next few decades. While a fertile marriage in the early Middle Ages might produce two or three children (meaning that the population barely sustained itself), families in the high Middle Ages might consist of as many as six or seven children. At elite levels, the number of children per family could be even higher, since maternal diets were better and the use of wet nurses meant that mothers did not reap the contraceptive benefits of breastfeeding. Some noble families became quite large: Matrona, wife of Docibilus I of Gaeta (Italy) in the ninth to tenth centuries, had at least eight children, while her grandson and his wife were parents to nine or more.[42] Eleanor of Aquitaine had two children with Louis VII of France and a further eight with Henry II of England, while Eleanor of Castile, queen to Edward I of England, bore 16 children over 29 years. But townspeople and peasants might also have large families: Ugolino Martelli and his wife, citizens of Florence, had 14 children between 1435 and 1456, while the Penifader peasant family of late-thirteenth century Brigstock (England) consisted of at least eight children.[43] Within some towns and villages, the number of children correlated strongly with the family's wealth. In the English village of Halesowen in the late fourteenth and early fifteenth centuries, for instance, the richest peasant families produced an average of 3.6 children, the families of middling status had an average of 2.2 children, and the poorest couples averaged only 1.6 children.[44] Fifteenth-century Florentine families also varied in size according to wealth: the richest 1000 households contained a total of 873 children, while the poorest 1000 households had a total of 648 children among them.[45] Female fertility thus varied with social class, and this reflected, in part, the quality of women's diet.

Yet diet was not the only factor in predicting how many children a woman might have. Evidence suggests that medieval people knew more about contraception than we might expect. Granted, some contraceptive techniques would almost certainly have proven deficient. In the village of Montaillou in the French Pyrenees during the fourteenth century, for instance, Béatrice de Planissoles explained the efficacy of an unidentified herb wrapped in linen and placed at "the opening of [her] stomach" during lovemaking. According to her testimony, the priest with whom she had a lengthy affair told her that it would prevent conception. Yet whether through good fortune or through the priest's infertility (he seemed to have no children despite racking up dozens of illicit affairs), Beatrice did not conceive and her faith in the girdle was reinforced.[46] Ample evidence of coitus interruptus (in which the man withdraws from the woman before ejaculating) survives in medieval texts: although more effective than magic girdles, this practice is also notorious for its unreliability. Other medieval contraceptive techniques, however, were more reliable. Manuscripts from as early as c. 800 provide recipes for concoctions to "move the menses" for "women who cannot move themselves." In other words, the combination of herbs and spices they prescribed were sufficient to produce an abortion in a woman who was not long pregnant. Pregnant women today are urged to avoid large, regular quantities of certain herbs, such as rue, tansy, or pennyroyal, since these can lead to miscarriage: some medieval women, at least, were well aware of the effects of these herbs. Such a termination of pregnancy was not considered to be an abortion per se, since medieval people did not regard the fetus as a true entity until after the first three months. Until the child "quickened," or moved in the womb, it was not believed to have a soul, and first-trimester abortions were typically seen as no more sinful than taking herbs that would prevent pregnancy.[47] Surgical tools to induce early abortions survive from early medieval Byzantium, along with texts explaining their use. In some cases these were used to remove a fetus that had died in the womb and threatened the life of its mother; in other instances they were used to abort viable fetuses, although herbal concoctions remained more popular. People often assume that the medieval church and state were strongly opposed to abortion and contraception. In fact, it was not until 1803 that the first law against abortion was passed by the English parliament and not until 1869 that the Catholic church adopted the position that ensoulment began at conception rather than at the point when a fetus quickened or became recognizably human. Medieval people—at least some of them—knew about contraceptive methods and accepted them as part of family planning.[48]

Women who decided to go ahead with their pregnancies faced a daunting task, since childbirth in the Middle Ages was a considerably more daunting experience than it is today. Even the discomforts of pregnancy were lamented by medieval commentators, men and women alike. One thirteenth-century homilist, in an effort to dissuade young women from marriage, spelled out the woes of the pregnant woman:

> Your rosy face shall become lean and green as grass. Your eyes shall become dusky and underneath pale, and from the giddiness of your brain, your head aches. Within your belly, your swelling uterus bursts forth like a water bag. Your bowels hurt, pains are in your flanks, and always abundant in your loins, heaviness is in every limb. Your chest is burdened with your two breasts and the milk streams that trickle from you. All withers; your beauty is overthrown. Your mouth is bitter and everything you chew nauseous, and whatever your stomach disdainfully receives it, with dislike, throws it up again.

The prospect of childbirth in an era without anesthetics made the plight of the pregnant woman even worse. The homilist above continued by lamenting how pregnant women could not sleep due to their "anxiety about the torment of labor."[49] Surviving medical texts demonstrate very real concern for the suffering that women would experience in childbirth, and religious authors reminded people to honor their mothers for the pain experienced in labor.[50]

Childbirth was one of the few experiences faced similarly—if not identically—by women of all social classes. As Osbert of Clare, prior of

Westminster, put it in the twelfth century, "nor does the wife laden with gold and jewels conceive and give birth any differently in her palace than the poor and ragged woman in her hovel."[51] Osbert was right to an extent: not even the rich could avoid the pain of childbirth. But those with greater means could afford amulets, charms, and other devices that might have granted some psychological ease. Amulets often consisted of a rolled or folded piece of parchment containing texts of prayers, charms, or symbols such as the cross. Especially popular in late medieval France, England, and the Low Countries, texts were written either in Latin or in the vernacular. Most consisted of a single piece of parchment, folded or rolled tightly to make it more portable and easy to wear but also to hide it from the scrutiny of the clergy, who condemned the use of such quasi-magical devices as superstition. Some might be worn inside specially-made leather or linen pouches, while others were tied directly around a woman's belly or knee or slid next to her skin. The contents of the amulets themselves varied. Some, for instance, included charms thought to staunch the flow of blood. Some listed the names of the famous "Seven Sleepers of Ephesus" who were protected from persecution during the Roman era as they slept in a cave: the inclusion of these names was thought to help a pregnant or post-partum woman to get the sleep she needed. Amulet rolls also often included lists of powerful names, such as the variety of names by which Jesus or God might be called. Typically commissioned by noblewomen and wealthier townswomen, the texts of amulets sometimes promised relief from pain during childbirth. Although such promises were doubtless unfulfilled, the popularity of these devices shows that they must have offered some degree of comfort to women as they prepared to undergo a painful and dangerous experience.[52] In addition to amulets, relics associated with saints could sometimes help women in childbirth. As chapter 1 explains, books containing the legend of St. Margaret were thought to ease childbirth pains and ensure safe deliveries. Girdles (belts) purportedly worn by saints were also popular among the rich: Eleanor, wife of the thirteenth-century Henry III of England, took comfort from a girdle said to be that of the Virgin Mary, presented to Westminster Abbey by King Edward the Confessor.[53] Other women made pilgrimages while pregnant to sites associated with saints. Cecily Neville, Duchess of York in the fifteenth century, visited the famed shrine of the Virgin Mary at Walsingham in an effort to ensure an easier labor.[54] Pilgrimages were more difficult for poorer women, especially serfs, although they might well have used charms and spells passed on by word of mouth.

Osbert's claim that all women experienced childbirth in the same way regardless of social class might also be challenged by the physical conditions in which women gave birth. For the rich, birth took place in specially prepared birthing chambers to which a woman might withdraw for several weeks prior to and after delivery. These rooms were elaborately decorated

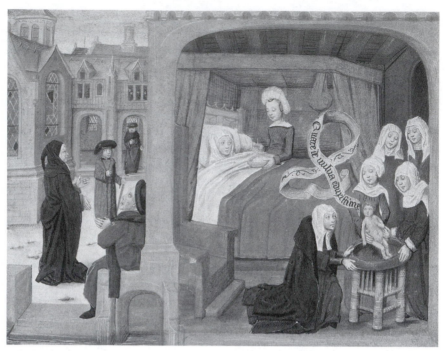

Women take care of a newborn baby and its mother in this fifteenth-century French manuscript illumination. © Bibliothèque de L'Arsenal, Paris, France/Archives Charmet/The
Bridgeman Art Library

and typically contained portable altars at which the pregnant woman would
pray. Christine de Pisan is particularly scornful about the extravagance of
birthing chambers prepared for mothers from rich merchant classes: from
Christine's perspective, the provision of ornate tapestries, silk pillows, fine
sheets, and embroidered rugs denoted immodesty and pride rather than
deserved comfort.[55] Birthing chambers served to seclude the expectant
mother: with the exception of priests, men were banned and mothers-to-be
were instead surrounded by friends, female servants, and—when the time
came—midwives. Poorer women, on the other hand, had little choice but
to work for as long as possible up until the beginnings of labor pains, and
their physical surroundings were far less pleasant.

Rich and poor alike remained mostly in the company of women throughout the labor and delivery. Surgeons and male doctors might be on hand
to attend to noblewomen if they ran into particular difficulties, but for the
most part childbirth was a woman's preserve. Caesarian sections were performed only when the mother had died or was about to die, since survival
was rare for either mother or child. The aim of the Caesarian in such cases
was twofold: to enable the child to be baptized, if it were to survive for any

time at all, so that it could be considered Christian, and to enable the dying mother to be blessed and cleaned so that she could be buried in consecrated ground. Midwives were also trained to administer emergency baptisms of infants who seemed unlikely to survive. Medieval views of contamination and pollution meant that stillborn infants and women dying with fetuses inside them were considered unclean and were thus unable to be buried in consecrated ground. One exception could be found at Büren, in Switzerland, where an image of the Virgin Mary was thought to have granted life to stillborn babies for sufficient time for them to be baptized: 250 skeletons of stillborn infants were found in recent excavations.[56]

The weeks following the birth also varied according to the social status of the mother. Among the rich, this period of lying-in was one in which new mothers might enjoy a well-earned rest of four to six weeks while other women cared for the baby. Rich Florentines sometimes hired a special servant, called a *guaradonna*, to care for the mother during her lying-in.[57] Even among poorer women, a period of bed-rest was expected, although economic necessity and the needs of older children may have forced her out of bed sooner. Mothers seldom, therefore, attended the baptisms of their children, which usually occurred within a week of the birth. Instead, new mothers were surrounded by other women; husbands, male relatives, and priests were kept away. Women of higher social statuses might expect to receive lavish gifts, both practical (such as the cape and pieces of damask cloth given to Lisa Guidetti by a female friend in 1483) and commemorative (such as a small painted plate known as a *desco da parto* often presented to postpartum Italian women).[58]

Among rich and poor alike, sexual intercourse was prohibited until the new mother had undergone the ceremony of churching or purification. Sex prior to purification was equated with sex during menstruation, and medieval scholars believed that sex during menstruation would result in the conception of a child with leprosy or deformities. The churching ceremony, derived from a Hebrew tradition, was one that cleansed the mother and welcomed her back into the community after the uncleanness of childbirth. For Christians, it echoed the Purification of the Virgin Mary, or Candlemas, an important medieval feast day occurring on February 2. For her own churching, a woman would finally emerge from the birthing chamber (if rich) or house (if poor) and be accompanied to the church by her female friends and relatives. Kneeling at the church door, she would be sprinkled with holy water by the priest. New mothers typically made offerings of candles in thanks for their safe delivery, and they sometimes sat in special pews. They were first to receive the blessed bread at the end of mass, and they joined the procession out of the church as the service ended. The ritual was subject to regional variations: a manuscript illustration from fifteenth-century France shows the woman led into the church by the priest by holding onto one end of his stole, enabling the priest to avoid touching the unclean woman, but it is unclear whether this practice took place elsewhere. Wealthier families followed the churching ceremony with a lavish feast to which they would invite those of high status and present guests with gifts. The lying-in period and the churching ceremony may be interpreted in two ways: on the one hand, they seem misogynous in excluding women from the Christian community immediately following childbirth and treating them as temporarily unclean or impure; on the other, however, they enabled a period in which a woman could take a break from her usual duties, enjoy the company of her friends, and participate in a ritual that focused attention on women. Whether imposed by men or encouraged by women, the ceremony of churching was popular particularly in the high to late Middle Ages, and it was clearly seen as important. Men and women alike often remembered churching ceremonies and feasts many years later: when called upon to attest to the age of an heir about to inherit land, many consciously recalled the purification of the heir's mother. In 1304, for instance, William de la Haye of Gloucestershire (England) remembered the purification feast for Maud, wife of Robert de Stallinge, 21 years earlier because he still resented the fact that he had not been invited.[59] People today sometimes have an image of medieval mothers giving birth in the fields then getting up immediately to resume work. Surviving sources, however, paint a different picture: although the length and degree of comfort enjoyed during lying-in varied by social class, all regarded it as a time in which women needed extra rest and consideration and as a time in which they should enjoy the company of other women.

Among the poor, especially, women were expected to breastfeed their children themselves. Wet nurses were certainly popular for the rich, although some commentators scorned women who sent their children to be wet-nursed, condemning them as unnatural mothers. Medical authors were uncertain about the substance of breast milk. Some saw it as purified blood that had been boiled, whitened, and sweetened in the mother's breasts. Some were concerned that the colostrum produced by a woman immediately after birth was not sufficiently purified and that a woman should hire a wet nurse until her milk came in (an unfortunate practice, since the colostrum is, in fact, particularly nutritious for a newborn). Most commentators insisted that the diet of a lactating mother or wet nurse be ample and free of spicy or bitter foods. Impure milk, it was believed, was the major cause of illness in the child.[60] On the other hand, pure breast milk could serve as a powerful symbol: especially by the late Middle Ages, recurrent images depicted the baby Jesus suckling at the breast of Mary, and nuns sometimes imagined themselves nursing him too. Jesus himself was even imagined as nursing his followers as a metaphor for spiritual nourishment. As Julian of Norwich (1342–c. 1416) described it, "The mother may give her child suck her milk, but our precious mother Jhesu, he may feed us with him self, and doth full courteously and full tenderly with the precious sacrament, that is precious food of very life."[61] Babies were typically breastfed until they were somewhere between 18 months and two years, although the length of feeding varied according to time, place, social class, and the gender of the baby. In Iceland, for instance, women breastfed their children for at least two years throughout most of the Middle Ages. During the late medieval period, however, they shifted to a shorter period of nursing—perhaps only three to four months before children were weaned onto cows' milk and solid foods. Infant mortality rates in late medieval Iceland were, in consequence, remarkably high.[62]

The practice of wetnursing also varied over time: it does not seem to have been common in early medieval Italy, for instance, but had become common there by the late Middle Ages. Wet nurses to wealthy families sometimes enjoyed considerable esteem: Adelina, wife of Adam, was given pieces of land by King Roger of Sicily for her services as wet nurse to his son Henry. Spanish wet nurses to royal families were similarly rewarded.[63] Wet nurses frequently received bequests in wills from fourteenth-century Crete, either from mothers whose children they had nursed or from the grown children themselves. This suggests that the bond between child and wet nurse sometimes persisted beyond infancy and became a lifelong connection.[64] In late medieval Florence, however, wetnursing had become a more commercial arrangement, and children were sent from the town out to nurse in the countryside. For the wet nurse, this could be a risky business. If anything happened to a child while it was in her care, she would be held responsible. Like mothers who breastfed their children, wet nurses were accused of overlying (or inadvertently crushing) babies who died in the night. Children who died in the night without an apparent cause might well have been victims of Sudden Infant Death Syndrome, but medieval people assumed that the fault was with the caregivers.[65]

As explained above, a mother was responsible for her child's moral and intellectual development in its first few years of life. Noble mothers often taught children the basics of literacy and numeracy. For instance, in the mid-thirteenth century, Denise de Montchensey of Essex (England) taught her children French.[66] Yet the proportion of women who were able to read well enough to teach their children was small indeed. More significant, then, were the foundations of religious observance and morality that mothers were also expected to impart. Peasant mothers, especially, also taught their children the rudiments of the tasks they would carry out as adults. Thus girls learned to cook, weave, mind younger children, and tend animals. The lives of saints sometimes pay testament to the ways in which their mothers taught them crafts and instructed them in religion.[67]

The final major task of a medieval mother was to see her child married to an appropriate spouse. Among the nobility, mothers frequently played an important role in negotiating marriages for their children. Indeed, the chance to broker such arrangements provided women with some rare opportunities to exercise power. The fourteenth-century Violant of Bar, for instance, who had been married into the royal family of Aragon (Spain) as a 15-year-old, participated actively in the marriages of her stepdaughter and daughter. Surviving letters show her concern to find good mates for her children, even at the cost of sending them far away. Violant's daughter (also called Violant) was married at the age of eleven to Louis II of Anjou. Because of her youth, the younger Violant stayed at home for another eight years, but once she was sent to live with Louis in Provence (France) she only saw her mother on one other occasion, two decades later.[68] Similarly, Adela, Countess of Blois in the late eleventh and early twelfth centuries, made astute arrangements for the marriage of her children in which she balanced carefully the political needs of her family.[69] Mothers of lower social status seem to have played a less active role in choosing spouses for their children, although church court depositions reveal that many children hoped for the approval of both parents in their selection of a mate.[70]

While discussions of motherhood emphasized their biological role, various medieval cultures also recognized the importance of adoption and fostering. Women's wills, where they existed, sometimes made explicit mention of non-biological children raised in their households. Marudalena Bonohomo, of Venetian Crete, left her adopted daughter Margarita various items of clothing along with a bed and wardrobe and rights to a house.[71] Among the nobility, informal fostering was common in order to forge and maintain social connections. Children from lesser noble families were often sent to the houses of more powerful nobles under the surrogate motherhood of the mistress of the household. The fourteenth-century Italian Margherita Datini, for instance, was infertile, but her house was constantly filled with children whom she fostered or served as guardian. Included among these children was the illegitimate daughter of her husband, Francesco. Although Margherita clearly wanted a biological child of her own and did everything in her power to conceive, she also seemed to enjoy her role as foster-mother to those in her care.[72] Clearly close bonds often developed between foster-mothers and their charges: when the English Mary Basset spent several years with a French noble family in the early sixteenth century, her foster-mother wrote, "I could not cherish her more tenderly were she were my own daughter."[73]

Attitudes toward motherhood shifted throughout the course of the Middle Ages. In line with the emphasis on virginity, early medieval writings often represent childbirth as filthy and motherhood as a distraction from a highly focused Christian life. During the high Middle Ages, however, representations of the Virgin Mary became extremely popular. Depicted in art, poetry, and sermons, Mary suckled her son and—by extension—came to be seen as the mother of all humanity. As Anselm of Canterbury wrote in the eleventh century, "The mother of God is our mother. The mother of him in whom alone we hope and who alone we fear is our mother. The mother, I say, of him who alone saves us, alone damns us, is our mother."[74] Yet Christian authors also emphasized Mary's virginity and insisted that she gave birth without pain or indignity (the particulars of how she managed this were seldom spelled out). Thus Mary's maternity was carefully distinguished from that of ordinary women. Later medieval representations of motherhood tended to be warmer toward all mothers, not just the Virgin Mary. Whereas married women and mothers had been extremely rare among saints during the early and high Middle Ages, a number of mother-saints were canonized during the thirteenth to fifteenth centuries. The fourteenth-century Brigid of Sweden, for instance, was mother of eight children and was praised for her diligence and devotion in raising her children. Other mother-saints were more ambivalent about their role, perceiving their children as distractions from the holy life. Society as a whole, however, seemed more approving of maternity and family, and manuscript illuminations and carvings increasingly represented domestic scenes, especially those in which the baby or child Jesus was tended by his mother.[75]

As with so many of women's roles, therefore, attitudes toward motherhood involved a great deal of ambivalence. On the one hand, some religious authors condemned childbirth as disgusting; on the other, popular culture celebrated motherhood and acknowledged the significance of the bond between mother and child. Yet while attitudes toward motherhood varied, many of the experiences of motherhood did not: throughout the Middle Ages, women coped with pregnancy, birth, and child-rearing. Although some of these experiences were easier for women of higher social status, other experiences—such as giving birth without the aid of anesthetics—were common to all mothers. Most medieval women became mothers, and motherhood formed a central part of the identity of women of all social classes.

WIDOWS

In one of the versions of the Noah's Ark play performed in England in the late Middle Ages, Noah's wife tells her husband that she wishes she was a widow and would gladly pay for his funeral. For some women, like Noah's wife, widowhood represented independence and autonomy. Yet for others, it was a period of poverty, vulnerability, and loneliness. Just as women anticipated motherhood as a normal consequence of marriage, most expected that they would eventually become widows. While some women certainly did die before their husbands—in childbirth, perhaps—the chances were that a wife would live longer than her spouse. Women were usually a few years younger than their spouses and, as today, they might expect to live a little longer than men. Surveys of wills, for instance, show that husbands died before their wives in about 65 to 80 percent of cases. Moreover, a widowed woman was less likely to remarry than a widowed man. As a result, households headed by widows were quite common: some historians estimate that one-quarter of all households in some late medieval towns were headed by widows.[76] In Florence in 1427, the numbers were not quite so high, but they were still significant: widows headed 13.6 percent of households, whereas only 2.4 percent were headed by widowers.[77] Even at the time of marriage, it was assumed that a woman would eventually become a widow, since marriage contracts specified dower lands to provide for her after her husband's death. While the death of her husband might seem momentous for an individual woman, therefore, society as a whole anticipated her new role as widow.

Widowhood was expected, then, but how were widows regarded? As with so many other situations of women, widows were met with considerable ambivalence. Two major stereotypes of widows existed. One of these stereotypes was that of the pious widow, freed from her responsibilities to her husband and thus able to spend her days in prayer and performance of charitable deeds. Such a widow greeted her widowhood as a kind of second virginity. Indeed, as religious authors repeated, a virgin was blessed one hundred fold in the eyes of God, a widow sixty fold, and a wife thirty fold. While her virginity could not be restored completely, therefore, a chaste and holy widow could go at least partway to reclaiming it. Such widows might, if they had the means, become anchoresses or vowesses (discussed in chapter 1), or they might retire to a part of a nunnery set aside for widows of means and try to live a devout and simple life. Those who remained in the world were urged by clerics to be bounded by a metaphorical cloister whose four walls were the cardinal virtues of prudence, justice, fortitude, and temperance. They were urged to emulate the example of Anna, daughter of Phanuel, described in the Bible in the book of Luke. Anna had been married only seven years before being widowed, but she lived as a widow for another 84 years (or, in some versions, she was 84 years old when she died). During this time, she dedicated herself to prayer and prophesized the coming of Jesus. Among the poor, widows who were chaste and pious, especially if they had young children, were viewed as the most deserving of charity.

Yet the stereotype of the pious widow was countered by her polar opposite: the lusty, wanton, and greedy widow. This so-called bad widow, according to the stereotype, saw widowhood as a release from a boring husband and an opportunity to exercise her own autonomy in all matters. In late medieval poems and stories, bad widows such as La Vieille in the

prologue

The Wife of Bath, widowed five times over, from Geoffrey Chaucer's late fourteenth-century *Canterbury Tales*, printed by William Caxton and illustrated with woodcuts in the fifteenth century. © Private Collection/The Bridgeman Art Library

Roman de la Rose, the Wife of Bath in Chaucer's *Canterbury Tales*, and the widow in William Dunbar's "Treatise of the Two Married Women and the Widow," lead young wives astray by telling them how to deceive their husbands and how to get their way in all things. Such a stereotype was perhaps anticipated by St. Paul's first letter to Timothy, in which he condemned idle widows who gadded about. Paul's words were still being repeated 1,400 years later, when treatises on widowhood reminded women of the apostle's words and warned them not to "roam about hither and thither from house to house nor from town to town but be a widow ever stable in good manners and sad of countenance and of few words and to abide at home."[78] The much-repeated fable of the "Widow of Ephesus" tells of a recent widow apparently distraught at her husband's death who vows to remain at his tomb until her own death. Her fickleness is demonstrated by the fact that, while still at her husband's tomb, she falls in love with a soldier who has been entrusted with guarding the body of a hanged thief. While the soldier flirts with the widow, the body of the hanged thief is stolen away, and the soldier realizes he will be in great trouble when its absence is discovered. The widow suggests replacing it with the body of her own husband, and the soldier and the widow then marry. This story emphasizes how quickly the widow gets over her grief—even to the point of abusing her late husband's body—once a new possibility appears. Variations on the theme of the easily consoled widow appear in many French fables and stories. In some, the widow and her new mate even have sex on the tomb of her late husband. These stories underline widows' alleged inconstancy, greed, and lust.[79] In the centuries immediately following the Middle Ages, such stereotypes would have dangerous consequences for women: poor, elderly widows were more likely than any other group to be accused of witchcraft. While pious widows may indeed have been viewed as the most deserving among the poor, they were also seen as a burden to society.

Just as stereotypes varied, so too did the experiences of real widows. Socioeconomic status, in particular, made a huge difference in the lives of widows. Widows left without property or income—especially if they had children—were truly destitute, since they had little hope of earning a sufficient income from their own labor. Unfortunately for historians, such widows are often invisible in surviving sources since they did not make wills and are often absent from tax records due to insufficient income. We catch glimpses of them in records detailing the foundation of charitable institutions for widows and orphans, in wills of wealthier people leaving money for widows, or in coroners' rolls recording untimely deaths. Richard Wartere, a merchant of York (England), for instance, left 12d. to each poor woman or widow with children in the parish of St. Saviour in his will of 1458.[80] Others supported poor widows by lending them property: Matilda Sherlok of Pinchbeck, along with two young sons and a daughter, was a beggar in Spalding (England), living in a house lent to them by John Herney. Her name appears in surviving records only because the house burned down and Matilda and her family were killed.[81]

More is known about widows in both the town and the countryside who controlled property of their own. Some of these women seem to have relished their role as newly independent individuals, just as Noah's wife claims that she would. Others, however, proved more reticent. Widows in some towns were entitled to carry on their husbands' workshops and guild memberships, but this could sometimes prove more of a burden than a boon. Inheritance customs varied too: as chapter 4 explains, most (but not all) widows of propertied men were entitled to the return of their dowries, along with a dower consisting of one-third or one-half of their husbands' land. Even where laws and customs stipulated such inheritances, however, they did not always happen automatically. In London, where widows were entitled to free bench (lifelong tenancy in the couple's home) and legitim (one-third of their husband's chattels), widows sometimes needed to go to court in order to gain these rights. Most widows ultimately won their cases, either in court or in settlements reached outside of court, but the cases themselves could be costly and time-consuming, and many employed attorneys to help them through the quagmire of legal complexities.[82] Peasant widows used the courts, too. Some, like Alice, widow of Peter Avice of Brigstock (England), appeared far more frequently in courts after their husbands died. Before Peter's death in 1316, Alice usually relied on him to pursue any cases or answer for any debts. After his death, however, she was much more assertive. In addition to answering for her own debts and coming to court to pay rents and fees, Alice used the courts to bring cases against other villagers. She even, on three occasions, served as a pledge for others (a system that guaranteed that others would pay their fines or otherwise meet their legal obligations). Yet not all widows responded the same way: Alice Penifader, from the same village as Alice Avice, avoided appearance in court and sent in excuses on the occasions on which she was expected to attend.[83] Widows such as Alice Avice and Alice Penifader possessed land, but they lacked sufficient labor with which to work land. Some widows responded by hiring laborers, some remarried, and some rented out the land for a fixed income or made arrangements by which they signed over rights to the land in return for a pension. In some cases, maintenance agreements were drafted even before a husband's death. John Whytyng of Wymondham (England), for instance, summoned court officials to his deathbed to record the agreement he had made with Simon Wellyng. According to this contract, Wellyng received Whytyng's house and land in return for his promise to provide Whytyng's widow with food and drink, including 16 bushels of malt each year. He was also required to maintain six hens, one goose, and one cow for her and to cultivate an acre of land to provide grain for her. Clothing and shelter were included in this agreement too: she was to receive a new pair of shoes each Easter, along with three shillings of clothing allowance, and she was to be allowed free entry into the house along with a bed and a place by the fire. Other widows made similar bargains after their husbands' deaths in order to ensure their own maintenance.[84] For peasant women and townswomen who inherited property from their husbands, widowhood could thus be a period of independence, even if it were also accompanied by new responsibilities and obligations that some found onerous.

A similar mixture of autonomy and obligations characterized widowhood among the nobility. In some periods and places, noble widows were especially vulnerable to manipulation by the king: English and French noblewomen of the high Middle Ages, for instance, often found themselves forced into remarriage at the whim of their kings who could effectively sell them to the highest bidder. In other places, widows faced pressure to remarry from their families of origin. In Florence, for instance, young noble widows were quickly reclaimed by members of their birth family who saw an opportunity to forge a second series of political alliances with a second marriage. Yet such women were not permitted to take their children with them: instead, the children remained in the families of their widowed husbands while their mothers married into new families.[85] Some noble widows faced other family pressures too, finding themselves in conflict with their sons or stepsons for control over their late husbands' estates; others, whose husbands had rebelled against the king, might be deprived of their inheritance due to their husbands' alleged treachery. Yet still others found themselves in an enviable position. Widows like the fifteenth-century Elizabeth de Burgh and Euphemia, daughter of Ralph Neville, enjoyed widowhoods of 40 and 48 years respectively, during which they enjoyed considerable control over their properties. Indeed, dowagers who lived for many years could often cause considerable frustration for sons waiting to inherit. Long-lived noblewomen could also play an important role within families as grandmothers. The fifteenth-century Englishwoman Agnes Paston, for instance, was clearly a formidable figure. During the last 37 years of her life, Agnes served as grandmother to a growing brood. Letters among family members make it clear that her role was far from passive: she participated in the family's legal business, enmeshed herself in family quarrels, and insisted that her grandsons send her regular news of their doings.[86] For women of means, widowhood might be a time of vulnerability, but it might also be an era of independence and familial esteem.

From the high Middle Ages onward, the life expectancy of women exceeded that of men. Medieval societies recognized that women were likely to outlive their husbands and tried to ensure that widows were provided for from the moment of their marriage. Despite the expectation of widowhood, the experience of being a widow varied widely. In both economic and legal terms, widows were among the most independent of women yet they were also among the most vulnerable. They were viewed as pious and humble yet also as lascivious and wanton. When the character of Noah's wife claimed that she would prefer to be a widow, therefore, she desired a status that was fraught with contradictions.

Indeed, contradictions and ambivalence have been important themes in this chapter. At every stage of a woman's life, she encountered both advantages and disadvantages associated with her familial position. In fact, no single familial role—girl, maiden, lifelong single woman, married woman, mother, or widow—can be indisputably regarded as superior or inferior to any other familial role. Familial position was hugely important in defining the way in which medieval societies regarded women, yet each role brought with it both advantages and liabilities.

NOTES

1. Philip Gavitt, "Infant Death in Late Medieval Florence: The Smothering Hypothesis Reconsidered," in *Medieval Family Roles: A Book of Essays*, ed. Cathy Jorgensen McItnyre (New York: Garland, 1996), 137–53.

2. Christiane Klapisch-Zuber, *Women, Family, and Ritual in Renaissance Italy* (Chicago: University of Chicago Press, 1985), 102.

3. Emily R. Coleman, "Medieval Marriage Characteristics: A Neglected Factor in the History of Medieval Serfdom," *Journal of Interdisciplinary History* 2 (1971), 205–19; Barbara A. Hanawalt, *Growing up in Medieval London: The Experience of Childhood in History* (New York: Oxford University Press, 1995), 57–58.

4. Cited in John Eastburn Boswell, "*Expositio* and *Oblatio:* The Abandonment of Children and the Ancient and Medieval Family," *American Historical Review* 89 (1984), 10–33; reprinted in Carol Neel, ed., *Medieval Families: Perspectives on Marriage, Household, and Children* (Toronto: University of Toronto Press, 2004), 242–43.

5. Klapisch-Zuber, *Women, Family, and Ritual in Renaissance Italy,* 155.

6. *Women's Lives in Medieval Europe: A Sourcebook,* ed. Emilie Amt (New York: Routledge, 1993), 190.

7. Barbara A. Hanawalt, *The Ties that Bound: Peasant Families in Medieval England* (New York: Oxford University Press, 1986), 157–59.

8. *Women in England, c. 1275–1525,* ed. and trans. P.J.P. Goldberg (Manchester: Manchester University Press, 1995), 266.

9. Johanna Maria van Winter, "The Education of the Girls of the Nobility," in *The Empress Theophano: Byzantium and the West at the turn of the First Millennium,* ed. Adelbert Davids (Cambridge: Cambridge University Press, 1995), 86–98.

10. Felicity Riddy, "Mother Knows Best: Reading Social Change in a Courtesy Text," *Speculum* 71 (1996), 66–86.

11. Ann Marie Rasmussen, "Good Counsel for a Young Lady: A Low German Mother-Daughter Poem," *Medieval Feminist Forum* 28 (1999), 28–31.

12. Anna Dronzek, "Gendered Theories of Education in Fifteenth-Century Conduct Books," in *Medieval Conduct,* ed. Kathleen Ashley and Robert L. A. Clark (Minneapolis: University of Minnesota Press, 2001), 135–59.

13. Nicholas Orme, *Medieval Children* (New Haven: Yale University Press, 2001), 318.

14. Judith M. Bennett, *A Medieval Life: Cecilia Penifader of Brigstock, c. 1295–1344* (Boston: McGraw Hill College, 1999).

15. Kim Phillips, *Medieval Maidens: Young Women and Gender in England, 1270–1540* (Manchester: University of Manchester Press, 2003), 9.

16. Phillips, *Medieval Maidens,* 185–94; Katherine L. French, "Women in the Late Medieval English Parish," in *Gendering the Master Narrative: Women and Power in the Middle Ages,* ed. Mary C. Erler and Maryanne Kowaleski (Ithaca: Cornell University Press, 2003), 156–73.

17. John Mirk, *Mirk's Festial: A Collection of Homilies,* ed. Theodor Erbe, EETS, Extra Series, vol. 96 (London: Kegan Paul, Trench, Trübner & Co., 1892), 229–30.

18. Christine de Pisan, *A Medieval Woman's Mirror of Honor: The Treasury of the City of Ladies,* trans. Charity Cannon Willard, ed. Madeleine Pelner Cosman (New York: Persea, 1989), 202–3.

19. Orme, *Medieval Children,* 322.

20. Judith M. Bennett and Amy M. Froide, "A Singular Past," in *Singlewomen in the European Past, 1250–1800,* ed. Judith M. Bennett and Amy M. Froide (Philadelphia: University of Pennsylvania Press, 1999), 1 and 28, n.1.

21. Fiona Harris Stoertz, "Young Women in France and England, 1050–1300," *Journal of Women's History* 12 (2001), 22–46.

22. Phillips, *Medieval Maidens,* 23–51; van Winter, "The Education of the Girls of the Nobility," 90–91.

23. Phillips, *Medieval Maidens,* 23–51.

24. Bennett and Froide, "A Singular Past," 2.

25. Maryanne Kowaleski, "Singlewomen in Medieval and Early Modern Europe: The Demographic Perspective," in *Singlewomen in the European Past*, 38–81.

26. Sharon Farmer, "'It is not good that [wo]man should be alone': Elite Responses to Singlewomen in High Medieval Paris," in *Singlewomen in the European Past*, 82–105 at 84–85.

27. Jacqueline Murray, "Twice Marginal and Twice Invisible: Lesbians in the Middle Ages," in *Handbook of Medieval Sexuality*, ed. Vern L. Bullough and James A. Brundage (New York: Garland, 1996), 191–222.

28. Sharon Farmer, "Persuasive Voices: Clerical Images of Medieval Wives," *Speculum* 61 (1986), 517–43.

29. de Pisan, *A Medieval Woman's Mirror of Honor*, 210.

30. de Pisan, *A Medieval Woman's Mirror of Honor*, 220.

31. *Paston Letters and Papers of the Fifteenth Century*, ed. Norman Davis, 2 vols., (Oxford: Clarendon Press, 1971), v. 1, 662–65.

32. Stanley Chojnacki, "The Power of Love: Wives and Husbands in Late Medieval Venice," in *Women and Power in the Middle Ages*, ed. Mary Erler and Maryanne Kowaleski (Athens: University of Georgia Press, 1988), 126–48.

33. Jennifer Ward, *Women in Medieval Europe 1200–1500* (London: Longman, 2002), 29.

34. *Women's Lives in Medieval Europe*, 317–18.

35. Theresia de Vroom, "In the Context of 'Rough Music': The Representation of Unequal Couples in Some Medieval Plays," *European Medieval Drama* 2 (1998), 237–60.

36. Carol Lansing, "Concubines, Lovers, Prostitutes: Infamy and Female Identity in Medieval Bologna," in *Beyond Florence: The Contours of Medieval and Early Modern Italy*, ed. Paula Findlen, Michelle M. Fontaine, and Duane J. Osheim (Stanford: Stanford University Press, 2003), 85–100.

37. Geneviève Ribordy, "The Two Paths to Marriage: The Preliminaries of Noble Marriage in Late Medieval France," *Journal of Family History* 26 (2001), 323–36.

38. Linda Guzzetti, "Separations and Separated Couples in Fourteenth-Century Venice," *Marriage in Italy, 1300–1650*, ed. Trevor Dean and K.J.P. Lowe (Cambridge: Cambridge University Press, 1998), 249–74.

39. Margaret McGlynn and Richard J. Moll, "Chaste Marriage in the Middle Ages: 'It were to hire a great merite'," in *Handbook of Medieval Sexuality*, 103–22.

40. Louis Haas, "Women and Childbearing in Medieval Florence," in *Medieval Family Roles*, 87–99, at 88.

41. *Women's Lives in Medieval Europe*, 145–46.

42. Patricia Skinner, "'The Light of My Eyes': Medieval Motherhood in the Mediterranean," *Women's History Review* 6 (1997), 391–10, at 393.

43. Haas, "Women and Childbearing in Medieval Florence," 87; Bennett, *A Medieval Life*.

44. Ward, *Women in Medieval Europe*, 52–53.

45. Haas, "Women and Childbearing in Medieval Florence," 87.

46. Emmanuel LeRoy Ladurie, *Montaillou: The Promised Land of Error* (New York: Vintage Books, 1979), 172–73.

47. John M. Riddle, "Contraception and Early Abortion in the Middle Ages," in *Handbook of Medieval Sexuality*, 261–77.

48. Anne L. McClanan, "'Weapons to Probe the Womb': The Material Culture of Abortion and Contraception in the Early Byzantine Period," in *The Material Culture of Sex, Procreation, and Marriage in Premodern Europe*, ed. Anne L. McClanan and Karen Rosoff Encarnación (New York: Palgrave, 2002), 33–58; Riddle, "Contraception and Early Abortion in the Middle Ages," 273–74.

49. *Hali Meidenhad*, quoted in and translated by Fiona Harris Stoertz, "Suffering and Survival in Medieval English Childbirth," in *Medieval Family Roles*, 101–20 at 101–2.

50. Stoertz, "Suffering and Survival in Medieval English Childbirth," 101–20.

51. Quoted in Carole Rawcliffe, "Women, Childbirth, and Religion in Later Medieval England," *Women and Religion in Medieval England*, ed. Diana Wood (Oxford: Oxbow Books, 2003), 91–17, at 92.

52. Don C. Skemer, "Amulet Rolls and Female Devotion in the Late Middle Ages," *Scriptorium* 55 (2001), 197–227.

53. Stoertz, "Suffering and Survival in Medieval English Childbirth."

54. Ward, *Women in Medieval Europe*, 55.

55. de Pisan, *A Medieval Woman's Mirror of Honor*, 194–95.

56. Rawcliffe, "Women, Childbirth, and Religion in Later Medieval England."

57. Haas, "Women and Childbearing in Medieval Florence," 93.

58. Haas, "Women and Childbearing in Medieval Florence," 95.

59. Becky R. Lee, "The Purification of Women after Childbirth: A Window onto Medieval Perceptions of Women," *Florilegium* 14 (1995–6), 43–55; Becky R. Lee, "Men's Recollections of a Woman's Rite: Medieval English Men's Recollections Regarding the Rite of the Purification of Women after Childbirth," *Gender & History* 14 (2002), 224–41; Paula M. Reider, "Insecure Borders: Symbols of Clerical Privilege and Gender Ambiguity in the Liturgy of Churching," in *The Material Culture of Sex, Procreation, and Marriage in Premodern Europe*, 93–113.

60. William F. MacLehose, "Nurturing Danger: High Medieval Medicine and the Problem(s) of the Child," in *Medieval Mothering*, ed. John Carmi Parsons and Bonnie Wheeler (New York: Garland, 1996), 3–24.

61. Quoted in Andrew Sprung, "The Inverted Metaphor: Earthly Mothering as *Figura* of Divine Love in Julian of Norwich's *Book of Showings*," in *Medieval Mothering*, 183–99 at 190.

62. Jenny Jochens, "Old Norse Motherhood," in *Medieval Mothering*, 201–22 at 211–12.

63. Skinner, "'The Light of My Eyes'," 395.

64. Sally McKee, "Households in Fourteenth-Century Venetian Crete," *Speculum* 70 (1995), 27–67 at 29, 56.

65. Gavitt, "Infant Death in Late Medieval Florence."

66. Orme, *Medieval Children*, 243.

67. Skinner, "'The Light of My Eyes'," 396; Judith M. Bennett, *A Medieval Life: Cecilia Penifader of Brigstock, c. 1295–1344* (Boston: McGraw Hill College, 1999), 44.

68. Dawn Bratsch-Prince, "Pawn or Player? Violant of Bar and the Game of Matrimonial Politics on the Crown of Aragon (1380–1396)," in *Marriage and Sexuality in Medieval and Early Modern Iberia*, ed. Eukene Lacarra Lanz (New York: Routledge, 2002), 59–89.

69. Kimberly A. LoPrete, "Adela of Blois as Mother & Countess," in *Medieval Mothering*, 313–33.

70. Shannon McSheffrey, "'I Will Never Have None Ayenst My Faders Will': Consent and the Making of Marriage in the Late Medieval Diocese of London," in *Women, Marriage, and Family in Medieval Christendom: Essays in Memory of Michael M. Sheehan, C.S.B.,* ed. Constance M. Rousseau and Joel T. Rosenthal (Kalamazoo: Medieval Institute Publications, 1998), 153–74.

71. McKee, "Households in Fourteenth-Century Venetian Crete," 57.

72. Joseph P. Byrne and Eleanor A. Congdon, "Mothering in the Casa Datini," *Journal of Medieval History* 25 (1999), 35–56.

73. Barbara A. Hanawalt, "Female Networks for Fostering Lady Lisle's Daughters," in *Medieval Mothering,* 239–58 at 247.

74. Quoted in Clarissa W. Atkinson, *The Oldest Vocation: Christian Motherhood in the Middle Ages* (Ithaca: Cornell University Press, 1991), 118.

75. Atkinson, *The Oldest Vocation,* 144–93.

76. Peter Fleming, *Family and Household in Medieval England* (New York: Palgrave, 2001), 84.

77. Klapisch-Zuber, *Women, Family, and Ritual in Renaissance Italy,* 120.

78. MS Bodleian 938 ff. 265r-267v. Modernization of English is mine.

79. Heather M. Arden, "Grief, Widowhood, and Women's Sexuality in Medieval French Literature," in *Upon My Husband's Death: Widows in the Literature and Histories of Medieval Europe,* ed. Louise Mirrer (Ann Arbor: University of Michigan Press, 1992), 305–20.

80. *Women in England, c. 1275–1525,* 163.

81. Hanawalt, *The Ties that Bound,* 225.

82. Barbara A. Hanawalt, "The Widow's Mite: Provisions for Medieval London Widows," in *Upon My Husband's Death,* 21–46.

83. Bennett, *A Medieval Life,* 125.

84. Elaine Clark, Some Aspects of Social Security in Medieval England," *Journal of Family History* 7 (1982), 307–20.

85. Klapisch-Zuber, *Women, Family, and Ritual in Renaissance Italy,* 117–31.

86. Joel T. Rosenthal, "Looking for Grandmother," in *Medieval Mothering,* 259–77.

SUGGESTED READING

Atkinson, Clarissa W. *The Oldest Vocation: Christian Motherhood in the Middle Ages.* Ithaca: Cornell University Press, 1991.

Bennett, Judith M. and Amy M. Froide, eds. *Singlewomen in the European Past, 1250–1800.* Philadelphia: Pennsylvania University Press, 1999.

Bullough, Vern L. and James A. Brundage, eds. *Handbook of Medieval Sexuality.* New York: Garland, 1996.

Dean, Trevor and K.J.P. Lowe, eds. *Marriage in Italy, 1300–1650.* Cambridge: Cambridge University Press, 1998.

Hanawalt, Barbara A. *Growing up in Medieval London: The Experience of Childhood in History.* New York: Oxford University Press, 1995.

Hanawalt, Barbara A. *The Ties that Bound: Peasant Families in Medieval England.* New York: Oxford University Press, 1986.

Klapisch-Zuber, Christiane. *Women, Family, and Ritual in Renaissance Italy.* Chicago: University of Chicago Press, 1985.

Lanz, Eukene Lacarra, ed. *Marriage and Sexuality in Medieval and Early Modern Iberia.* New York: Routledge, 2002.

McItnyre, Cathy Jorgensen, ed. *Medieval Family Roles: A Book of Essays.* New York: Garland, 1996.

Mirrer, Louise, ed. *Upon My Husband's Death: Widows in the Literature and Histories of Medieval Europe.* Ann Arbor: University of Michigan Press, 1992.

Orme, Nicholas. *Medieval Children.* New Haven: Yale University Press, 2001.

Parsons, John Carmi and Bonnie Wheeler, eds. *Medieval Mothering,* New York: Garland, 1996.

Phillips, Kim. *Medieval Maidens: Young Women and Gender in England, 1270–1540.* Manchester: University of Manchester Press, 2003.

4

꠷

Women and the Law

Medieval people were subject to multiple, overlapping systems of law, and almost all of these legal systems disadvantaged women. In theory, women were usually under the guardianship of men (whether their male relatives or their husbands). In theory, most married women could not own property, could not take cases to court, and had few (if any) rights over their children when they became widowed. Medieval law codes were clear that adult men were to be regarded as the basic legal subjects of society and that women were mere hangers-on. Yet in practice, some of these legal restrictions were mitigated on a day-to-day level. A peasant wife may not have had the right to sue her neighbor for refusal to repay a debt, but she could certainly pressure her husband to bring the case before the local manorial court. A noblewoman may not always have had the legal standing to appear before a church court to complain against a heretic, but she could be regarded as a legitimate witness on matters of genealogy. And a queen like the twelfth-century Melisende of Jerusalem may have understood that she should relinquish the throne when her son reached the age of majority, but she did not necessarily comply. For some women, then, restrictions on their legal status and rights to inheritance could be overcome. The law served as an instrument of patriarchy—that is, it served to support the overall system which privileged men at the expense of women—but individual women were sometimes still able to find ways of getting around it.

WOMEN AS LEGAL SUBJECTS

In theory, women's legal status was very much inferior to that of men. Throughout much of medieval Europe, women were expected to stay out of courts and leave any legal business to their husbands, fathers, and other male guardians. In many medieval jurisdictions, indeed, they were regarded as the property of men, and any threat or injury to women was expected to be pursued by their male guardians. Their theoretical status under the law, in other words, was much like that of children. In practice, however, individual women were sometimes able to circumvent the laws and customs that limited women's legal participation. Although women used law courts far less often than men, they were often able to find ways to ensure that their voices were heard.

Medieval law, like medieval society in general, evolved from the mingling of Roman, Germanic, and Celtic influences in the early Middle Ages. The two most dominant traditions—Roman and Germanic—offered different approaches, however, to the status of women. By the last centuries of the Roman Empire, Roman women's legal status was quite high. Although certainly not equal to men, Roman women were permitted to inherit and transmit property in their own right. While theoretically under the control of male guardians, they could dismiss or change these guardians with relative ease. Women were not allowed to hold public offices or exercise the same degree of power that a Roman paterfamilias (male head of household) held over his family, but they fared relatively well under the law nonetheless. Germanic law, on the other hand, placed much more value on the concept of *mundium,* or guardianship, in which women were regarded as being under the protection of their husbands, fathers, or other male relatives.

Germanic law codes of the early Middle Ages provide some of the earliest data on the ambivalent legal status of women. As groups such as the Visigoths, Ostrogoths, and Franks moved into the ailing Roman Empire and established independent kingdoms within its borders, they began to record laws that had previously existed only orally. Early Germanic law codes thus represent many of the values of the Germanic peoples expressed in a Roman format. For instance, laws recorded the *wergild,* or "blood money" that one had to pay for killing or injuring another person. The Bavarian and Aleman law codes, compiled in the eighth century but based on earlier rules, set the *wergild* for women as double that of men. According to the Bavarian Code, this was because women were unable to protect themselves in the same way that men could—in fact, if a woman did take up arms, her *wergild* was forfeited.[1] The Law of the Salian Franks, recorded during the reign of King Clovis in the early sixth century, also established a high *wergild* for women, but this varied according to her age. The following laws provide interesting data on the relative value of a Frankish woman's life in comparison with the value of Frankish boys and men:

24:1. If any one have slain a boy under 10 years—up to the end of the tenth—and it shall have been proved on him, he shall be sentenced to 600 shillings.

24:3. If any one have hit a free woman who is pregnant and she dies, he shall be sentenced to 700 shillings.

24:6. If any one have killed a free woman after she has begun bearing children, he shall be sentenced to 600 shillings.

24:7. After she can have no more children, he who kills her shall be sentenced to 8,000 denars, which make 200 shillings.

41:1. If any one shall have killed a free Frank, or a barbarian living under the Salic law, and it have been proved on him, he shall be sentenced to 200 shillings.

41:3. But if any one has slain a man who is in the service of the king, he shall be sentenced to 600 shillings.

41:15. He who kills a free girl before she is able to bear children shall be liable to pay 200 shillings.[2]

As the laws show, a woman's *wergild* was highest (suggesting that her value to society was highest) when she was pregnant. Each child represented a potential warrior, someone who could be of great value in a society still struggling to maintain itself in a new and hostile environment. A woman of childbearing age was also valuable—as valuable as a boy under the age of 10 or a Frankish man of high status (that is, one who served the king). Before and after her childbearing years, however, her value to society was diminished, and her *wergild* was the same as that of ordinary Frankish men. Women in Frankish society, therefore, were certainly valued, but they were prized largely for their reproductive capacities. Salic Law offers other glimpses into women's status too: the highest of the fines for insults (45 shillings) was reserved for anyone who called a woman a harlot, suggesting that a woman's sexual chastity was seen as particularly important.

The Angles and the Saxons, Germanic tribes who established independent kingdoms in England, give less specific data on women's *wergild* in their law codes. The earliest of their law codes do show, however, that women were regarded as being under the *mundium* of men, no matter what their stage of life. Crimes against women, such as rape or abduction, were regarded as offenses against women's guardians (their husbands or fathers) or against society rather than as offenses against the women themselves. The seventh-century code of Ethelbert of Kent lists fines for violating women, but these vary according to the rank of her guardian and suggest that women were seen as property. In fact marriage, in Ethelbert's code, was seen as a purchase in which a woman was "bought for a price" and could be returned if the bargain between the purchaser (her husband) and the bride's family was not kept.[3]

Irish laws demonstrate similar concerns to limit the legal capacity of women and tie their status to that of their guardians. Ireland, dominated by Celtic rather than Germanic law, used the terms *lóg n-enech* or *dire* in preference to *wergild,* but the concept was similar. A woman's *lóg n-enech* was usually about half of that of her guardian. As an eighth-century legal tract explained, a woman was never without a guardian: her father watched over her when she was a girl, her husband watched over her when she was a wife, her sons watched over when she was a widow, and her family watched over her if she was widowed without a father or adult sons. Women's legal status, in other words, was the same as that of children.[4]

The notion of *mundium* persisted into the high and later Middle Ages. The *Sachsenspiegel,* a collection of laws recorded in the thirteenth century, justified women's legal inferiority with the story of a woman named Calefurnia whose outrageous anger and disrespect in the courtroom had apparently led to women's banishment from the courtroom and the requirement that all women be represented by male guardians.[5] In England after 1066, *mundium* evolved into the convention of coverture, which subsumed women's legal identity into that of her husband. A wife, therefore, was a *femme covert,* a woman whose legal status was covered by her husband's representation. This meant that wives could not, in theory, own any personal property during their marriages; instead, all would belong to their husbands. Nor could married women bring cases to court without their husbands' participation. Married women were not held responsible for their own debts. As legal commentators of the seventeenth century put it, "Every *Feme Covert* is a sort of infant ... It is seldom, almost never, that a married woman can have any action to use her wit only in her name: her husband is her stern, her prime mover, without whom she cannot do much."[6] Single women and widows had a little more leeway in that they were permitted to represent themselves in court.

Almost all jurisdictions agreed that—no matter what a woman's marital status—she was not permitted to serve as an officer of the court or as a juror. Certainly women did not serve as justices in the royal courts, and their status in church courts was especially low given the all-male nature of the church hierarchy. But, as chapter 6 explains, even local courts very seldom recognized any authority on the part of women. As they elected bailiffs, aletasters, reeves, chamberlains, jurors, and other local officials, peasants and townspeople seem not to have considered women for the jobs. A woman might, very rarely, serve as a pledge for someone else, a position similar to standing bail since it involved guaranteeing that a fine would be paid or that a person would show up to the next court session. For instance, of the thousands of pledges offered on the English manor of Brigstock in the late thirteenth and early fourteenth centuries, only 46 were offered by women, and many manors and towns never recorded female pledges at all.[7] Occasionally, too, a woman might serve as a procurator, or advocate, in borough courts of late medieval Scotland, but examples are rare and they acted usually on behalf of family members.[8]

In theory, then, a woman's legal status was very much limited. Seen as children or as incompetents whose interests had to be represented by men, women's access to any kind of justice system would seem to have been almost nil. Many jurisdictions, in fact, forbade women from initiating criminal charges for crimes committed against them or limited the circumstances in which a woman could bring a claim. Thirteenth-century English royal justices, for example, told Juliana de Holeworth and Edelina, mother of Peter, that they were not allowed to bring charges against William Pech for the deaths of their sons because "a woman cannot make an appeal except for the death of her husband or rape done to herself."[9] Wives who attempted to sue others in the courts of the town of Exeter were similarly admonished and told that they should be represented by their husbands.[10] Social conventions often reinforced laws preventing women from appearing in courts. In fifteenth-century Lucca (Italy), it was considered unseemly for women of high status to appear in courts, where they might have to mingle with men. On the few occasions when a woman might have to come before the court, she could ask to have her testimony heard in a private house or a church in order to protect her modesty.[11] Even the fifteenth-century French author Christine de Pisan argued that women should avoid the courts. In answer to the question of why women did not plead law cases and were unfamiliar with legal disputes, Christine responded, "because of the integrity to which women are inclined, it would not be at all appropriate for them to go and appear so brazenly in the court like men, for there are enough men who do so." As one of the few medieval authors whose writings can be considered pro-woman, she added, however, that women's lack of participation in the courtroom was not due to their inability to understand the law.[12] Instead, she saw the courtroom as a place of brazen and unfeminine behavior which women would best avoid. The message was clear: whether because women needed protection or because of their legal incapacity, the courtroom was supposedly out-of-bounds.

Yet in practice this theory did not always hold. Some courts and some justices were much more receptive toward cases brought by women. Most medieval people were subject to several jurisdictions—often the church courts, the royal courts, and the local courts (courts of the manor or borough), although the types of jurisdictions varied from one area to another. In some situations, people could decide where best to pursue their cases, choosing the court most likely to give them a favorable outcome. Studies of fifteenth- and early-sixteenth-century cases brought before the

English royal courts of King's Bench and Common Pleas show that about 5 percent of cases were brought by women, apparently without reference to the prohibition against litigation by women. More women took their cases to the equity court of Chancery, another English royal court established to try cases that did not fit easily or equitably into the jurisdiction of ordinary courts. About 15 percent of litigants in the English equity court of Chancery were women, suggesting that women saw this court as a more favorable venue in which to pursue a case.[13] Variations also occurred within jurisdictions: although justices refused to hear the cases brought by Juliana de Holeworth and Edelina, mother of Peter, for instance, other women fared better in the same court system. When Alice, mother of Margery, brought a case against two men who had allegedly killed her daughter and fled, Alice's case was taken seriously and the two accused men were declared outlaws.[14] A similar gap between theory and practice existed in the courts of southern Italy. In some regions, women were theoretically banned from representing themselves in courts, whereas in others they were expected to limit their actions to cases that involved them personally. Yet examination of court cases shows that there were exceptions to these rules. For instance, at Amalfi, an active port city, women often came to court on behalf of their husbands and sons when their menfolk were away on sea voyages. In some regions of southern Italy, abbesses were regarded as honorary men in a legal sense, bringing cases on behalf of their convents.[15] The general legal maxim that women were not supposed to bring cases to court was, therefore, one that was often overlooked.

Similarly, the status of women as witnesses could be ambivalent. As legal inferiors, their testimony in the courtroom was often assumed to be lacking. Roman law, usually fairly tolerant of women, had banned them from acting as witnesses. The sixth-century Byzantine law codes reiterated this view, and most Germanic law codes seem also to have assumed that women would not normally have acted as witnesses.[16] Irish law forbade women from being witnesses, while Welsh law accepted women's testimony against other women but not against men. In most areas within France, women's testimony had to be corroborated by other accounts in order to be credible since, in the words of a legal commentator from Toulouse in the late thirteenth century, "women always give varying and changeable testimony."[17]

Yet women were sometimes judged to be credible witnesses in particular situations, especially situations involving knowledge or expertise deemed womanly in nature. The thirteenth-century French lawyer Philippe de Beaumanoir claimed that a woman's status as witness was like that of a bastard, serf, or leper: while her word was usually to be doubted, she might be trusted on certain matters. A woman might not speak on behalf of her husband or son, for instance, because everyone would assume her testimony to be false, but she would be more credible and hence admissible in court if giving evidence *against* one of her male relatives. Similarly, a woman's word might be trusted on matters of a child's age, since—according to Philippe—women often remember children's ages better than men do. She might also be trusted to give evidence in matters concerning another woman's virginity (for instance, in a rape trial). In most other situations, however, a woman's word was to be doubted unless it could be supported by other, male, witnesses.[18] Philippe was not alone in acknowledging women's reliability when it came to proof of virginity and the age of children. Elsewhere, women's knowledge of so-called female matters was also recognized. At Zamora (Spain), women's testimony was believed when they certified that another woman had been pregnant, and in the Spanish cities of San Sebastián and Estella, women were permitted to testify to the last wishes of women who died in childbirth. Several Spanish towns allowed women charged by their husbands with adultery to summon "juries" of women (really witnesses rather than jurors per se) to help clear their names.[19] Female witnesses were especially likely to be called upon when the court needed to decide whether or not a woman was pregnant. In such cases a "jury of matrons," composed of 12 or more women, might be empanelled to examine a woman's belly for fetal movements and inspect the size of her breasts for the heaviness that might accompany pregnancy. For instance, when the childless William Constable of Merton died in 1220, his brother Peter assumed he was the rightful heir. William's widow Muriel, however, claimed to be pregnant, and since her child would become William's heir she argued that she should be examined by a jury of matrons. (In Muriel's case, things did not work out: although the jury of matrons declared her to be pregnant, no child was ever born, so Peter ended up inheriting his brother's estate and Muriel was forced to admit that she had been mistaken about the pregnancy.) In places in which convicted female felons might have their executions postponed if they were pregnant, the court might similarly ask juries of matrons to decide whether pregnancy could be verified. A woman who was successful in "pleading the belly" might be fortunate enough to be granted a reprieve altogether, as was the case for several thirteenth-century English women whose pregnancy was confirmed by juries of matrons.[20]

Church courts, too, paid extra heed to women's testimony on particular occasions. Church courts governed marriage in the Middle Ages, and this involved adjudicating the grounds on which a marriage might be annulled (the medieval equivalent of divorce). Women were called upon as witnesses with regard to two grounds in particular: consanguinity and impotence of husbands. The issue of who could marry whom was a complex one, especially prior to 1215, since the laws of the church insisted that no one could marry within seven degrees of blood relationship. These rules of consanguinity meant that one could not share a pair of great-great-great-great-great-grandparents with one's spouse, and in effect meant that there could be thousands or even tens of thousands of people whom one was forbidden to marry. (After 1215, the rule was reduced to four degrees of separation, which still made for a sizable group of prohibited potential spouses.) In order to enforce these laws, the church needed to draw on as many witnesses as possible in order to trace family relationships, and since many cultures regarded women as genealogical experts, women's testimony on consanguinity was often heard. Another of the grounds for annulment involved sexual impotence on the part of either partner, and a woman who alleged that her husband was impotent was allowed to testify in court.[21] Sometimes other women (occasionally prostitutes) were invited to examine the man's penis in order to try to arouse him. If he was unable to become sexually aroused, it was assumed that he was indeed impotent and an annulment might be granted.[22] In church courts, as in secular jurisdictions, women's testimony was thus permissible—and even sought after—in specific circumstances.

LEGAL PROTECTIONS FOR WOMEN

Women were not regarded as equal under the law, yet the law could also serve to protect them. Indeed, in some cases the presumption of women's fragility afforded them particular protection. Since biblical times, moralists had reminded people that widows, especially, needed special protection in courts of law, as in other matters, and widows—as well as single women and wives—were willing to make use of this presumption. A woman taking a case to court, like Elizabeth Gambylfelde in 1539, might describe herself as a "poor maiden" or "friendless girl" in an effort to cultivate sympathy among justices.[23] Courts also frequently overlooked wives' participation in the crimes of their husbands since, in the words of the thirteenth-century English judge and legal commentator Henry Bracton, "whether or not [a woman] was privy to the crime, she was under her husband's rod." Bracton, following Anglo-Saxon traditions, also argued that a wife was not responsible for stolen goods found in her house, since the house was not under her control, unless the goods were found in a storeroom, chest, or cupboard to which she possessed keys. Thirteenth-century English cases show that a wife who argued that she acted on the orders of her husband would often (though not invariably) be acquitted.[24]

The impulse to protect women can also be seen in situations in which hues and cries were adjudicated in English manorial and borough courts. Hues and cries were raised when someone—either the victim or a bystander—saw an offense being committed. Such offenses might include a physical assault, robbery, or damage to property. The witness to the crime was obliged to shout out to those nearby to pursue the offender, and those nearby were required to obey the hue and cry and make chase. Each of these hues and cries was later considered in the local court: if a hue and cry was judged to have been justified, the person on whom it was raised paid an extra fine, in addition to that levied for his or her crime. If the hue and cry was judged unjust, however, the court punished the hue-raiser for raising a "false hue." In the years when hue-raising as a means of communal policing was most common, the thirteenth and early fourteenth centuries, it was a system that protected women disproportionately. Of nearly 1,200 hues and cries raised in eight manorial and borough jurisdictions, women were responsible for raising half. Yet women were only rarely the targets of hues and cries: in 82 percent of cases, hues and cries were raised on men. Moreover, women were judged slightly more reliable than men when the validity of their hues and cries was considered in court. Most jurisdictions either found women's and men's hues and cries equally reliable or they were slightly more inclined to believe women. Overall, then, the system of the hue and cry was one that disproportionately provided protection for women and punishment for men.[25]

Yet despite this overall impulse to protect women, prosecutions for rape and domestic violence—two crimes that often victimized women— were typically low. The term *rape* was used by medieval courts, but its precise meaning was somewhat different from the way it is used today. The crime of rape included abduction of women, and the issue of a woman's consent to sexual intercourse, which is so important in the way the crime is constructed today, was not always considered relevant in the medieval courts. In fact, rape was often seen as a crime against property rather than a crime against the person. A rapist was considered to have stolen the property of another man: a daughter, a wife, or a woman under his guardianship. A woman could thus consent to her abduction, and to sexual intercourse, yet her abductor might still be charged with rape by her male relatives. In other situations, the term rape might be applied to illicit sexual intercourse in a more general sense. For instance, priests who had consensual sexual relationships with their parishioners might find themselves charged with rape as a way to punish them for engaging in sexual intercourse (since they were supposed to be celibate). These charges were seldom brought to trial, but the fact of the indictment and imprisonment prior to trial served as a kind of punishment.[26]

Both rape and abduction were taken seriously under Germanic law, even though the distinction between the two crimes was not always clear. A man who raped a free girl, according to the law of the Salian Franks, had to pay—presumably to her family—the amount of her bride price (that is, the amount that would have been paid to her family by a potential husband). If an abductor had sex with her in secret, the fine was only about three-quarters as high, perhaps because the woman would still have been considered marriageable. The Lombard code of the seventh to eighth centuries imposed the high fine of 900 shillings on a man who violently seized a woman and married her without her consent. None of this money went to the woman herself, though: half was paid to the king and half to her relatives. Some Germanic codes were stricter still: the law code of the Visigoths, for instance, allowed a rapist to be killed by his victim's family.[27] Although some of the codes did acknowledge the importance of a woman's consent, most regarded the rape or abduction of a woman as an offense against her family rather than an offense against the woman herself.

In some instances, a man accused of rape could free himself from punishment if he was to marry his victim. In fact, evidence suggests that women and men sometimes colluded to use this provision as a way of avoiding the need for parental consent. That is, if a woman and a man wanted to marry but her family would not agree, the man might rape (or, in other words, abduct) her so that the option of marriage became automatic and parental consent was not needed. The term *rape* thus became a means of elopement. In other instances, a woman might choose to marry her rapist, or might be pressured into such a marriage by her family, because her marital prospects had been so damaged by the rape that she was viewed as damaged goods and the bride price she could command would be lower. The laws of Valencia and of Tortosa (Spain), for instance, decreed that a man who raped a virgin might marry her if she was of the same social status as he or of a higher social status (if the woman was of a lower social status, he might instead give her money for a dowry).[28]

The term *rape* was thus often used to refer to situations quite different than those connoted today. Where it was used in the same sense as today, however, it is clear that the crime was frequently under-reported and that those accused were seldom found guilty. Only 142 rape cases were heard in records of 20 English Eyre courts between 1202 and 1276, compared with 3,492 homicide cases, and only 6 percent of alleged rapists were convicted. Conviction rates were slightly higher in the early fourteenth century, when 10 percent of indictments resulted in conviction, but the numbers were still very low overall.[29] Only eight cases of rape were heard by the officiality of Cerisy (France) between 1314 and 1414, suggesting that many more rapes were never brought into the court.[30] Part of the reason for the low rates of accusation and conviction may have been the legal and social obstacles that an accuser faced. A twelfth-century English legal theorist described the steps a rape victim must take: as soon as the rape is over she must take herself to the nearest village or town and "show to trustworthy men the injury done to her, and any effusion of blood there may be and any tearing of her clothes. She should then do the same to the reeve of the hundred. Afterwards she should proclaim it publicly in the next county court." Other commentators specified the exact formula that a woman should use in making her accusation: the words used in accusation had to be exactly right or the case could be thrown out on a technicality. Spanish laws stipulated that a woman who was raped had to bring charges by the next day in order for her case to be taken seriously. Moreover, if the victim became pregnant as a result of the rape it was assumed that she had consented to sex. Thus a man from the English county of Kent was acquitted of rape in 1312–13 because his alleged victim became pregnant.[31]

Just as the law did little to protect women against rape, it also did little to punish men culpable of domestic violence. Husbands expected to be allowed to use physical force in the so-called governance of their wives, and courts were generally reluctant to intervene unless the force was clearly excessive. Prosecutions for wife-beating were thus rare. Indeed, references to domestic violence in the context of other crimes help to show the ways in which it was under-reported. For example, when Richard Scharp, a wool merchant of London, beat his wife Emma so seriously that she miscarried, he was indicted only for the death of his stillborn son and not for the injury to his wife.[32] Violence was seldom seen as sufficient grounds for marital separation unless it was of a particularly serious nature. More typically, courts remonstrated with wife-beaters and sometimes bound them over with a threatened fine or penalty that they might incur if the violence was to continue. For instance, Ingerrand Douin, of the officialty of Cerisy (France), was told that he might beat his wife if there was just cause, but he was also warned that he would face a fine of £40, plus be sentenced to time in the pillory, if he abused her "excessively."[33] The courts of York (England) made a similar distinction between reasonable and excessive force when they refused the petition of Margaret Neffield in 1395–96 for separation from her husband. Margaret argued that her husband, Thomas, had broken her arm, attacked her with a knife, and beaten her. Thomas (along with his witnesses) agreed that these events had occurred, but said that his behavior was necessary in order to discipline Margaret sufficiently. Thomas, like Ingerrand, was told by the court that he might beat his wife as needed to correct her faults but that he must avoid cruelty and excessive force.[34]

While violence toward wives was widely accepted in Christian regions, Jewish communities were generally less tolerant of wife-beaters. The extent of acceptance among Jewish communities varied according to their location: rabbis in Muslim regions of Spain condemned domestic violence less harshly than those elsewhere. In northern Europe, many rabbis saw it as a serious offense and as grounds for divorce, especially if the violence was repeated. In fact, the great thirteenth-century Talmudic scholar Rabbi Meir ben Baruch of Rothenberg (Germany) described the practice of wife-beating as "the way of the gentiles" and said that wife beaters should be boycotted, excommunicated, beaten, and subject to having their hands cut off.[35]

Of course, domestic violence did not always involve men beating their wives. Rare cases show charges being brought against men who beat other relatives, such as their daughters-in-law or sisters-in-law. Rarer still were cases in which women were charged with beating men. In fact, scenes of women beating men were often considered humorous in medieval literature and art. In the late medieval play of the building of Noah's ark, for instance, the wife of Noah is sometimes depicted as an obstreperous woman who clouts Noah and defends herself physically against his blows. Similarly, small wood carvings known as misericords, located on the underside of seats in the choir area in medieval cathedrals and larger parish churches, often depicted the scene of a woman beating a cowering man. In many such depictions, she beats the man with her distaff (a piece of equipment used in spinning). The context of these images make it clear that they were intended to be humorous rather than serious: a woman beating a man represented a reversal of the supposedly natural order of things, and medieval people seem to have taken particular delight in such inversion of hierarchies.

The various law codes of medieval Europe did offer some protection to women, but this protection was often theoretical rather than practical. Women, as the fragile property of men, were not supposed to be damaged or violated. Social norms, however, often worked against the theoretical protections laid out in law codes, and the under-reporting of crimes such as rape and domestic violence show that women's rights were often undermined by the expectation that they stay remote from the masculine, public world of the law courts.

WOMEN AND CRIME

Despite the fact that medieval commentators on women's behavior so often typecast them as immoral and poorly behaved, women were charged with crimes far less often than men. In the courts of medieval England, men were charged with about nine times as many felonies, or serious crimes, as women.[36] Among violent criminals in particular, women were even scarcer: in the French officialty of Cerisy, women accounted for only about 8 percent of violent crimes. They numbered only 7 percent of accused murderers in the king's courts of fourteenth-century England and 11 percent of those charged with assault in the manorial court of Wakefield (England).[37] Clearly, then, there was a large discrepancy between the ways that women's morality was presented in literary and moral texts and the extent to which they were prosecuted in courts. Yet despite this discrepancy, there were certain crimes closely associated with women, crimes in which women either made up the majority or a significant minority of the accused. The most common of these were the offenses of prostitution, adultery, scolding and defamation, and theft of foodstuffs.

Prostitution was a crime overwhelmingly associated with women. Women made up the large majority of those accused as prostitutes and were often involved in other aspects of the trade, such as running brothels. Young women migrating to towns from the countryside were at greatest risk of becoming prostitutes: prostitution was, after all, an occupation requiring little initial capital and few formal skills. Of the 55 prostitutes who appear in the court records of Exeter (England) between 1373 and 1393, for instance, all came from poor backgrounds, 85 percent were single, and many had no family within the area (suggesting that they were recent immigrants to the town).[38] Women who worked part-time in other low-status and poorly-paid occupations, such as domestic service, laundry, or textile work, might turn to prostitution in the hope of earning a little extra income to make ends meet. Prostitution was almost exclusively a female crime, but in very rare instances we know of men, too, charged with having sex for money. John Rykener, who went by the name of "Eleanor," was convicted in 1394 in London for having sex with another man in the street. Rykener was wearing women's clothing, and at least some of his sexual partners thought he was a woman.[39] Rykener's case, however, is very much the exception to the rule; medieval commentators, lawmakers, and officials assumed that prostitutes were women.

Attitudes toward prostitutes and prostitution fluctuated over time. For much of the Middle Ages, prostitution was regarded as a necessary evil, an abhorrent practice yet one that could never completely be eradicated. Romans had been relatively tolerant of prostitution, although ex-prostitutes were never able to escape the stigma that came with the job: once a woman had been registered with local authorities in the Roman Empire as a prostitute, she found it hard to put her past behind her. Because of the church's teaching on repentance, medieval ex-prostitutes were encouraged to confess their sin and receive forgiveness. Mary Magdalene, described by the church as the prostitute who befriended Jesus of Nazareth, served as an example for repentant prostitutes, and houses for former prostitutes who wished to become respectable were sometimes named for her. In late medieval Avignon (France), for instance, the so-called repenties houses organized themselves on a model similar to that of convents and expected their members to follow strict rules. Vienna's Magdalene house was less successful: ex-prostitutes were expected to repent and marry, but the house was closed down in the late fifteenth century after rumors that prostitution continued within its walls.[40]

Ironically, at the same time that some late medieval towns provided options for ex-prostitutes, many French, Italian, German, Spanish, and English towns licensed prostitutes in municipal brothels. In Toulouse (France), for instance, the town established a brothel at least as early as the 1360s or 1370s, the theory being that licensed prostitutes were more readily regulated and kept under control.[41] Red-light districts were established and prostitutes were even given limited rights. In Montpellier (France), for instance,

Prostitutes with their clients. From a French manuscript (c. 1403) of Boccaccio's *Des Claires et Nobles Femmes (De Claris Mulieribus)*. © Bibliothèque Nationale, Paris, France/Archives Charmet/The Bridgeman Art Library.

a document of 1285 designated a particular street as the home for prostitutes, and the women were promised that they could live there peacefully without being harassed by bailiffs or by their neighbor.[42] London's brothels (known as *stews*) were housed in the district of Southwark, across the Thames from the main part of the city. In fact, the land on which they were built was under the jurisdiction of the Bishop of Winchester, suggesting that the church, as well as the city of London, was to some extent complicit in the existence of these brothels. Fifteenth-century regulations of the Southwark stews show a concern to keep law and order (the brothels were to be closed down on holy days between 6 and 11am and 1 and 6pm, for instance), but also a concern to protect the prostitutes. Brothel keepers were warned not to beat prostitutes, nor to overcharge them for food. The regulations also aimed to protect customers: neither brothel keepers nor prostitutes were permitted to harass potential clients in the street, for instance. Prostitutes afflicted with what was called *burning sickness* were expelled from the stews in an attempt to protect clients from contracting what was presumably a venereal disease.[43] Many municipal brothels established in the late Middle Ages would be disbanded in the sixteenth and seventeenth centuries.

Why would town legislators and members of the church condone and even facilitate prostitution by setting aside space for prostitutes and granting them limited rights? Historians' answers to this question vary, but most claim that medieval people saw prostitution as the "lesser evil." The alternate evils, which organized prostitution was supposed to prevent, included concerns about threats to public decency if prostitutes were allowed to wander freely throughout towns and the contamination of so-called decent women that was feared if prostitutes and respectable women were allowed to intermingle. Some towns cited even more specific reasons: in fifteenth-century Florence, for example, the brothels were encouraged in part because young men were allegedly engaging in homosexuality, resulting in a lower marriage and birthrate. By luring them back to heterosexuality with the help of a city-sponsored brothel, it was hoped that the birthrate might increase again. Other cities seemed less concerned about the sexuality of their young men and more concerned about protection of respectable young women who, it was thought, might be vulnerable to rape if men had no outlet for their sexual urges. The limited protection provided to prostitutes by municipal brothels was thus seldom motivated by concern about their own safety or morality and was grounded more in the desire to shield public order and so-called respectable women.[44] As the thirteenth-century monk and scholar St. Thomas Aquinas put it, prostitution was as necessary to medieval life as sewers were to palaces: without sewers, palaces would become backed up with filth, and without prostitutes, lust would overcome decency. Moreover, the protection to prostitutes provided by medieval regulations came at a price: prostitutes were often expected to keep to the section of town set aside for their use (resulting in prostitutes' ghettoes) and in some towns they were required to wear particular clothing so that prostitutes could be distinguished at a glance from so-called respectable women. In fourteenth-century Avignon (France), they were prohibited from wearing coats, silk veils, amber rosaries, or gold rings. English prostitutes were not permitted to wear fur-lined hoods but were instead required to wear unlined, striped hoods so that they could easily be identified.[45] Prostitutes came to be seen as symbols for female sin in a more general sense, justifying the control of all women's sexuality.

Medieval people assumed that prostitutes were all women, but their pimps could be either women or men. In many places, such as late medieval

Ghent, brothels were often owned by a married couple. While the husband and wife would both be cited as co-owners, it was the wife who became known as the madam and dealt with both clients and prostitutes on a regular basis. Regulations governing the Southwark stews required that all brothel owners be men, yet court convictions show that this rule was often ignored and that women also held this position.[46]

The crime of prostitution was often linked to those of fornication (sexual intercourse outside of marriage) and adultery (sexual intercourse outside marriage in which at least one partner was married). In fifteenth-century Spain, for instance, several law codes equated prostitutes and adulteresses, some even insisting that all adulteresses be forced to join the public brothel.[47] Both men and women were convicted of sex outside marriage, in both church courts and civil courts, but the sexes were not always punished equally. Germanic law codes tell us that adultery on the part of women was punished more harshly than that of men. According to the Anglo-Saxon law codes of King Cnut, for instance, a woman who committed adultery was mutilated and forced to give up all her property to her husband. A man who committed adultery, on the other hand, was punished only by fine.[48] Extra-marital sex was also punished unevenly in the fines for fornication known as *leyrwites* imposed on peasants by medieval lords and ladies during the high Middle Ages. Although a few cases have been found in which men, too, were forced to pay *leyrwites,* the vast majority of fines were paid by women. The *leyrwite* fine was imposed especially on serfs (as opposed to free peasants: see chapter 2 for a discussion of the differences among categories of peasants), and the amounts of the fines could be particularly high. The typical *leyrwite* was around 6 pence, equivalent to about six days' wages for an unskilled worker, although some could be as high as 32 pence. Such a sum would have been especially hard for a poor single woman, with low earning capacity, to raise.[49] In medieval Spain and Italy, too, the social and legal punishments for women engaging in sex outside of wedlock were considerably higher than for men. Husbands who murdered adulterous wives and their lovers in Spain were treated sympathetically by judges, whereas both secular and church authorities turned a blind eye to adultery on the part of men. In some towns, men were permitted by law to kill unfaithful wives, provided that at least three of the wife's relatives agreed that she had committed adultery. Adultery by a woman was seen as dishonorable not only to the husband but also to the family of the wife, and murder was viewed as a means of regaining this honor.[50] Statutes of fourteenth-century Italian city-states became increasingly harsh toward women committing adultery: whereas male adulterers faced fines and loss of their wives' dowries, adulteresses might find themselves sentenced to shaving, whipping, imprisonment, or even death.[51]

Other jurisdictions punished male and female fornicators and adulterers more equally. In the same era in which medieval lords and ladies singled out female serfs for *leyrwites,* for instance, English church courts imposed roughly equal penances on men and women who had sex outside of wedlock. Men were sometimes regarded, in fact, as particularly guilty. Statutes of the Danish town of Ribe in 1269 directed that both male and female adulterers should be forced to run together through the streets, with the woman dragging the male by his penis, since it was this organ that was responsible for their joint crime.[52] Punishments in the Belgian courts were less dramatic, but men were convicted far more often than women: 79 percent of those convicted in adultery cases in the secular courts of Bruges, Ghent, and Ypres in the fourteenth to sixteenth centuries were men. Men were also overrepresented in the same proportion in charges laid in fifteenth-century Belgian church courts.[53] Attitudes toward responsibility for sex outside wedlock thus seem to have varied across time, place, and even jurisdiction. While women were punished more often and more harshly in some places, men were identified as the key culprits in others.

Attitudes towards illicit speech also varied considerably over time and place. Whereas women were always regarded in literature and popular culture as particularly liable to gossip and defamation, they were not always predominant among those charged with illicit speech in the courts. For example, men outnumbered women by about two to one among those charged with defamation in both church courts and secular courts in England in the thirteenth and fourteenth centuries. In the French officiality of Cerisy between 1314 and 1346, the proportion was even lower: women accounted for only 15 percent of alleged defamers. Yet attitudes towards female speech varied over time. By the fifteenth century, women accounted for more than half of those accused as defamers in English courts, making defamation a particularly female-associated crime.[54]

Other types of disruptive speech were also increasingly associated with women in late medieval England. Women greatly outnumbered men among those charged with the crime of scolding, an offense which involved talking too much or having loud, public arguments. Scolding was a new crime, prosecuted particularly from the late fourteenth century onward. Although men could sometimes be accused as scolds too, more than 90 percent of those charged were women. Nor were these women necessarily disreputable or disorderly. For instance, Margery, wife of Thomas del Mulne (mentioned in connection with ale brewing in chapter 2), was accused of scolding in the small town of Middlewich (England) in 1426. According to the bailiff, Margery had scolded Isabel, widow of Thomas Dun, calling her a "whore and other dishonest words" and saying that Isabel's mother, father, and late husband were thieves. The people of Middlewich, however, knew Margery del Mulne as an industrious and respectable woman: she was a regular brewer and baker and was married to a man who had served his town as bailiff. Yet this respectability was not enough to prevent her being charged with scolding and fined the heavy sum of 12 pence. Isabel, in her turn, called Margery a whore and said that Margery's parents were thieves (Isabel, perhaps due to her higher social status, was fined twice as much, an extremely stiff penalty). Had Margery and Isabel had their argument a century earlier, the chances are that the townspeople of Middlewich would have regarded it as disruptive and annoying but not worth punishment in the courts. By the early fifteenth century, however, attitudes toward female speech had changed, and the insults traded between the two were regarded as worthy of criminal charges. Margery and Isabel might have counted themselves lucky, at least, that they did not live in a town that operated a cucking stool. These devices, used by some towns and manors to punish convicted scolds, along with cheating brewsters and bakers, consisted of chairs strapped to the ends of long beams. A convicted offender was forced to sit in the chair while it was dunked in a lake, river, or water-filled pit. Such a punishment would not only have been uncomfortable but also humiliating, since scold-dunkings were regarded as popular entertainment. Punishments of scolds became even more gruesome in the early modern era with the invention of scolds' bridles or branks, small metal cages that fit over the head of the alleged scold and forced a barb into her mouth, making it impossible for her to talk.

In addition to crimes associated with prostitution and with illicit speech, women in some places and periods found themselves charged more often than men with stealing foodstuffs. In the English manor of Brigstock in the late thirteenth and early fourteenth centuries, for instance, women accounted for two-thirds of those charged with stealing small amounts of grain and illegal gleaning. Gleaning, or gathering the fragments of grain left behind after harvesting, was a right that manors often reserved to those who were especially poor, elderly, or disabled. In committing petty thefts in the fields, then, women may have been trying desperately to feed their families during the particularly difficult economic conditions of the early fourteenth century.[55] Some judges seem to have recognized poverty as a mitigating factor in theft of food. In Carlisle in northern England in 1331, for instance, a woman who stole two geese from her neighbor was sentenced to a short prison sentence, while another who stole various items of clothing was sentenced to be hanged.[56] For many crimes, in fact, judges seem to have been ever so slightly more lenient toward women than toward men. Among alleged felons in fourteenth-century England, for instance, women were acquitted in 84 percent of cases compared with only 70 percent of men.

In general, then, women committed crimes far less often than men. Yet some crimes, such as those involving prostitution, illicit speech, and theft of foodstuffs, were seen as especially feminine offenses. The extent to which each was regarded as an actionable crime varied significantly over time and place, however. Prostitutes in late medieval Montpellier, for example, were given limited rights as long as they stayed within a specified part of town, whereas prostitutes in thirteenth-century Castile (Spain) might be flogged, banished from towns, or forced to carry a red-hot iron rod in order to try and prove their innocence. Women committing adultery in late medieval Italy or Spain might be sentenced to death, whereas those committing adultery in late medieval Ghent might not even face prosecution. Women who spoke ill of others in thirteenth-century Cerisy were likely to find their words largely ignored, whereas those uttering the same words in four-teenth- or fifteenth-century England could be charged with defamation or scolding. And women who stole foodstuffs in periods of extreme poverty might find their judges a little more lenient than those committing similar thefts in less desperate periods.

LAWS REGARDING MARRIAGE AND WIDOWHOOD

Even if a woman never went near a courtroom, much about her life was still shaped by the law of the region in which she lived. In particular, women who married (the large majority of women, after all) found that local laws and customs determined the extent to which they could participate in the choice of their marriage partners, their control over property they brought into the marriage and inherited after their husbands' deaths, and their control over their children.

Medieval marriages, particularly those of the elite, were typically arra-nged by parents in accordance with the best interests of the family as a whole. Theoretically, at least, a woman needed to give her consent before the marriage ceremony took place. In fact, the church, which oversaw marriage litigation, came to emphasize consent and consummation (hav-ing sex) as the two major components of a valid marriage, although chaste marriages, without sex were sometimes possible too. The Fourth Lateran Council of 1215 strongly encouraged "present consent," that is, consent expressed in the present tense (e.g., "I consent to marry you") rather than in the future tense (e.g., "I will marry you"). A valid marriage could also be established, however, by consent in the future tense followed by sexual in-tercourse. Both parties had to have reached the age of puberty (arbitrarily defined as 12 for girls and 14 for boys) at the time that they articulated their consent. Problems arose, however, when it came to witnesses. According to the church, a marriage could take place anywhere and witnesses, though certainly desirable, were not absolutely necessary. The church increasingly encouraged people to have their intent to marry read aloud at mass and to conduct wedding ceremonies at the church door, but neither practice was essential in order for a marriage to be valid.

Marriage as the church preferred it: witnessed by a priest. From a thirteenth-century French manuscript of *Decrets de Gratien*. © Bibliothèque Municipale, Laon, France/The Bridgeman Art Library.

A woman's consent was necessary in theory, but in practice it was often taken for granted. Men did not always fare much better: their marriages, too, were often arranged to suit the family's political ambitions, although they were sometimes able to wriggle out of a marriage agreement with more ease. In some societies, betrothal arrangements were made when the children were as young as two or three years old, even though the official wedding ceremonies were not carried out until they reached puberty. Members of the aristocracy, since they had the most to lose or gain by marital alliances, were especially likely to contract marriages for their children when they were young. Princess Margaret of France (1158–97), for instance, was betrothed (or promised) to Prince Henry of England when she was only two or three years old and he was only five. The formal wedding did not take place until 12 years later. Had either Margaret or Henry tried to back out of the marriage in the meantime, they would have found it very difficult. Their fathers (kings of France and England respectively) would certainly have applied pressure for them to keep to the arrangement. Even among members of the lesser nobility, pressure to marry could be extreme. As seen in chapter 1, Christina of Markyate (c. 1096–post 1155), faced extreme pressure from her parents when she took a vow of chastity and refused to marry her betrothed. And as chapter 2 pointed out, Elizabeth Paston (1429–88), daughter of an English family trying to establish themselves among the gentry (lower nobility), was beaten regularly for refusing to marry a widower twice her age until she yielded and agreed. Scandinavian societies similarly assumed that the major responsibility for arranging marriages lay with a woman's family, and that the woman's consent played little to no role. Icelandic law codes of the twelfth and thirteenth centuries describe marriage negotiations as taking place between the groom and the family of the bride, with no mention of the women's consent. Similarly, thirteenth-century Danish law sought a woman's consent only if her father was dead and no relatives could step into his place.[57] Although the twelfth-century church lawyer Gratian had insisted that "no woman should be married to anyone except by her free will," therefore, the reality was often different.[58]

Women who chose to marry without parental support were rare, and they typically had a difficult time. In the French towns of Montpellier and Carcassonne, for instance, unmarried daughters were prohibited from marrying without their parents' consent.[59] By the late Middle Ages, most Italian city-states similarly prevented daughters from marrying without consent, at least until they reached a certain age. This age varied from one city to another: at Vercelli, an unmarried woman could choose her own spouse at fifteen; at Piacenza, Perugia, and Mirandola she did not have this right until the age of twenty-five. Those who broke the law would be punished with significant fines that would have seriously constrained the budget of any young couple. Elizabeth Paston's niece, Margery (c. 1448–82) proved more stubborn in the face of family pressure than her aunt. Margery chose to marry the family's bailiff, Richard Calle, to the horror of her socially climbing family who saw Calle as beneath her in status. Margery found herself subject to pressure from all sides, including the Bishop of Norwich, who summoned her and reminded her "what rebuke and shame and loss it should be to her if not guided by [her family]." By this stage, however, it was too late, for Margery and Richard had already secretly exchanged marital vows in the present tense. Margery was ostracized by her family, who clearly considered that the ultimate control over consent to marry should have lain with them.

When women were regarded as feudal wards of kings, they were particularly vulnerable to pressure to marry. When the vassal of a king died without a male heir old enough to inherit his fief (a piece of land granted by his overlord in return for specific duties), his widow and daughter might become wards of the king. This meant that he was responsible for their protection and well-being, but it also meant that he had the power over their marriage or remarriage. Since the man marrying an heiress or a wealthy widow stood to gain much power and profit, the king could effectively auction off the right to marry her to the highest bidder. Alternatively, he might use the right to marry her as a way to reward his loyal followers or gain some other political advantage. Henry II of England, for instance, gave the right of marrying a young girl to his loyal supporter William Marshall. William Marshall may have intended to marry her once she was of age but eventually decided to marry someone else and thus passed her on again.[60] Women could sometimes resist being moved around as pawns in such a way by purchasing licenses from the king to make their own marriage choices, but the cost of such licenses weakened their estates. The right of kings to force the marriage of heiresses and the remarriage of widows was unpopular, and kings repeatedly promised that they would not insist upon it, only to renege. In England, the eleventh-century King Cnut and twelfth-century Henry I vowed not to force marriage of heiresses and remarriage of widows, but both broke their promises. The forced remarriage of widows was still an issue at the time of the thirteenth-century Magna Carta, in which King John promised that "No widow shall be forced to marry so long as she wishes to live without a husband, provided that she gives security not to marry without [the king's] consent."[61] In France, too, Philip Augustus had a reputation for making money from the forced marriage of heiresses and remarriage of widows.

Peasants and townspeople typically had more say in choosing marriage partners, but they too were influenced heavily by their families and friends. Although they may not have had spouses chosen for them from an early age, they nonetheless consulted their parents and guardians in making their decisions. For some young women, the consent of their parents was a condition on which they accepted an offer of marriage. As Margery Sheppard of London said in 1486, "I will do as my fader will have me. I will have none ayenst my faders will." Maude Gyll of London sought her mother's permission as well as her father's: when asked by Laurence Wyberd to marry him, she agreed only, "with my faders leve and my moders."[62] In the case of serfs, who were not permitted to leave the manor without the permission of their lords, the situation could be more complicated. French and German serfs often had to pay fees or seek the permission of their lords, especially if they chose to marry someone who was subject to a different lord. By the twelfth century, English female serfs who wished to marry had to pay the lord a fee called a *merchet* which functioned as a marriage license. In some cases, the woman herself paid this fee; in others it was paid by her father or by her prospective husband. If she wanted to marry someone from outside the manor, the fee was typically higher because it meant that she would leave and that any children she might have would not be subject to the lord's governance. Occasionally, manorial lords could become quite directive about whom their serfs should marry, but evidence suggests that their wishes were not always followed. When the lord of the manor of Horsham (England) tried to have the marriages of his serfs determined by a group of village elders in the late thirteenth century, he faced considerable protest and resistance from his tenants.[63] *Merchet* payments and efforts by manorial lords to direct the marriages of their serfs became less common in the fourteenth and fifteenth centuries, partly in response to changing economic conditions and the gradual breakdown of manorialism and partly because of the church's increasing insistence that the power of consent lay with the couple alone.

Once consent was obtained (or coerced), a woman's power within marriage also varied according to her status and the time and location in which she lived. The exchange of gifts upon marriage was commonplace, but the types of gifts and the control that a woman could exercise over them varied. Three main types of gifts were exchanged between grooms, brides, and brides' families. First, from Roman tradition, came the custom of the dowry, presented by a bride's family to her new husband. Usually this dowry was returned to the wife on her husband's death and helped provide for her in widowhood. The dowry was often acknowledged as a woman's inheritance from her family, meaning that she would not receive any further inheritance (or might receive only a very small portion) when her parents died. Second, Germanic customs involved the provision of a "bride price" or *wittamon*, paid by the groom to the bride's family. In regions such as France and Spain in the early Middle Ages, the bride price evolved into a "bride gift" (or *dos*) paid not to her family but to the newly-widowed wife herself on her husband's death. In some legal traditions, the widow inherited the property outright only if she had no children; otherwise, she inherited the use of the bride gift but was expected to pass it on to her children upon her own death. Third, some regions under Germanic influence also provided for a *morgengabe,* or "morning gift," given by the husband directly to his new

wife on the morning after their marriage as compensation for her relin-
quishment of her virginity. The amount of the morning gift was sometimes
restricted by law: eighth-century laws from Lombardy (Italy), for instance,
insisted that the morning gift not constitute more than one-quarter of a
groom's estate and that it not be larger than the dowry. Of course, since
husbands had the right to manage the property of their wives, a woman's
control over these gifts was very much restricted while he was alive. Nevertheless, most law codes stipulated that husbands could not sell property
that was part of their wives' dowry, bride gift, or morning gift without their
wives' explicit consent.[64]

During the high Middle Ages, the bride gift and morning gift became less
common, and widows in many areas relied on their dowries and on dowers,
which consisted of either one-third or one-half of the land owned by their
husbands. Since women typically lived longer than men and had far fewer
opportunities for making an independent income, the provision of dowers and dowries was especially important to their welfare. In some places,
the dower lands were nominated at the time of marriage (and sometimes
even needed to be stipulated as part of the marriage settlement); in others, women were entitled to a third or a half of the land owned at the time
of their husbands' deaths. Widows had the right to use and take profits
from their dower lands, but again they were often prohibited from selling
them outright; instead, they were obliged to pass on these lands to their
husband's heirs.[65] Jewish law made similar kinds of provisions: a widow was
entitled to the return of her dowry, to a *ketubbah* (or marriage portion)
as stipulated in the marriage contract, and often to a *tosefet ketubbah*, or
supplemental *ketubbah*, also specified in the contract. A husband's entire
estate was pledged as security for the return of the dowry and payment of
the *ketubbah*; in other words, the widow's portions would be paid before
anything else.[66]

Individual cities and towns developed their own customs of inheritance,
too. London widows, for instance, were entitled not only to dower but also
legitim (the term for one-third of their husbands' chattels or movable property) and free bench, or the right to live in the marital household for as
long as they wished, provided that they did not remarry. Medieval Dublin
had similar rules: if a couple had children, the widow received one-third of
his movable goods at the time of his death, one-third went to his children,
and the remaining third paid for his funeral. If the couple was childless, the
widow received half of the man's movable goods.[67] Quite a different custom
evolved, however, in late medieval Douai (Flanders; now part of France).
In Douai, possessions and properties of both the husband and wife were
controlled absolutely by the husband during his lifetime (which meant that
he even had the right to sell the wife's dowry if he saw fit). After his death,
however, a widow inherited absolute control over all the property so long

as she had children; if she did not have children, she inherited half of the estate and the other half went to the parents or family of her husband.[68]

Property was not the only thing that concerned a widow on the death of her husband. If she was a mother, she was also anxious to ensure the welfare of her children. In most medieval societies, women were not necessarily or automatically named sole guardians of their children. In some areas of Anglo-Saxon England, for instance, a widow was given custody of her children, but her husband's relatives controlled his estate, effectively giving them a bargaining tool with which to ensure that the children were raised as they wished.[69] In Lucca (Italy), children typically had several guardians named, of whom their mother was only one. Often, however, men stipulated in their wills that their widows were to have a special position among the guardians and that any decisions must be made with their widows' consent. The situation was similar in Florence, in which two-thirds of men making wills included their wives among their children's guardians.[70] In the kingdom of Jerusalem, in which the rights of women were usually a little stronger than in Western Europe, women were routinely granted the right to act as their children's guardians. In the case of noblewomen whose children would inherit lands or titles, this meant that they served as regents and temporarily held the positions and administered the lands that their children would inherit upon reaching the age of majority.[71] Queen Melisende, for instance, ruled the Kingdom of Jerusalem between 1143 and 1145 while her son Baldwin was still a minor. In fact, after he reached his majority in 1145, she continued to hold onto authority for the next seven years, and only gradually yielded to pressure from her son to allow him to participate in power. Guardianship over their children, therefore, was not always an automatic right of widows. In fact, men sometimes included in their wills stipulations that their widows' inheritances would be less or that their guardianship would cease if they remarried: although this sounds controlling and harsh, the primary intention may have been to protect the children of a man's first marriage, since the inheritance of these children could be diminished if a woman was to remarry and have more children.

Widowhood could thus bring plenty of legal restrictions. A widow was often prohibited from selling land she inherited, because of her obligation to pass it on to her children, and her rights to guardianship could be curtailed if other guardians did not approve of her actions or if she remarried. Yet the rights of a widow were considerably broader than that of a wife. A widow could usually represent herself in court, was responsible for her own debts, and could make a will (married women made wills only seldom, since their husbands had ultimate rights over their property anyway).

Medieval laws, complicated and contradictory as they were, seldom served to empower women. At their best, law codes might protect women from those who sought to exploit them; at the worst, they treated women as little more than children or criminals who could not be expected to act responsibly. By looking at law codes alongside the actual legal strategies and practices of men and women, however, we can see that many of the restrictions on women were mitigated by the realities of their lives. Women who were theoretically restricted from bringing law suits might find ways to have their cases heard anyway, and wives who wished to give gifts of foodstuffs or jewels probably only seldom found their husbands denying them the right to do so. The law certainly served as one element within the broader patriarchal system of medieval Europe, but it was an element which medieval women were sometimes able to find ways to transcend.

NOTES

1. Suzanne F. Wemple, *Women in Frankish Society: Marriage and the Cloister, 500 to 900* (Philadelphia: University of Pennsylvania Press, 1981), 28–29.

2. The complete text of the Salic Law is available online at http://www29.homepage. villanova.edu/christopher.haas/lex_salica.htm.

3. Anne L. Klinck, "Anglo-Saxon Women and the Law," *Journal of Medieval History* 8 (1992), 107–21 at 109.

4. Lisa M. Bitel, *Women in Early Medieval Europe 400–1100* (Cambridge: Cambridge University Press, 2002), 70–71.

5. Sarah Westphal, "Bad Girls in the Middle Ages: Gender, Law, and German Literature," *Essays in Medieval Studies* 19 (2002), 103–19, at 105.

6. T. E., cited in Emma Hawkes, "'[S]he Will . . . Protect Her Rights Boldly by Law and Reason …': Women's Knowledge of Common Law and Equity Courts in Late-Medieval England," in *Medieval Women and the Law*, ed. Noël James Menuge (Woodbridge, U.K.: Boydell Press, 2000), 145–61.

7. Judith M. Bennett, "Public Power and Authority in the Medieval English Countryside," in *Women and Power in the Middle Ages*, ed. Mary Erler and Maryanne Kowaleski (Athens: University of Georgia Press, 1988), 18–36 at 26.

8. Elizabeth Ewan, "Scottish Portias: Women in the Courts in Mediaeval Scottish Towns," *Journal of the Canadian Historical Association* 3 (1992), 27–43 at 35–36.

9. Patricia R. Orr, "*Non Potest Appellum Facere:* Criminal Charges Women Could Not—But Did—Bring in Thirteenth-Century English Royal Courts of Justice," in *The Final Argument: The Imprint of Violence on Society in Medieval and Early Modern Europe*, ed. Donald J. Kagay and L. J. Andrew Villalon (Woodbridge, U.K.: Boydell Press, 1988), 141.

10. Maryanne Kowaleski, "Women's Work in a Market Town: Exeter in the Late Fourteenth Century," in *Women and Work in Preindustrial Europe*, ed. Barbara A. Hanawalt (Bloomington: Indiana University Press, 1986), 145–64 at 146.

11. Christine Meek, "Women Between the Law and Social Reality in Early Renaissance Lucca," in *Women in Italian Renaissance Culture and Society*, ed. Letizia Panizza (Oxford: European Humanities Research Centre, University of Oxford, 2000), 182–93 at 189.

12. Cited in Ewan, "Scottish Portias," 27–28.

13. Hawkes, "'[S]he Will. . . Protect Her Rights Boldly by Law and Reason . . .'"

14. Orr, *"Non Potest Appellum Facere,"* 146.

15. Patricia Skinner, "Disputes and Disparity: Women at Court in Medieval Southern Italy," *Reading Medieval Studies* 22 (1996), 85–105.

16. Elisabeth van Houts, "Gender and Authority of Oral Witnesses in Europe (800–1300)," *Transactions of the Royal Historical Society* 6th Series, 9 (1999), 201–20.

17. Ewan, "Scottish Portias," 31–32.

18. van Houts, "Gender and Authority of Oral Witnesses," 210–12.

19. Heath Dillard, *Daughters of the Reconquest: Women in Castilian Town Society, 1100–1300* (Cambridge: Cambridge University Press, 1984), 154.

20. Thomas K. Forbes, "A Jury of Matrons," *Medical History* 32 (1988), 23–33.

21. James A. Brundage, "Juridical Space: Female Witnesses in Canon Law," *Dumbarton Oaks Papers* 52 (1998), 147–56 at 149–51.

22. Ruth Mazo Karras, *Common Women: Prostitution and Sexuality in Medieval England* (Oxford: Oxford University Press, 1996), 97.

23. Hawkes, "'[S]he Will. . . Protect Her Rights Boldly by Law and Reason . . .'," 154.

24. Margaret H. Kerr, "Husband and Wife in Criminal Proceedings in Medieval England," in *Women, Marriage, and Family in Medieval Christendom: Essays in Memory of Michael M. Sheehan, C.S.B.*, ed. Constance M. Rousseau and Joel T. Rosenthal (Kalamazoo: Medieval Institute Publications, 1998), 211–51 at 234–36.

25. Sandy Bardsley, *Venomous Tongues: Speech and Gender in Late Medieval England* (Philadelphia: University of Pennsylvania Press, 2006), 38–9, 70–75.

26. R. L. Storey, "Malicious Indictments of the Clergy in the Fifteenth Century," in *Medieval Ecclesiastical Studies in Honour of Dorothy M. Owen*, ed. M. J. Franklin and Christopher Harper-Bill (Woodbridge, U.K.: Boydell Press, 1995), 221–40.

27. Suzanne F. Wemple, "Consent and Dissent to Sexual Intercourse in Germanic Societies from the Fifth to the Tenth Century," in *Consent and Coercion to Sex and Marriage in Ancient and Medieval Societies*, ed. Angeliki E. Laiou (Washington D.C.: Dumbarton Oaks Research Library and Collection, 1993), 227–44, at 229–31.

28. Rebecca Lynn Winer, "Defining Rape in Medieval Perpignan: Women Plaintiffs before the Law," *Viator: Medieval and Renaissance Studies* 31 (2000), 165–83 at 167, n. 8; 168.

29. Barbara A. Hanawalt, "Whose Story was This? Rape Narratives in Medieval English Courts," in *"Of Good and Ill Repute": Gender and Social Control in Medieval England* (New York: Oxford University Press, 1998), 142–57 at 131–32.

30. Andrew Finch, "Women and Violence in the Later Middle Ages: The Evidence of the Officialty of Cerisy," *Continuity and Change* 7, 1 (1992), 23–45.

31. Hanawalt, "Rape Narratives," 126–27; Winer, "Defining Rape in Medieval Perpignan," 173.

32. Kerr, "Husband and Wife in Criminal Proceedings in Medieval England," 215, n. 7.

33. Finch, "Women and Violence in the Later Middle Ages," 31.

34. Emma Hawkes, "The 'Reasonable' Laws of Domestic Violence in Late Medieval England," in *Domestic Violence in Medieval Texts*, ed. Eve Salisbury, Georgiana Donavin, & Merrall Llewelyn Price (Gainesville: University Press of Florida, 2002), 57–70 at 63–64.

35. Avraham Grossman, "Medieval Rabbinic Views on Wife-Beating, 800–1300," *Jewish History* 5 (1991), 53–62.

36. Barbara A. Hanawalt, "The Female Felon in Fourteenth-Century England," *Viator* 5 (1974), 253–68.

37. Hanawalt, "The Female Felon in Fourteenth-Century England"; Finch, "Women and Violence in the Later Middle Ages."

38. Kowaleski, "Women's Work in a Market Town," 154.

39. Ruth Mazo Karras and David Lorenzo Boyd, "'Ut cum muliere': A Male Transvestite Prostitute in Fourteenth Century London," in *Premodern Sexualities*, ed. Louise Fradenburg and Carla Freccero (New York: Routledge, 1996), 99–116.

40. Joëlle Rollo-Koster, "From Prostitutes to Brides of Christ: The Avignonese 'Repenties' in the Late Middle Ages," *Journal of Medieval and Early Modern Studies* 32 (2002), 109–44 at 117; Vern L. Bullough and James Brundage, *Sexual Practices and the Medieval Church* (Buffalo: Prometheus Books, 1982), 183.

41. Leah Lydia Otis, *Prostitution in Medieval Society: The History of an Urban Institution in Languedoc* (Chicago: University of Chicago Press, 1985), 11, 31.

42. Otis, *Prostitution in Medieval Society*, 25–26.

43. Karras, *Common Women*, 37–40.

44. Ruth Mazo Karras, "Prostitution in Medieval Europe," in *Handbook of Medieval Sexuality*, ed. Vern L. Bullough and James A. Brundage (New York: Garland, 1996), 243–60 at 245–46.

45. Rollo-Koster, "From Prostitutes to Brides of Christ," 112; Karras, *Common Women*, 21–22.

46. Marianne Naessens, "Judicial Authorities' Views of Women's Roles in Late Medieval Flanders," in *The Texture of Society: Medieval Women in the Southern Low Countries*, ed. Ellen E. Kittell and Mary A. Suydam, 51–77 at 58–63; Karras, Common Women, 44.

47. Eukene Lacarra Lanz, "Changing Boundaries of Licit and Illicit Unions: Concubinage and Prostitution," in *Marriage and Sexuality in Medieval and Early Modern Iberia*, ed. Eukene Lacarra Lanz (New York: Routledge, 2002), 158–94 at 166.

48. Klinck, "Anglo-Saxon Women and the Law," 111.

49. Judith M. Bennett, "Writing Fornication: Medieval Leyrwite and its Historians," *Transactions of the Royal Historical Society* 6th Series, 13 (2003), 131–62.

50. Lanz, "Changing Boundaries of Licit and Illicit Unions, 165–6; Dillard, *Daughters of the Reconquest*, 205.

51. Trevor Dean, "Fathers and Daughters: Marriage Laws and Marriage Disputes in Bologna and Italy, 1200–1500," in *Marriage in Italy, 1300–1650*, ed. Trevor Dean and K.J.P. Lowe (Cambridge: Cambridge University Press, 1998), 85–106 at 86.

52. Inger Dübeck, "Women, Weddings, and Concubines in Medieval Danish Law," *Scandinavian Journal of History* 17 (1992), 315–22 at 319.

53. Naessens, "Judicial Authorities' Views of Women's Roles in Late Medieval Flanders," 63.

54. Bardsley, *Venomous Tongues*, 77–81; Finch, "Women and Violence in the Later Middle Ages."

55. Judith M. Bennett, *Women in the Medieval English Countryside: Gender and Household in Brigstock before the Plague* (New York: Oxford University Press, 1987), 41.

56. Cynthia J. Neville, "War, Women and Crime in the Northern English Border Lands in the Later Middle Ages," in *The Final Argument*, 163–79 at 163.

57. Jenny Jochens, "'Með Jákvæði Hennar Sjálfrar': Consent as Signifier in the Old Norse World," in *Consent and Coercion to Sex and Marriage in Ancient and Medieval Societies*, 274–75, Dübeck, "Women, Weddings, and Concubines in Medieval Danish Law," 316.

58. Cited in Michael M. Sheehan, "Choice of Marriage Partner in the Middle Ages," in *Medieval Families: Perspectives on Marriage, Household, and Children*, ed. Carol Neel (Toronto: University of Toronto Press, 2004), 157–91 at 164.

59. Jennifer Smith, "Unfamiliar Territory: Women, Land, and Law in Occitania, 1130–1250," in *Medieval Women and the Law*, 19–40 at 32.

60. Cited in Fiona Harris Stoertz, "Young Women in France and England, 1050–1300," *Journal of Women's History* 12 (2001), 27.

61. Janet Senderowitz Loengard, "*Rationabilis Dos:* Magna Carta and the Widow's 'Fair Share' in the Earlier Thirteenth Century," in *Wife and Widow in Medieval England*, ed. Sue Sheridan Walker (Ann Arbor: University of Michigan Press, 1993), 59–80.

62. Shannon McSheffrey, "'I Will Never Have None Ayenst My Faders Will': Consent and the Making of Marriage in the Late Medieval Diocese of London," in *Women, Marriage, and Family in Medieval Christendom*, 153–74 at 156, 161.

63. Judith M. Bennett, "Medieval Peasant Marriage: An Examination of Marriage License Fines in *Liber Gersumarum*," in *Pathways to Medieval Peasants*, ed. J. A. Raftis (Toronto: Pontifical Institute of Mediaeval Studies, 1981), 193–246; Elaine Clark, "Decision to Marry," *Mediaeval Studies* 49 (1987), 496–516, at 500–502.

64. Wemple, *Women in Frankish Society*, 44–45; Barbara M. Kreutz, "The Twilight of 'Morgengabe'," in *Portraits of Medieval and Renaissance Living: Essays in Honor of David Herlihy*, ed. Samuel K. Cohn Jr. and Steven A. Epstein (Ann Arbor: University of Michigan Press, 1996), 131–47 at 135.

65. Janet Senderowitz Loengard, "'Of the Gift of Her Husband': English Dower and its Consequences in the Year 1200," in *Women of the Medieval World: Essays in Honour of John H. Mundy*, ed. Julius Kirschner and Suzanne F. Wemple (Oxford: B. Blackwell, 1985), 215–55.

66. Elka Klein, "The Widow's Portion: Law, Custom, and Marital Property Among Medieval Catalan Jews," *Viator: Medieval and Renaissance Studies* 31 (2000): 147–63.

67. Lynda Conlon, "Women in Medieval Dublin: Their Legal Rights and Economic Power," *Medieval Dublin: Proceedings of the Friends of Medieval Dublin Symposium* 4 (2002), 172–92 at 175.

68. Martha C. Howell, "Fixing Movables: Gifts by Testament in Late Medieval Douai," *Past and Present* 150 (1996), 3–45 at 19–25.

69. Klinck, "Anglo-Saxon Women and the Law," 110.

70. Meek, "Women Between the Law and Social Reality in Early Renaissance Lucca," 188; Isabelle Chabot, "Lineage Strategies and the Control of Widows in Renaissance Florence," in *Widowhood in Medieval and Early Modern Europe*, ed. Sandra Cavallo and Lyndan Warner (Harlow, U.K.: Longman, 1999), 127–44 at 138.

71. Sylvia Schein, "Women in Medieval Colonial Society: The Latin Kingdom of Jerusalem in the Twelfth Century," in *Gendering the Crusades*, ed. Susan B. Edgington and Sarah Lambert (Cardiff: University of Wales Press, 2001), 144.

SUGGESTED READING

Ewan, Elizabeth. "Scottish Portias: Women in the Courts in Mediaeval Scottish Towns," *Journal of the Canadian Historical Association* 3 (1992): 27–43.

Finch, Andrew. "Women and Violence in the Later Middle Ages: The Evidence of the Officialty of Cerisy," *Continuity and Change* 7, 1 (1992): 23–45.

Hanawalt, Barbara A. "The Female Felon in Fourteenth-Century England." *Viator* 5 (1974): 253–68.

Karras, Ruth Mazo. *Common Women: Prostitution and Sexuality in Medieval England.* Oxford: Oxford University Press, 1996.

Klinck, Anne L. "Anglo-Saxon Women and the Law," *Journal of Medieval History* 8 (1992): 107–21.

Loengard, Janet S. "Common Law for Margery: Separate but not Equal," in *Women in Medieval Western European Culture.* ed. Linda E. Mitchell. New York: Garland, 1999.

Menuge, Noël James, ed. *Medieval Women and the Law.* Woodbridge, England: Boydell Press, 2000.

Skinner, Patricia. "Disputes and Disparity: Women at Court in Medieval Southern Italy," *Reading Medieval Studies* 22 (1996): 85–105.

Wemple, Suzanne F. *Women in Frankish Society: Marriage and the Cloister, 500 to 900.* Philadelphia: University of Pennsylvania Press, 1981.

5

⊶∾

Women and Culture

Throughout the Middle Ages, women's interaction with art, literature, and music was multifaceted. First, they sometimes served as creators of these art forms. Women were not typically assigned a creative role in medieval culture, but there were certainly instances in which they could and did paint, write, compose, and design. Second, women found themselves depicted in works created by both men and women. Such images could be both positive and negative, and they sent important and influential messages about women's role in medieval society (although women did not necessarily interpret them in the ways intended). Third, women served as patrons for works composed and executed by others. In doing so their role was often very active: some female patrons were quite explicit in their directions to authors, artists, and musicians and quite mindful of the ways in which commissions reflected their power and authority. Women's exclusion from many of the creative trades did not, therefore, prevent them from engaging in the creative process.

WOMEN AS CREATORS

Female Artists

Prior to the Renaissance era, artists were not accorded any special status in society—rather, they were seen as ordinary craftspeople. Since men dominated crafts and trades in general, the majority of artists were almost certainly men. Moreover, medieval artists—whether women or men—did

The mythical St. Marcia paints a self-portrait. Illumination from a fifteenth-century manuscript of Giovanni Boccaccio's *De Claris Mulieribus.* © Bibliothèque Nationale, Paris, France/Giraudon/The Bridgeman Art Library

not typically sign their works, so identifying work executed by a woman is difficult. Yet the names of a few female artists have survived. These include Anastaise, a fifteenth-century manuscript illuminator employed (and much praised) by Christine de Pisan; Mabel of Bury St. Edmunds, an embroiderer who worked for the English court in the thirteenth century; and Bourgot, a female illuminator employed along with her father to illustrate a book for Yolande of Flanders, countess of Bar, in 1353.[1] Although creative arts were dominated by men, there were also frequent exceptions to the rule.

As with other trades, women might learn from their husbands and fathers and thus participate as miniaturists, calligraphers, illuminators, or embroiderers even though they seldom established independent workshops. Women accounted for 10 of 229 sculptors and painters from the Parisian guild lists from around 1300, for example, but at least five of these were widows of men who had once run workshops of their own. Glimpses of the rank-and-file craftswomen are sometimes hard to find: embroiderers of large projects, for instance, were often hired in groups or teams, and the names of individual embroiderers have been lost. An exception which seems to prove this rule is the contract for embroidering counterpanes for Queen

Philippa of England in 1330. Among the 112 embroiderers working on the project, 42 were women (although the women were paid at two-thirds the rate of the men). Moreover, both male and female embroiderers worked to the design of a professional artist, paid twice as much, and hence had little room for artistic license.[2] Other sources attesting to women's role in artistic crafts include court cases in which women are mentioned as professional craftspeople and contracts. Surviving thirteenth-century contracts from the Italian city of Bologna, for instance, mention several women who are identified as miniaturists, calligraphers, or copyists of books. Tula, a widow from the German city of Cologne, was described in the thirteenth century as a professional *rubeatrix,* one who applied the red color used to highlight important words in manuscripts. A few women worked in the metal trades, too, such as Sancia Guidosalvi of Spain who, in the early twelfth century, created a large silver cross decorated with figures.[3] Women illustrators and painters appear occasionally in small sketches in the margins of other works, too. Surviving copies of Boccaccio's *Famous Women* include several illuminations showing women painting frescoes, copying and decorating manuscripts, and sculpting tombs. Anastaise, Mabel, Bourgot, Tula, and Sancia are, however, the exceptions to the rule. The vast majority of medieval female artists have disappeared without any record of their names.

Despite this anonymity, we can also attribute other works to groups of women. Nuns, in particular, were often responsible for producing embroideries, manuscript illuminations, and drawings. For example, the embroidery of the eleventh-century Bayeux Tapestry, commemorating the Norman Conquest of England, is often attributed to Anglo-Saxon nuns. Measuring 230 feet long, the Bayeux Tapestry served as a piece of propaganda justifying and celebrating the Conquest from the Normans' perspective, so it must have rankled with the nuns to expend so much labor in its production. Other nuns may have found outlets for their own creativity while producing works-to-order for others. Dominican convents in southern Germany and northern Switzerland, for instance, were famed for producing both tapestries and manuscripts. Tiny images of nuns weaving, included in the margins of two surviving tapestries from the late medieval era, suggest that the nuns might have wanted to leave a kind of signature on their works of art and display their reverence by placing themselves near the biblical scenes depicted in the main section of the tapestries.[4] This focus on textile art was not new: complaints by church officials and church councils in the early Middle Ages that certain nunneries spent too much time producing embroideries point to a long-standing association between nuns and embroidery.[5] Their complaints were clearly unheeded, since embroidery had become so closely associated with certain nunneries by the late Middle Ages that the technique of brightly colored wool embroidery was known as *Klosterstich* (convent stitch). In the nunnery of Lüne in Saxony

(Germany), for instance, nuns produced over 900 square feet of *Klosterstich* between 1492 and 1508.[6] Textile art, long connected with women, served as a source of both income and occupation for cloistered nuns.

Nuns also turned to the copying and illustration of manuscripts as a source of income. Diemud of Wessobrun, a German nun of the eleventh to twelfth centuries, was known to have copied around 45 manuscripts and to have acquired a certain fame for the beauty of her work. Another, Guta of Schwarzenthann, signed her name on a book she copied in 1154.[7] Other nunneries served as workshops for the production of books with multiple (anonymous) sisters contributing. Like nuns who worked at textile art, nuns engaged in copying and illustrating religious manuscripts were not only performing works of devotion but also generating income for their houses.

Other nuns were able to direct their creative efforts toward their own communities. An unknown nun or nuns from the Convent of St. Walburg in Bavaria (Germany), for instance, produced a series of drawings that were used as part of devotional practices. Powerful in their visual appeal, the drawings have typically been neglected by art historians because they lack the size and sophistication of altarpieces or statues. Nonetheless they provide insight into the ways in which the nuns of St. Walburg's organized their religious lives by encouraging a strong, almost mystic, connection between the images and the viewers. A drawing of the Consecration of Virgins, for instance, depicts the Virgin Mary and the baby Jesus blessing a group of kneeling women. The ceremony in which virgins were consecrated was presided over by a bishop, but in this instance the nun-artist has placed Mary in the role of consecrator. Moreover, in the consecration ceremony, nuns were typically married in a spiritual wedding to an adult Christ; here, however, Christ is still a baby, and in the inscription the baby Jesus instructs the virgins to "suckle me!" Thus the nuns are not only blessed by Mary but are also encouraged to identify with her in her role as nurse to Jesus.[8] Nuns who created images for their own communities could thus tailor them to fit their communities' religious needs. Similarly, some nunneries were able to accumulate substantial libraries from the work of nuns who copied books by hand: the library of St. Katherine's in Nuremberg (Germany) numbered over 500 books by the fifteenth century.[9] The prolific nun Kunigunde Niklasin, for instance, copied out 31 manuscripts, among them the Bible, saints' lives, and books of sermons. Sparsely illustrated, the books copied by the nuns of St. Katherine's demonstrate that their primary interest was in the message of the text.[10]

Women's role in the creation of the visual arts, therefore, was important, even if it is sometimes difficult to uncover. In part this is due to the fact that craftspeople seldom attached their names to their works; many surviving works of painting, sculpture, metalwork, embroidery, and more might actually have been created in whole or in part by family workshops that included women, but we have no way to detect their role. And in part the difficulty of finding medieval female artists is due to the conventions of medieval trade which relegated women to lesser roles in the production of any item, whether it be a piece of woven cloth or an embroidery. While women participated in making such objects, their role was often confined to the less creative aspects of the task, carrying out the needlework, for instance, rather than designing the embroidery.

Female Authors

Women artists of the Middle Ages are hard to find; women writers, however, are a little easier to identify, and in the last three decades they have been the subject of a great deal of scholarship by literary scholars. Women wrote plays, poems, medical treatises, histories, letters, spiritual and moral literature, academic discourses, and more. Female writers can be found among nuns, elite women and—although rarely—townswomen. Writing by women can also be found from throughout the Middle Ages, but (as with writing by men) more survives from the late Middle Ages. As writing in Latin gave way to writing in the vernacular, more women's voices were recorded. Indeed, just as scholarly Latin was associated with men, the vernacular—unscholarly, accessible to all—was often associated with women. Some well-educated women certainly wrote in Latin throughout the Middle Ages, but many more were silent until the proliferation of vernacular texts in the late Middle Ages. No matter the language in which they wrote, female authors had especially to be cautious not to claim too much authority through their writing. St. Paul had insisted that women were not to preach nor teach; through the act of recording her own thoughts, a woman might come dangerously close to defying his instruction. Thus female authors needed to find ways to justify their own writing and reassure their audiences that they were not overstepping their bounds.

Writing from the position of a mother, for instance, was a strategy that some female authors employed. A heart-wrenching example of an advice manual written by a mother comes from the ninth-century Dhuoda, a noblewoman separated from her sons at the orders of her husband, Duke Bernard of Septimania. In the prologue to her *Liber Manualis,* Dhuoda explains why she wrote this book for her older son:

> I am well aware that most women rejoice that they are with their children in this world, but I, Dhuoda, am far away from you, my son William. For this reason I am anxious and filled with longing to do something for you. So I send you this little work written down in my name, that you may read it for your education, as a kind of mirror. And I rejoice that, even if I am apart from you in body, the little book before you may remind you, when you read it, of what you should do on my behalf.[11]

The contents of Dhuoda's advice are both practical and devout. William, in his mid-teens when Dhuoda wrote her book, is advised to pray frequently, act nobly toward widows and orphans, collect and read books, serve his lord faithfully, and more. Dhuoda's *Liber Manualis* not only provides insight into the relationship between a noblewoman and her son; it also provides information about the extent of her education. Most agree that her Latin was awkward and contained a number of errors, yet the contents of her book show that she knew of the ideas of several other authors. Through close analysis of her language, scholars have shown that Dhuoda was very familiar with the Bible, especially the psalms, and that she was also aware of the works of a number of classical and early medieval authors. For instance, she had clearly read or heard about the *Rule* of St. Benedict (see chapter 1), which served as a model for her discussion of humility and obedience.[12] The extent to which Dhuoda's education was typical for a laywoman of her era remains an issue of debate among scholars: some see her as exceptional, while others disagree. Dhuoda's *Liber Manualis* is in some ways a radical book, since she clearly regards maternal advice as worthy of being recorded and as a way to compensate, if only a little, for the separation from her sons that her husband had imposed. For Dhuoda, motherhood grants her the right to give her son advice. As she tells William, "My son, my firstborn son—you will have other teachers to present you with works of fuller and richer usefulness, but not anyone like me, your mother, whose heart burns on your behalf."[13]

Later authors similarly spoke from their position as mothers. Christine de Pisan, one of the best-known medieval authors, took up professional writing after the death of her husband and father. Mother of three, Christine supported herself through her pen, a rare feat in fourteenth- and fifteenth-century Paris. Among her many works were two books written ostensibly for her son, *Moral Teachings* and *Moral Proverbs,* in which she recorded words of maternal advice. But Christine also wrote advice books intended for a wider audience, especially for an audience of young women. Her *Book of the City of Ladies* and its sequel *Treasure of the City of Ladies* included advice for women of all social ranks (although its contents do show that the author was more familiar with the lives of the elites than those of craftspeople or peasants). Christine's advice deals with both the ethical and the practical. Women who live at court and serve princesses, for example, are warned not to fraternize with too many men. Christine first explains how excessive friendliness toward men might undermine the courtly woman's honor, along with that of the princess whom she serves. She then gives the more practical reasons: men who become too friendly, she warns, will vie for a woman's affection and make fun of her behind her back if she is not forthcoming. Reputation matters, and Christine does not want to see young women defamed through their own naïveté.[14] Similar kinds of advice were doled out to young women through poems that included a mother's voice. The English "How the Good Wife Taught her Daughter" and the German "Die Winsbeckin" poems, for instance, feature a mother advising her daughter on both morality and practical matters. The authorship of these poems, however, is uncertain: even though the poems take the perspective of a mother, they may well have been written by men.

A related genre in which women authors often wrote was that of devotional literature. Mystics, visionaries, nuns, and lay women found that religious writing allowed them a voice—as long, that is, as they were careful not to claim too much authority. Negotiating St. Paul's prohibition on preaching and teaching, female authors often justified their writing by claiming that they had been compelled by God to record their visions and messages. The twelfth-century nun Elisabeth of Schönau, for instance, was reluctant to record her visions but forced physically to do so by a fearsome angel:

> In order that I might avoid arrogance, however, and that I might not be perceived as the author of novelties, I strove to hide these things [visions] as much as possible. Therefore . . . an angel of the Lord stood before me saying 'Why do you hide gold in mud?' . . . And having said this he lifted a scourge over me, which he struck me with most harshly five times . . . so that for three days I lay with my whole body shattered by this beating.[15]

Elisabeth's fear that she might be perceived as arrogant was well-founded. When accounts of some of her visions were circulated without her knowledge or permission, she was ridiculed and dismissed as a fraud. The fifteenth-century English anchoress Julian of Norwich sought also to offset the risks involved in recording her visions:

> But God forbid that you should say or understand that I am a teacher, for I do not mean that, and I never meant that; for I am a woman, ignorant, feeble and frail. But I know well, this that I say, for I have it from the revelation of He who is sovereign teacher . . . Because I am a woman, should I therefore believe that I should not tell you of the goodness of God, since I saw at the same time that it is His will that it be known?[16]

By denying that she was a teacher per se and arguing that she merely transmitted the teachings of God, Julian was able to write of visions that seem quite radical today. As chapter 1 explains, Julian emphasized the maternal nature of Jesus and wrote of him feeding worshippers with the Eucharist as a mother might breastfeed her child. Writing by mystics such as Julian emphasizes closeness, even union, with God. It seeks to prompt an emotional response in the reader, emphasizing, for instance, the agony of Jesus on the cross or the intense pleasure of a mystical union with him. Some scholars have argued that texts by female visionaries can be distinguished from those of male visionaries by their emphasis on emotions; others, however, find fewer differences between male- and female-authored mystical writings.[17]

In keeping with their reluctance to be seen as teaching or preaching, female mystics and writers of devotional material often focused primarily on their own experiences. That is, rather than purporting to lecture their audiences about morality or make sweeping claims about the ways in which people should behave, they frequently structured their writing around personal accounts of what they saw in the course of their visions. As such, their writing tended toward the autobiographical. The first autobiography in the English language, *The Book of Margery Kempe*, originates from this tradition. Margery, who came from the town of King's Lynn in the early fifteenth century, dictated the details of her life, travels, trials, and visions, to a scribe. Margery's references to the work of Julian of Norwich, Brigid of Sweden, Marie d'Oignies and others show that she was familiar with the genre of visionary literature.

Women could, in fact, play a significant role in the authorship of ostensibly male-authored texts too. The male writer of the thirteenth-century *Ancrene Wisse*, for instance, claimed to have written it for the edification of three sisters who sought to become anchoresses. Recent scholarship has, however, pointed out that it was clearly composed as a result of close conversations with these young women in which they explained their needs and sought advice. While these women were not authors per se, then, they nonetheless played an important role in shaping the contents of this devotional text.[18]

Fewer concerns were sparked about women preaching or teaching when they confined their writing to letters. While letters could still be powerful in content, like St. Catherine of Siena's fourteenth-century letters to the pope and others (see chapter 1), they were generally intended for a much smaller audience than were mystical and devotional writings. Some of the most famous letters written by a woman are those of Heloise, a twelfth-century abbess of the French nunnery known as the Paraclete. Prior to her entry into the convent, Heloise had had a love affair with Peter Abelard, one of the most widely known scholars and intellectuals of his day. The affair produced a child, and both Abelard and Heloise were forced to take refuge in religious houses from the wrath of Heloise's family. Heloise's subsequent letters to Abelard show that she continued to love him; Abelard's responses, however, became more distant and pious as time went on. Heloise's letters are unusual for the emotion conveyed in them, since medieval letters were often terse and business-like, conveying only glimpses into the personality of the authors. Because men of the gentry and noble classes were frequently away from home, their wives wrote letters to order provisions, seek advice, and pass on news. Several important collections of family letters survive from late medieval England, most notably those of the Paston,

Stonor, Plumpton, and Cely families. Yet even business letters occasionally went beyond the strictly practical, providing wonderful insights into the emotional lives of their authors. While letters by four women of the Paston family survive, those of Margaret Paston (c. 1426–84) are especially interesting. Margaret certainly uses letters in their traditional function, updating her husband, John, on the status of the estate and the deeds of their children. She also, however, uses the medium persuasively. When she wants a new belt, for example, Margaret implies to her husband that her father thought him too cheap to buy it. She adds "but I suppose that is not so—he said it but for an excuse. I pray you, if ye dare take it upon you, that ye will vouchsafe to [have it made before] ye come home." Margaret also conveys genuine love and emotion in her letters, lamenting one Christmas Eve that her husband will not make it home for Christmas and hoping he will return soon: "I pray you that ye will come as soon as ye may; I shall think myself half a widow because ye shall not be at home."[19] The letters of the Italian widow Alessandra Macinghi Strozzi, dating from the middle of the fifteenth century, are even more confident in tone. In her letters to her sons, Strozzi does not hesitate to advise on matters of business nor those of ethical behavior. Strozzi's letters are influenced by the tradition of advice literature: they are like a cross between Dhuoda's *Liber Manualis* and traditional business correspondence.

Women who composed fictional literature faced barriers too. Scholars have estimated that women accounted for about 20 of the more than 400 troubadours writing in southern France in the twelfth and thirteenth centuries. Troubadour poetry, an important literary genre of the high to late Middle Ages, typically focuses on the theme of courtly love. Very often it centers on an illicit, adulterous passion which may or may not be consummated. In many such poems, the object of the poet's love is not even aware of the poet's passionate feelings, and the verse thus focuses on the agony of unrequited love. Much troubadour verse places women on a pedestal, imagining them as perfect, chaste, beautiful, and inaccessible. Yet this did not necessarily make life any easier for real women. Just as images of the Virgin Mary (discussed below) could frustrate women by their inapproachability, so too the remote, worshipped image of the lady in courtly literature may have done little for real women's status. Biographies of troubadours composed in the mid- to late thirteenth century list several female names (female troubadours were sometimes called *trobairitz*), but little verifiable information survives about these women.[20]

We know most about the twelfth-century poet Marie de France, and even our knowledge of her is very little. Marie herself tells us at the end of her Fables that "Marie is my name, and I am of France." Finding this information too brief, scholars have sought more information on Marie's identity, and various hypotheses have been raised about exactly who Marie might have been. Some think she may have been a nun or abbess of French birth living in an English convent; others are not so sure. What is clear from Marie's writings is that she expected her name to be remembered. Indeed, she tells us that she will name herself, "for posterity . . . It may be that several clerks would lay claim to my work. I do not want anyone to appropriate it. To allow oneself to be forgotten is to act as a fool."[21] Marie wrote especially in two genres: fables (or *fabliaux*), which tended to be more bawdy, and lays (or *lais*), which were short stories with themes of courtly love. Like the stories of other authors of her time, Marie's fables were seldom truly original: instead, she borrowed from the tales in circulation and gave them her own unique spin. Marie's stories differ from those of her fellow troubadours, however, in that she avoided the more misogynous tropes about the faults of women. For instance, when she adapts a Latin fable from the first century C.E. that concluded that women were never satisfied and always wanted more, Marie shifts the moral so that it applies to both women and men. Even in stories in which women seem to be at fault, Marie resists the temptation to draw conclusions about all women (as her fellows often did) and instead makes her moral more generalizable. In one of her fables, for instance, a peasant woman deceives her husband by making him think that his glimpse of her with a lover is a trick of his eyes. Marie concludes not by condemning the trickery of women but rather by claiming, "By this example we learn that sense and quick wit are often worth more than wealth or family."[22] While not perhaps feminist in a modern sense, Marie de France nonetheless supported women by avoiding explicitly anti-female sentiments.

Little enough is known about Marie de France, but even less is known about other female troubadours. The paucity of background information, indeed, can make it very hard for scholars to fully understand their works. For example, a late thirteenth-century poem attributed to Na Bieris de Roman consists of 24 lines of verse praising another woman (Lady Maria) and hoping to win her heart. "For you I have whatever happiness I have," she writes, "and for you I often go about sighing." Does this love for another woman mean that Na Bieris de Roman was a lesbian? Or did she write this poem as if it were voiced by a man?[23] Scholars are undecided on how to interpret her poem, but one thing is clear: social norms did not permit female troubadours to address such poems to men in the same way that male (or female) troubadours could address them to women. No poems exist detailing how a woman obsessed on a man and how, for his sake, she often went about sighing. Female troubadours could avoid the overt misogyny present in many male-authored texts, but they needed to follow other conventions of the genre.

Women who wrote in other genres were similarly careful not to stray too far from convention. Hrotswita of Gandersheim, a German canoness of the tenth century, drew on classical models in her epics, poems, and plays, but she carefully shaped these for the Christian context. Her plays, in particular, take inspiration from the Roman comic playwright Terence. As Hrotswita herself notes, however, she attempts to apply Christian morality to his so-called immoral (i.e., pagan) works. Six dramas of Hrotswita's survive, and these are generally acknowledged as her most important work, although she also wrote poems and histories. The prolific eleventh-century abbess Hildegard of Bingen also wrote in many different genres. In addition to accounts of her own visions, Hildegard wrote an encyclopedia of science and medicine, lives of saints, works of theology, and music. Among her most famous compositions is her *Ordo Virtutum* (Play of Virtues), a drama set to music which she composed for the nuns in her convent known as the Rupertsberg.

Women like Hildegard occasionally composed works that might today be classified as scholarly, although their opportunities for doing so were rare indeed. Trota, a twelfth-century healer from southern Italy, for instance, recorded some of her treatments and medical advice. Over the following centuries, more works were attributed to her under the name Trotula, creating a compendium of medical advice only parts of which can reliably be attributed to the original Trota.[24] Women wrote histories, too: Anna Comnena, daughter of the Byzantine Emperor Alexius, compiled a history of her father's life and reign during the early twelfth century. The *Alexiad*, as the work is known, draws upon a number of classical models, demonstrating Anna's broad education. It also serves as one of historians' major primary sources for understanding the Byzantine Empire in the eleventh and twelfth centuries, an era of considerable change. Anna describes, for instance, the Byzantine response to the Western European crusaders who traipsed through Constantinople en route to the Holy Land.[25] Anna cannot, however, be regarded as typical: her impressive education and position as daughter and sister of emperors made her exceptional.

Another exceptional woman, Christine de Pisan, was important not only for the extent and range of her works but also for their subject matter. Christine's contributions to the advice genre are noted above; she was also, however, an important participant in a debate raging in early fifteenth-century Paris about women's status and abilities. The *querelle de la Rose*, or debate over the book known as the *Roman de la Rose*, took the form of a series of letters exchanged among members of Paris's intellectual elites. The original manuscript of the *Roman de la Rose* had been composed by Guillaume de Lorris in the 1230s and consisted of about 4,000 lines describing a lover who hoped, through brave completion of quests, to win a rose symbolizing his beloved. The text was continued, however, by Jean de Meun in the 1260s and 1270s. De Meun's addition of 17,000 lines of verse took the story in a different direction, and in the process he gave several of his characters lines that belittled and defamed women. Over a century later, Jean de Montreuil praised de Meun's additions. Christine de Pisan responded by pointing out its failings, especially its ill-treatment of women. Jean de Montreuil and his friend, Gontier Col, defended Jean de Meun's work and in turn attacked Christine, asking her to withdraw her criticisms. Christine refused, and she published the contents of the debate. Others became involved, most notably Jean Gerson, chancellor of the University of Paris, who supported Christine. Eventually the flurry of letters died down, but the pro-female sentiments they sparked certainly influenced Christine's best-known works, the *Book of the City of Ladies* and *Treasure of the City of Ladies.* Christine insisted, for instance, that women were not innately inferior in intellectual ability to men; rather, she said, their lack of education accounted for the fact that women typically played a lesser part in public affairs. Like Marie de France, Christine de Pisan updated misogynist stories as she retold them. A popular medieval legend was that of the patient and obedient Griselda, a peasant woman who married a lord and promised him absolute obedience. The lord tested her promise by taking away her two children and saying that he would kill them and by sending her away. Despite these humiliations, Griselda remained loyal to him and so—eventually—he reinstated her to her position. Griselda, like the Virgin Mary and the courtly women of troubadour literature, was thus an impossibly good woman whose obedience showed up the flaws in ordinary women. Christine's spin on the Griselda legend is different: when she retells the story, she places less emphasis on Griselda's virtue and more on the kinds of abuse that married women must often suffer at the hands of cruel husbands.[26]

Women authors thus ranged over a wide array of literary genres. In each case, however, they needed to pay particular attention to tone and audience so as not to violate the proscription against female teachers. Women tended to position themselves very carefully, in fact, in order to make clear that they did not intend to claim too much authority for themselves. Indeed, the proscription against female teachers may have caused other texts by women to disappear. Since manuscripts survived only if they were copied out by hand, less popular or more radical texts might well have suffered the fate of being lost or destroyed without copies made. Perhaps other Dhuodas, Hrotswitas, or Christines once recorded their thoughts too. Even if only a fraction of their writings survive, however, the corpus of literature written by medieval women is both diverse and impressive.

Female Musicians

St. Paul not only banned women from preaching or teaching; he also insisted that they should be silent in church. This limited the extent to which they could participate in the singing of divine services. In the first few centuries after the death of Jesus, women did sing as part of church services, but they were increasingly silenced from the fourth century onward. Gradually, devotional singing became the preserve of men and boys. Yet women did continue to sing in nunneries and, sometimes, as part of dances or sing-alongs outside the context of the church. Medieval dramas were often sung or put to music, and women sometimes participated in these, too. In nunneries, for instance, women had little choice but to play both male and female roles themselves. Outside of the convents, however, parts were typically played by men (although female characters were sometimes played by boys dressed as women).

Among composers, women's names are very rare. A few are known to have composed Byzantine Christian chant. Most of these were nuns, such as the ninth-century Kassia, who composed at least 23, and perhaps as many as 50, chants. One of Kassia's hymns, about Mary Magdalene, is still sung as part of services on Holy Wednesday in the Greek Orthodox church.[27] But just as the names of female artists have very often been lost, so too have the names of female composers.

The best-known female composer of the Middle Ages is undoubtedly Hildegard of Bingen. Similar to other mystics, who claimed divine inspiration for their works so as to avoid charges that they were asserting authority, Hildegard cited God's instructions in recording her music and visions. Her two musical works are the *Ordo Virtutum* (the morality music-drama, mentioned above) and the *Symphonia Armonie Celestium Revelationem* (Symphony of the Harmony of Celestial Revelations). The *Symphonia,* a chant cycle, contains 75 pieces of her own poetry which were intended originally for her nuns at the Rupertsberg. Hildegard's compositional style was unconventional: her songs often include notes from two octaves or more, for instance. Her lyrics especially focused on female saints: over one-third of the chants in her *Symphonia* are dedicated to the Virgin Mary or to St. Ursula. Hildegard's music has been rediscovered in recent years and has undergone a new popularity.

Outside the religious sphere, women appeared occasionally as singers. Female troubadours, considered above, wrote lyrics that were accompanied by music and may have been performed by their authors. Female minstrels seem to have been especially prominent in Spain, where many minstrels were of Islamic descent. The thirteenth-century palace account books of King Sancho IV of Castile, for instance, show payments to two Arabic women among the 27 minstrels. French courts often employed female minstrels, too: references attest to their employment by the thirteenth-century French king Louis IX and the fourteenth-century Mahaut d'Artois. The guild lists from Paris in 1341 include the names of 7 women along with 30 men.[28]

Female musicians, therefore, are few and far between in surviving sources from medieval Europe. As with artists and authors, however, we must remember that we are perhaps seeing only the tip of the iceberg: many more compositions by women or performances by female musicians may well have been lost or attributed to anonymous composers. No traces may remain, for instance, of a peasant woman who improvised a song in the local tavern or a nun who created a variation on a chant. Remnants of female participation may be found in almost every creative genre from the Middle Ages, but only rarely can women's role be examined in detail.

DEPICTIONS OF WOMEN

Medieval women received conflicting messages about their role in society and about the ways that they should behave. They heard that they were by nature sources of evil and temptation, like the Biblical Eve, yet at the same time they were told they were capable of great piety, like the Virgin Mary. These conflicting messages are not perhaps as surprising as they seem at first: modern society is also riddled with contradictions in the messages that it sends to both women and men about their own natures and about how they should behave. Much literature and art aimed to warn women away from the image of the so-called bad woman and encourage them to follow the image of the so-called good woman. But women could also be resistant readers or viewers. That is, they did not necessarily interpret these images in the ways that they were intended.

Medieval philosophers and scholastic authors were not, on the whole, particularly positive about women. As men of the church, they saw women as distractions from the religious life and tended to portray them as evil temptresses. Beginning in the fourth century, the Church Fathers, or Patristic writers, established much important church doctrine by synthesizing the Bible with other early Christian writings and with Greek and Roman philosophy. As chapter 1 explains, St. Jerome, who had struggled with his own lust, advised that virginity was the best status from which to lead a devout life. Ambrose agreed: married men were distracted from devotion by their wives and the enjoyment of sex, so virginity was preferable. Augustine, although not as insistently anti-marriage, emphasized the lesser status of women as a result of Eve's sins in the Garden of Eden. Women were to be ruled by their husbands and must be obedient to them. Although marriage did at least produce children, the very process of childbirth was seen as dirty: Augustine commented that "we are born between urine and feces."[29] Jerome, Augustine, and Ambrose thus set the stage for the church's misogynistic views of women.

Attitudes toward women were reinforced in the high Middle Ages as various popes and other reformers sought to purge the church of clerical marriage. Clerical marriage involved priests, bishops, and other church officials abandoning celibacy and forming long-term relationships with women. Although churchmen could not officially marry these women, the women nonetheless functioned as de facto wives by living with these men, bearing children to them, and carrying out other expected wifely roles. In order to dissuade men from such relationships, the church preached about the evils of women and the ways in which women could act as temptresses. The tenth-century reformer and abbot Odo of Cluny, for instance, said that a woman was like a "sack of dung" and that if they could see beneath the superficial beauty of women, men would be nauseous.[30] Artists depicted women diverting clerics from their songs or distracting them so that they fell from the ladder of virtue. Women were increasingly associated with Eve, luring men away from pious lives.

In fact, Eve, as the original temptress who caused humanity's expulsion from the Garden of Eden by persuading Adam to eat the forbidden fruit, served as the symbol for all that was flawed in women. In enticing Adam away from purity, she was to blame for humankind's expulsion from paradise. Paintings and manuscript illuminations depict Eve naked or dressed in scanty clothing like a prostitute.[31] Artists and authors thus urged women to avoid behaving like Eve, and priests repeated these injunctions as part of their services. For example, women were instructed not to behave like the chattering Eve who could not resist speaking with the serpent, despite God's warnings. William Lichfield, a fifteenth-century London preacher, repeated an old motif when he advised his parishioners:

> Eve, our oldest mother in paradise, held long talks with the adder, and told him what God had said to her and to her husband about eating the apple; and by her talking, the fiend understood her feebleness and her unstableness, and found a way to bring her to confusion.

The Virgin Mary, on the other hand, represented purity and goodness and served as the model to which ordinary women were expected to aspire. Priests urged women to follow Mary's example not only in preserving their virginity but even in such matters as keeping good company and refraining from gossip. Mary's speech, as women were constantly reminded, was recorded in the bible on only four occasions and on each occasion she spoke "words of great discretion and great importance." Lichfield's sermon continues by contrasting Eve with the Virgin Mary:

> Our Lady Saint Mary did otherwise. She told the angel no tale, but asked him discretely things she did not know herself. Follow therefore Our Lady in discrete speaking and hearing, and not cackling Eve who both spoke and heard unwisely.[32]

From the high Middle Ages onward, both women and men strove to show their dedication to the Virgin Mary. Churches and cathedrals were frequently named for her, artists painted and carved representations of her with the baby Jesus, and writers imagined themselves in her presence. Bernard of Clairvaux, a very influential Cistercian monk of the twelfth century, envisioned himself directly nourished by the Virgin as he knelt in prayer; manuscript illuminations of Bernard's vision depict a stream of milk traveling from her breast to his mouth.[33] Images of Mary and Jesus became more common in the high Middle Ages, too, both in painting and in sculpture. Although these look less sophisticated than the many Renaissance images of the same theme, we must remember that medieval artists were less concerned about making their images as realistic as possible and more concerned about the messages they conveyed. Statues of Mary holding the baby Jesus that were made during the high middle ages, for instance, look stiff and awkward to modern eyes, but they often position Mary as a sort of throne surrounding and protecting her son. Such images might be kept in lady chapels, where people could come to offer their prayers to the Virgin Mary, or carried in processions on feast days. Although Christians in the medieval West resisted the notion that statues possessed any innate holiness, they nonetheless saw images of the Virgin as worthy of genuine respect. A story from the late Middle Ages told of an acrobat who wanted to leave an offering before a statue of Mary. Since he lacked money, he gave an acrobatic performance in front of the statue, and the Virgin rewarded him by coming to life. People thus interpreted images of the Virgin as important and directly relevant to their own lives. Indeed, later medieval depictions sometimes portrayed Mary and Jesus in domestic settings familiar to their viewers, encouraging identification with them. Miniatures from the fifteenth-century Book of Hours of Catherine of Cleves show, for instance, the Virgin weaving at a loom and cooking dinner while suckling her baby. Illustrations elsewhere show her knitting, feeding the child from a bowl of broth, or testing the temperature of the bathwater in which he will be bathed.[34]

For real women, this devotion to Mary could have both positive and negative consequences. Images of a woman protecting and nurturing her child must surely have sent the message that motherhood was a worthy vocation (although we must again remember that medieval artists were neither as capable nor as interested in depicting love between mother and child as artists would become during the Renaissance). Mary also served as a maternal figure who would potentially protect both women and men, an intercessor between humans and God who seemed more accessible to humans. Yet at the same time, the Virgin Mary represented an impossible standard for ordinary women. Because she was by definition a perfect and sinless woman, no ordinary woman could possibly measure up. Every impure thought and action reminded women how far they fell below Mary's level of purity and how much closer they came to the sinfulness of Eve.

Artists and authors seized on the contrast offered by Eve and Mary as exemplars of evil and good. Eve, they pointed out, brought death and sin, while Mary brought life and the hope of redemption. Manuscript illuminations sometimes show Eve and Mary together on opposite sides of the Tree of Knowledge. Eve, naked, accepts the fruit from the serpent, while surrounded by images of death and hell. Mary, on the other hand, is fully clothed, backed by an angel and by Jesus on the cross.[35]

Yet Mary and Eve were not the only examples of good and bad women. Mary was supported by a bevy of female saints, some of whom appealed particularly to women. As mentioned in chapter 2, St. Margaret was associated with protecting women during childbirth, and artistic and literary representations of her often emphasize this role. According to legend, St. Margaret had been swallowed by a dragon but had emerged unharmed from his stomach when she made the sign of the cross. Medieval physicians suggested that the story of St. Margaret should be read to women in labor, in the hope that their children, like the saint, might emerge from the belly unharmed. Sometimes a book containing St. Margaret's story was even placed on a laboring woman's stomach. Amulets and relics of St. Margaret were popular too: belts associated with the saint, for instance, were often worn by pregnant and laboring women. Although some medieval clerics insisted that St. Margaret was not swallowed by the dragon but merely threatened by him, representations of the saint on amulets and other paraphernalia for pregnant women clung steadfast to this aspect of the story since it offered hope for their safe delivery.[36] Women thus helped to shape the story of St. Margaret as she addressed an important need for them.

Another important model for women, especially women of the noble classes, was St. Anne, mother of the Virgin Mary. St. Anne appeared in several roles—as a supporter of family life, a patron of crafts (especially woodworking), and as a supplement to St. Margaret in protecting women during childbirth. One particular image of St. Anne, though, became especially common during the late Middle Ages: recurrent images showed her teaching her daughter to read, thus providing a strong role model for late medieval noblewomen who oversaw the instruction of their children. Scenes of St. Anne, the Virgin Mary as a child, and a book were common from the early fourteenth century onward. Wall paintings, manuscript illuminations, carvings, and other media attest to the popularity of the theme, despite the fact that it was not mentioned in the Bible. Indeed, the trinity of Anne, Mary, and Jesus (plus a book) provided an alternative to that of Joseph, Mary, and Jesus. At the same time as works of devotional literature became more commonly available in the late Middle Ages to those with the means to afford them, so women were provided with a strong role model for teaching their daughters to read.[37]

St. Anne tutoring the Virgin Mary, from a fifteenth-century manu-
script written and illuminated in Paris.© British Library, London,
UK/ © British Library Board. All Rights Reserved/The Bridgeman
Art Library

Saints, along with legendary women such as Griselda, provided models
of good behavior for ordinary women to follow. Very often, however, these
models were unrealistic ones: few real women could, like Griselda, will-
ingly relinquish their children in the name of obedience to their husbands.
The Virgin Mary's purity and virtue were especially unattainable. Real
women, according to authors and clerics, were far more likely to emulate
Eve in sin. In fact, women sometimes served as personifications for sins in
general. In representations of the seven deadly sins, for instance, lust was
sometimes represented by a mermaid or by a lascivious, Eve-like woman,
and pride was often symbolized by a woman looking in a mirror. Artists

and writers sometimes ridiculed women's fashions, especially the peculiar late medieval trend of wearing headdresses (like hats, except that hair was wrapped up in them too) shaped to look like horns. Wood carvings and wall paintings made fun of these horns by depicting devils peeping out from between them, while poems claimed that elaborate hairstyles made women look like cats, wolves, or snails.

Women were also strongly associated with gossip, chatter, and failure to pay attention to religious teachings. A misogynist theme popular throughout much of Europe was one in which women chattered in church, instead of listening to the service, and were overheard by a demon. The complete story was often told as part of a sermon as priests encouraged their parishioners to pay attention to the service, but parts of the story were represented visually in wood carvings and wall paintings. The sermon exemplum explained that the demon, sometimes named Tutivillus, recorded the words spoken by the women on a scroll. Because they gossiped so much, the demon ran out of space on which to record the women's words and thus tried to stretch the scroll by holding one end of it between his teeth and using his claws to tug on the parchment. In some accounts, the demon's teeth slipped; in others, his scroll snapped in half. Either way, he banged his head against the side of the church and caused the women's sin to be discovered. Although this story survives in many different versions, the gender of those talking is almost always female, in order to emphasize women's connection with excessive speech. Similarly, those depicted talking in wood carvings and wall paintings are almost always women. Lust, pride, and gossip were sins especially associated with women, and artistic and literary representations used these connections to send a message to both women and men. A man who gossiped, acted lustfully, or was vain about his appearance was not only sinful but also womanly.

Troubled gender relations could also serve as a metaphor for social disorder in a more general sense. Some images reversed the typical and expected gender order by displaying women dominating men. The theme of a world-upside-down was popular in the late Middle Ages: illustrations in the margins of manuscripts sometimes show scenes such as rabbits hunting humans, and the feast of Carnival—immediately before Lent—often featured a peasant being appointed lord for a day or a boy being temporarily raised to the position of bishop. Inverted hierarchies were thus amusing to medieval people. The inversion of the gender hierarchy fit this tradition, yet it became even more popular than most other world-upside-down motifs. Wood carvings, ivory carvings, paintings, embroideries, manuscript illustrations, ceramics, woodcuts, and even stained glass windows depict the theme of women dominating men. Often they are shown beating men with a rod or a pot as the men squirm beneath them; sometimes, the dominated men are shown cooking dinner or spinning yarn, activities associated with

A woman beats her husband with a distaff. Illumination from a man-
uscript begun prior to 1340 for Sir Geoffrey Luttrell (1276–1345).
© British Library, London, UK/ © British Library Board. All Rights
Reserved/The Bridgeman Art Library

women. Other illustrations refer more specifically to a story common from
the early thirteenth century onward: that of Phyllis riding the philosopher
Aristotle as if he were a horse. According to this story, Phyllis was the lover
of the young Alexander the Great, Aristotle's pupil. Aristotle, however, resented the extent to which Phyllis distracted his pupil from his studies and
tried to dissuade Alexander from spending time with her. Phyllis decided
to take revenge by tempting Aristotle himself. She thus showed up in the
garden outside his study and displayed herself to him in a provocative manner. Aristotle, charmed, begged her to have sex with him. Phyllis agreed on
the condition that he first allowed her to ride him like a horse (the scene
depicted in so many artistic representations). As Aristotle crawled around

the garden, Phyllis called out to Alexander to look out his window and see his teacher humiliated. Although the point of the story was initially to emphasize that young love ought not to be thwarted, it came to represent a larger point about the cunningness of women and the risk of men being dominated by women.[38] As Jacques de Vitry, a thirteenth-century preacher, put it in his sermon:

> If indeed the malice and cunning of the woman so prevailed that she deceived and held an old man captive, the most prudent of all mortals, and who has argued with many great masters, it demonstrated to me how much more power she might have over you [whom she could so much more easily] deceive, allure, and defraud, unless you guard against her [through] my example.[39]

Jacques de Vitry's sermon makes it clear how men were expected to interpret the image of the woman on top. But how did women interpret such a story or respond to such an image? We cannot know for certain, but it is possible that at least some women silently cheered Phyllis on when they heard the Aristotle story or identified with the women brandishing sticks or pots when they saw carvings of women dominating their husbands. At some level, then, such images might have proved empowering for women, even as they served to make the point that women were dangerous, deceptive, and in need of control. Ironically, some of the best sources we have for women as resistant readers come from male authors. Jehan le Fèvre, a fourteenth-century poet and translator, used the character of Lady Leësce to attack misogynistic views of women, among them the story of Aristotle:

> And if [Aristotle] allowed himself to be ridden like a horse,
> That was out of joy and out of pleasure . . .
> It shows well that one ought to love women
> Without saying anything hard or defamatory to them.[40]

Another male author, Geoffrey Chaucer, similarly makes the point that women did not necessarily interpret stories in the same way as men. In the prologue to the Wife of Bath's Tale, part of the *Canterbury Tales,* the Wife notes that male authors depict women in the way that suits them best, whereas female authors might see things differently:

> By God, if women had written stories,
> as clerks have in their oratories,
> they would have written more of men's wickedness
> than all of the sex of Adam can redress.[41]

Christine de Pisan makes a similar point. Rather than a female character written by a male author, her *Letter to the God of Love* of 1399 features a male character, Cupid, defending the perspective of women. After surveying conventional representations of women as treacherous and cunning, Cupid says:

> I know that they would read quite differently,
> For well do women know the blame is wrong.
> The parts are not apportioned equally.
> Because the strongest take the largest cut
> And he who slices it can keep the best.[42]

Jehan, Chaucer, and Christine thus seem to agree that women's interpretations of misogynistic stories and representations might have been quite different from that of men. While a man interpreted a wood carving of a woman beating her husband as a warning against allowing women too much power, his wife may have identified with the woman brandishing the stick and hoped to wield such power herself. Even images of saints might be interpreted differently than the way they were intended. The scene of Saints Elizabeth and Mary sharing with one another the news of their miraculous pregnancies, for instance, was generally represented by two women holding one another in an embrace. An ordinary woman might indeed be reminded of the Biblical story when she saw this image, but she might also see in it an affirmation of female friendship.

Whether they read with the text (i.e., in the way that authors and artists intended) or against the text, women of the noble classes certainly received and exchanged books with some frequency. When books were commissioned for women, they were often adapted to reflect women's interests and concerns and, frequently, the roles expected of them. Isabelle of France, for instance, was presented with a Psalter around the time of her marriage at age 12, in 1308, to the English king Edward II. Images in the margins and initial letters of the so-called Isabelle Psalter emphasize mothers and sons, making it clear to the young queen that she was expected to produce an heir. The Psalter also included depictions of a number of Old Testament heroines as models for Isabelle to emulate.[43] A similar message was sent by the Book of Hours of Jeanne d'Evreux, a small but elaborate manuscript probably presented to Jeanne upon her marriage to Charles IV of France in 1324. Jeanne was Charles's third wife, his first two wives having died without producing a male heir. For this reason, perhaps, the images in the book include recurrent symbols of sexuality and potency.[44] Images of wives and mothers are also apparent in a devotional picture book commissioned for a woman known as Madame Marie, tentatively identified as Marie de Rethel, who married Wautier d'Enghien in 1266. Marie is depicted 10 times kneeling in prayer before her favorite saints. Other scenes emphasize torture in the form of decapitation, flaying, disembowelment, and attacks on the nipples of female saints. Such scenes, it has been speculated, were designed to heighten compassion for the saints. The torturing of St. Agatha's nipples, for instance, may have caused Marie to think of the saint and identify with her as she nursed her own children.[45] Similarly gruesome (and yet apparently inspirational) were some of the images painted on panels commemorating the marriages of young women in fifteenth-century Italy. Several surviving panels depict the ancient story in which men from the city of Rome abducted and raped women from nearby tribes in order to produce children. The story tells how, after a few years, the Sabine men came to reclaim their womenfolk. At this point the women, along with the children they had produced, intervened and urged peace. This might seem like a peculiar theme to decorate a panel for a new bride, yet it reflects the demographic situation of fifteenth-century Italy. The Black Death hit many of the Italian cities particularly hard: in Florence, for instance, the population in 1441 was still less than one-third of what it had been a century previously. The message sent by the marriage panels was thus that childbirth was the civic duty of young women, even if it seemed like a sacrifice. The panels also reinforced the proper role for wives and mothers, that of supporting their husbands.[46]

Even if some of these messages were unwelcome to women (poor Isabelle and Jeanne, for example, must have felt considerable pressure from all sides to produce heirs), they clearly still regarded books as valuable. In the era before printing, when books had to be copied out by hand, manuscripts were often lent, traded, and gifted. Women played an especially important role in these networks of book circulation. Through tracing book ownership, literary scholars have been able to highlight connections between lay women and religious women. For instance, a laywoman might specify in her will that a particular book was to be given to a local anchoress or nunnery. Similarly, noble families sometimes donated books to nunneries at the time of a daughter's entry into the convent. Aristocratic women presented one another with books as gifts or bequests, too.

Those with particular wealth owned highly decorated Books of Hours, some of which were illuminated with portraits of those who commissioned them. Books of Hours, written in Latin, contained texts appropriate to the eight main church services of the day and were usually read in private or in family chapels. Portraits of owners in surviving Books of Hours often depict women reading, sometimes in the presence of the Virgin Mary. The Hours of Mary of Burgundy, for instance, executed sometime between 1467 and 1480, depicts the young Mary of Burgundy sitting reading in front of a window. Through the window, we see the interior of a church in which the Virgin Mary sits in front of the altar with the baby Jesus. Mary of Burgundy appears a second time in the picture, as one of the worshippers who kneel before the Virgin and child in the church. The image thus sends an important message: by reading holy books, Mary of Burgundy could place herself imaginatively in the presence of the Virgin and child.[47] Yet Mary of Burgundy, too, might have come up with an interpretation of her own:

perhaps she interpreted the image to mean that reading any kind of book, holy or not, was a worthwhile activity? Expensive books such as Books of Hours were often passed from mother to daughter, granddaughter, or other female relative, reaffirming important connections among women. Lady Margaret la Zouche, for example, bequeathed her "best Primer" in 1449 to her granddaughter, Elizabeth Chaworth.[48]

Women who could not afford such lavish and expensive books as Books of Hours nonetheless participated in the exchange of books. Especially by the late Middle Ages, when the amount of devotional literature available in the vernacular mushroomed, religious women and noble lay women read much the same kind of material. They might, for instance, read biographies of saints and conduct books which prescribed how to live a good and devout life. The *Ancrene Wisse,* an English text, was compiled in the thirteenth century with the intention of guiding anchoresses in leading a religious life. Yet versions also appeared in the libraries of nuns, laywomen, and men, none of whom were likely to become anchoresses. Some women also owned literature that was not primarily religious in focus, such as poems, histories, and Arthurian romances. These secular books can be harder to trace, however, because they were less often specified in wills. Evidence about book ownership by women is hard to find, but the data that survives points to the importance of books in women's lives and the importance of sharing books within female networks.

Medieval depictions of women in both art and literature were thus complicated and often contradictory. A few women, such as the Virgin Mary and other saints, were seen as completely virtuous. These women were, however, the exceptions to the rule: real women were far more likely to behave like the wicked temptress Eve. Indeed, sins in general were sometimes gendered feminine, and images of women dominating men could serve as metaphors for chaos and the inversion of proper social order. Yet despite receiving such messages about their innate sinfulness, real women may not have interpreted them in the way intended. Both male and female authors acknowledged that women might interpret stories differently from men.

WOMEN AS PATRONS

Elite women often participated in the creative process as patrons of works of art, music, or literature. Although this role was confined only to a few, it was nonetheless important in enabling the creation of cultural works, and it afforded them an active hand—should they choose to take it up—in designing the contents such works should take. For some women, such as the Byzantine Empress Theodora or Queen Blanche of Castile, patronage was both a source and a reflection of their power. Indeed, some historians

have regarded female patronage as a way in which women "acquired an au-
dible voice" and "were able to overcome at least some of the obstacles that
blocked their way to full participation in their own society."[49]

While patronage could indeed be empowering, it must be remembered
that the opportunity to serve as patrons was one open only to a very small
minority. Peasant women and townswomen had far fewer opportunities to
participate in cultural patronage than women of the elite classes. Nor could
every noblewoman fund creative enterprises: many were constrained by
having little or no access to money independent of that of their husbands.
The infrequency with which married women served as patrons can be seen
by an analysis of the account books of Neri di Bicci, a fifteenth-century Italian painter. Over a 22 year period, Neri listed 24 commissions by women.
Fourteen commissions came from nuns and 10 from secular women. Of
the 10 secular women, 5 were widows, 4 were listed without marital status,
and only 1 was identified as married. Although this sample is a small one,
it reflects a broader pattern in which married women were less visible as
patrons than were widows.[50] This decreased visibility doesn't necessarily
mean that married women played less of a role in patronage: rather, their
role as patrons was often hidden behind that of their husbands. In other
words, their husbands were listed as the major donors or patrons, when in
fact their wives may have been just as influential in deciding which artists,
authors, or causes to support. For instance, Duke Henry I of Silesia and his
wife, Hedwig, are known to have founded a number of religious institutions, but the nuns of Trebnitz (founded 1202) clearly regarded Hedwig,
rather than Henry, as their major benefactor. When they wrote about the
foundation of the convent, they explained that Hedwig "prevailed on her
husband" and that he endowed the convent "on the advice of his wife, the
holy Hedwig."[51] Women might have played a similarly active role in other
instances in which husbands alone are listed as patrons or in which husbands and wives are listed jointly. When artists came to include portraits of
the donors in their paintings and sculptures, men were almost always depicted on the right-hand side of holy figures in the image (the more powerful position in medieval conceptions of space) and women on the left-hand
side, thus underlining their secondary importance.

Wealthy widows, on the other hand, had the ability to make commissions in their own names. Some embarked on their role as patrons soon
after becoming widows, in fact, as they instructed artists and authors to
commemorate their recently dead husbands through a commission dedicated to the salvation of their souls. Lionarda del Pescaia of Florence, for
example, commissioned an altarpiece for the family chapel in 1463, following the instruction in her husband's will that she should furnish the chapel
after his death.[52] Others, such as Countess Ela of Salisbury and Marie de St.
Pol, were likely responsible for commissioning the elaborate tombs occu-

Flemish oil on panel "Triptych of Jean de Witte" (1473) showing the Virgin and Child along with the altarpiece donors, Jean de Witte and Maria Hoose. As is typical, the man is portrayed to the Virgin's right-hand side and the woman to the Virgin's left. © Musées Royaux des Beaux-Arts de Belgique, Brussels, Belgium/ Giraudon/The Bridgeman Art Library

pied by their knightly husbands.[53] Wealthy widows decorated their homes, commissioned the copying of books for themselves or others, and even founded colleges at universities. The fourteenth-century Elizabeth de Burgh of Clare (England), for instance, was an active patron of the arts. Widowed three times, Elizabeth had the right to control not only the substantial inheritance from her own family but also inheritances from her husbands. Among her staff she employed several goldsmiths, sculptors, and enamelers to execute commissions for her private chapel and household. She also paid for expensive and elaborate vestments for members of the clergy: Elizabeth's will lists a vestment embroidered with a thousand pearls, a cope (an ecclesiastical garment) with three silver crests on a red taffeta cloth of gold, a cope encrusted with pearls and elaborate embroidery, and two very expensive silk vestments embroidered with gold. She hired musicians, bought books, founded religious houses, and established Clare College at Cambridge University.[54] Elizabeth's patronage contributed substantially to the cultural environment of fourteenth-century England, but her contribution would likely have been smaller had she not been widowed for almost four decades after the death of her third husband. For Elizabeth de Burgh and others like her, the agency that came with patronage was possible in large part because of their widowhood.

Nuns and other holy women, also free from the constraints of marriage, might serve as patrons too. The French nun Heluis d'Ecouffans, for instance, commissioned a religious manuscript for her convent of Sainte-Benoîte-d'Origny in 1312.[55] The nuns of the wealthy convent of San Pier Maggiore in Florence put considerable resources into artistic patronage, purchasing a large, highly elaborate, altarpiece for their church.[56] In this instance, as in many when a religious community commissioned a work of art or a manuscript, we cannot tell who specifically decided what to depict. In a few cases, however, we have more information: Chiara Gambocorta of Pisa (Italy) played an important role, for example, in commissioning paintings for her convent of San Domenico. Prioress Chiara, seeking to inspire her nuns, particularly selected images of female saints such as Catherine of Siena and Brigid of Sweden. The experience of Heluis, Chiara, and the nuns of San Pier Maggiore in serving as patrons was, however, atypical: as chapter 1 explains, nunneries generally faced more financial pressures than monasteries, and most had little money available for the commissioning of literature or art.

When women commissioned or funded creative works that were seen by others, they sent important messages about their own power and status. When the Carolingian Empress Richildis (late ninth to early tenth centuries) created a seal of her own, for example, she demonstrated her authority in visual form. Seals were used to ensure privacy for letters and other written communications. Often attached to rings, they were used to imprint an image (in the case of Richildis her name and a profile bust of a woman) onto wax or soft clay. Once the image was broken, the contents of the message could no longer be guaranteed. In the early Middle Ages, seals were typically used only by men; Richildis was unusual in possessing a seal of her own. By owning and using such a seal she sent the message that her words deserved privacy and respect. If, as some art historians have proposed, the image on her seal was intended to portray the legendary Omphale, Queen of the Lydians and consort of Hercules, this message would have been stronger still.[57] The very public position of queens and other aristocratic women within their own courts offered other opportunities for exercising power through patronage, too. For example, Lady Margaret Beaufort, mother of the English king Henry VII, helped shape the cultural environment of late fifteenth-century England through her support of musicians. Margaret, who maintained a household separate from that of the king, employed professional choristers, both men and boys, in her large and well-staffed chapel. In addition to their religious duties in the chapel, her choristers also participated in plays and secular performances at Margaret's court. She especially rewarded those who composed new songs, either religious or secular. Margaret's musicians were often lent out to other courts or large households, helping to spread her patronage even further. Margaret's patronage of musicians thus enhanced her own power and influence, even rivaling that of the king, within late medieval English culture.[58] Perhaps even more influential was the twelfth-century Eleanor of Aquitaine, whose patronage of troubadours fostered the genre of courtly love literature in southern France. Eleanor passed on her interests to her children. One of her daughters, Marie of Champagne, sponsored the poet Chrétien de Troyes, famous for his retelling of Arthurian legends. Another, Leonor of England, welcomed troubadours along with her husband, Alfonso VIII, at their court in Castile (Spain). A third daughter, Matilda of Saxony, intro-duced the literature of courtly love into the court of her husband, Henry the Lion, resulting in the composition of German courtly epics.[59] In each case, personal prestige accompanied cultural authority.

Some women tailored the messages sent by the works they commis-sioned to underscore further their claims to power. A moralized Bible most likely commissioned by Blanche of Castile in the thirteenth century, for instance, emphasized scenes of women as rulers and authority figures. The Bible includes a number of scenes of women giving birth, underscoring the importance of motherhood, and it incorporates a disproportionate number of illustrations of biblical women. This emphasis on women, motherhood, and female authority makes sense given the fact that Blanche served as re-gent for her son, Louis IX of France, and played an active role in govern-ment even after he assumed the throne.[60]

Women's familial roles, indeed, often provided opportunities for them to exercise patronage. The English Queen Philippa (c. 1314–69), for instance, hired a minstrel to write songs memorializing her father, just as wealthy widows commissioned works in honor of their husbands. In addition, women sought manuscripts and artworks for their children. Following the impulse of Dhuoda, who wrote her own manual in order to guide her son, later mothers sometimes commissioned manuscripts with an eye to both education and moral training. Marguerite de Provence, for example, com-missioned Vincent of Beauvais in the thirteenth century to write a book to guide her children in appropriate reading, writing, and behavior. The ver-sion intended for her son Louis included a section on choosing a good wife, while his sister Isabelle's version explained how to be a good wife. When the fourteenth-century Marie de Bretagne commissioned an elaborate manu-script for her son depicting the Life of St. Eustace, she clearly gave instruc-tions to the illuminator to ensure that the right message was sent. For one thing, Marie chose to include in the donor portrait images of other saints relevant to her family history. For another, she guided the illuminator to emphasize acts of charity on the part of St. Eustace and others. The manu-script produced differed from other contemporary representations of St. Eustace: some of the typical scenes, such as Eustace's vision of Christ with a stag, were omitted, while other scenes depicting him as a husband and father were emphasized. Marie's active guidance as patron thus produced a version of St. Eustace best suited to serve as a role model for her son.[61] Isabelle of France, wife of the ill-fated Edward II of England, may similarly have commissioned books for her son, the future Edward III. Scholars have speculated that Isabelle's influence lay behind a treatise on the proper conduct of kings (a book that the prince may have needed if he was not to be murdered by his barons as his father would be). The so-called Milemete Treatise includes several images of queens alongside kings, suggesting the important role that women could play in government. It also emphasizes the kinds of activities that Isabelle likely regarded as appropriate pastimes for kings, such as hawking and hunting, and it warns repeatedly against listening to bad advice. Edward II's death was blamed on his unwillingness to listen to the counsel of the nobility, so Isabelle may have been trying to ensure that her son behaved more in the manner expected of a king.[62]

Marie de Bretagne and Isabelle of France were not unusual in trying to influence the contents of their commissions: works sponsored by and for women suggest that they often played an active role in the creative process. Some, for instance, used their patronage to soften or counterbalance the misogyny in the popular romance known as the *Roman de la Rose.* Some scribes, possibly influenced by female patrons, omitted the more misogynous passages when they copied the text. In other instances, illuminators included illustrations that downplayed the anti-feminist content of the book.[63] Anne of Bohemia (1366–94), wife of Richard II of England, was reportedly unhappy with the poet Geoffrey Chaucer for translating the *Roman de la Rose* into English and for his negative portrayal of Criseyde in *Troilus & Criseyde.* She thus either inspired or ordered him (depending on whose version of events one believes) to counterbalance them by writing his *Legend of Good Women.*[64] Women could thus use their patronage to influence the contents of art and literature and, in some cases, to produce more positive representations of women.

For wealthy women, the ability to sponsor works of art, music, or literature—and perhaps even to influence their contents—served as partial compensation for the social constraints keeping them from painting, carving, or writing their own works of art. In commissioning manuscripts, music, and art, women like Eleanor of Aquitaine, Margaret Beaufort, and Anne of Bohemia left their mark on the cultural landscape of their era. Women of lesser means, however, had fewer opportunities to play a role in the creative process. Although some women certainly served as artists, authors, and musicians, many were barred from these trades in the same way that they were kept from participation in other trades and crafts. Those who did participate were often relegated to minor, less prestigious roles, and their names have long since been forgotten. Even if they lacked opportunities to create works of art, however, women of all social classes exercised agency in their interpretation of such works. That is, they could (and presumably did) decide for themselves how to interpret the messages they received via wall paintings, poetry, stories, sermons, songs, and other media. Despite the fact that much medieval culture was misogynist, women could sometimes be creative in choosing how to understand the messages they received about appropriate female roles.

NOTES

1. Veronica Sekules, "Women and Art in England in the Thirteenth and Fourteenth Centuries," in *Age of Chivalry: Art in Plantagenet England 1200–1400,* ed. Jonathan Alexander and Paul Binski (London: Royal Academy of Arts, with Weidenfeld and Nicolson, 1987), 45; June Hall McCash, "The Cultural Patronage of Medieval Women: An Overview," in McCash (ed.), *The Cultural Patronage of Medieval Women* (Athens: University of Georgia Press, 1996), 1–49 at 32.

2. Annemarie Weyl Carr, "Women as Artists in the Middle Ages: 'The Dark is Light Enough'," in *Dictionary of Women Artists,* ed. Delia Gaze (London: Fitzroy Dearborn Publishers, 1997), v. 1; 3–21 at 6, 10.

3. Chiara Frugoni, "The Imagined Woman," in *A History of Women: Silences of the Middle Ages,* ed. Christiane Klapisch-Zuber (Cambridge: Belknap Press of Harvard University Press, 1992), 336–422 at 400–407.

4. Jane L. Carroll, "Woven Devotions: Reform and Piety in Tapestries by Dominican Nuns" in *Saints, Sinners, and Sisters: Gender and Northern Art in Medieval and Early Modern Europe,* ed. Jane L. Carroll and Alison G. Stewart (Aldershot, U.K.: Ashgate, 2003), 183–201.

5. Carr, "Women as Artists in the Middle Ages," 4.

6. Carr, "Women as Artists in the Middle Ages," 7.

7. Carr, "Women as Artists in the Middle Ages," 8–9.

8. Jeffrey Hamburger, *Nuns as Artists: The Visual Culture of a Medieval Convent* (Berkeley: University of California Press, 1997), 56–57.

9. Carr, "Women as Artists in the Middle Ages," 11.

10. Marie-Luise Ehrenschwendtner, "A Library Collected by and for the Use of Nuns: St. Catherine's Convent, Nuremberg," in *Women and the Book: Assessing the Visual Evidence,* ed. Lesley Smith and Jane H. M. Taylor (London: British Library, 1997), 123–32.

11. Dhuoda, *Handbook for William: A Carolingian Woman's Counsel for Her Son,* ed. and trans. Carol Neel (Lincoln: University of Nebraska, 1991), 2.

12. Steven A. Stofferahn, "The Many Faces in Dhuoda's Mirror: The 'Liber Manualis' and a Century of Scholarship," *Magistra: A Journal of Women's Spirituality in History* 4 (1998), 89–134 at 100.

13. Dhuoda, *Handbook for William,* 13.

14. Christine de Pisan, *A Medieval Woman's Mirror of Honor: The Treasury of the City of Ladies,* trans. Charity Cannon Willard, ed. Madeleine Pelner Cosman (New York: Persea, 1989), 155–56.

15. Quoted in Rosalynn Voaden, "God's Almighty Hand: Women Co-Writing the Book," in *Women, the Book, and the Godly,* ed. Lesley Smith and Jane H. M. Taylor (Woodbridge: D.S. Brewer, 1995), 55–65 at 57.

16. Quoted in Rosalynn Voaden, "God's Almighty Hand," 65, n. 47.

17. Kathleen Garay, "'A Naked Intent Unto God': Ungendered Discourse in Some Late Medieval Mystical Texts," *Mystics Quarterly* 23 (1997), 36–51.

18. Anne Savage, "The Communal Authorship of 'Ancrene Wisse'," in *A Companion to "Ancrene Wisse,"* ed.. Yoko Wada (Woodbridge, U.K.: D.S. Brewer, 2003), 45–55.

19. *Women's Lives in Medieval Europe: A Sourcebook,* ed. Emilie Amt (New York: Routledge, 1993), 171, 174.

20. Nadia Margolis, "Trobairitz," in *Women in the Middle Ages: An Encyclopedia,* ed. Katharina M. Wilson and Nadia Margolis (Westport, CT: Greenwood Press, 2004), 2 vols, v. 2, 902–3; Danielle Régnier-Bohler, "Literary and Mystical Voices," in *A History of Women,* 427–82 at 435–36.

21. Quoted in Karen K. Jambeck, "Reclaiming the Woman in the Book: Marie de France and the *Fables,"* in *Women, the Book, and the Worldly,* ed. Lesley Smith and Jane H. M. Taylor (Woodbridge, U.K.: D.S. Brewer, 1995), 119–37 at 119.

22. Jambeck, "Reclaiming the Woman in the Book," 119–37.

23. Francesca Nicholson, "Seeing Women Troubadours without the '-itz' and '-isms'," in *Troubled Vision: Gender, Sexuality, and Sight in Medieval Text and Image,* ed. Emma Campbell and Robert Mills (New York: Palgrave MacMillan, 2004) 63–76.

24. Monica Green, *Women's Healthcare in the Medieval West: Texts and Contexts* (Aldershot, U.K.: Ashgate, 2000).

25. David Larmour, "Comnena, Anna," in *Women in the Middle Ages: An Encyclopedia,* v. 1, 203–5.

26. Charity Cannon Willard, *Christine de Pizan, Her Life and Works* (New York: Persea, 1984); Roberta L. Krueger, "Uncovering Griselda: Christine de Pizan, 'une seule chemise,' and the Clerical Tradition," in *Medieval Fabrications: Dress, Textiles, Clothwork, and Other Cultural Imaginings,* ed. E. Jane Burns (New York: Palgrave MacMillan, 2004), 71–88.

27. Martha Furman Schleifer, "The Middle Ages and the Renaissance," in *From Convent to Concert Hall: A Guide to Women Composers,* ed. Sylvia Glickman and Martha Furman Schleifer (Westport, CT: Greenwood Press, 2003), 16–17.

28. J. Michelle Edwards, "Women in Music to ca. 1450," in *Women and Music: A History,* ed. Karin Pendle, 2nd ed., (Bloomington: Indiana University Press, 2001), 26–53.

29. Quoted in Jacques Dalarun, "The Clerical Gaze," in *A History of Women: Silences of the Middle Ages,* 15–42 at 22.

30. Quoted in Jacques Dalarun, "The Clerical Gaze," 20.

31. Christa Grössinger, *Picturing Women in Late Medieval and Renaissance Art* (New York: Manchester University Press, 1997), 7.

32. Quoted in G. R. Owst, *Literature and Pulpit in Medieval England: A Neglected Chapter in the History of English Letters and of the English People.* 2nd ed. (Oxford: B. Blackwell, 1961), 387.

33. Grössinger, *Picturing Women in Late Medieval and Renaissance Art,* 20.

34. Grössinger, *Picturing Women in Late Medieval and Renaissance Art,* 25–28.

35. Grössinger, *Picturing Women in Late Medieval and Renaissance Art,* 5.

36. Wendy R. Larson, "Who is the Master of this Narrative? Maternal Patronage of the Cult of St. Margaret," in *Gendering the Master Narrative: Women and Power in the Middle Ages,* ed. Mary C. Erler and Maryanne Kowaleski (Ithaca: Cornell University Press, 2003), 94–104.

37. Pamela Sheingorn, "'The Wise Mother': The Image of St. Anne Teaching the Virgin Mary," in *Gendering the Master Narrative,* 105–34.

38. Susan L. Smith, *The Power of Women: A Topos in Medieval Art and Literature* (Philadelphia: University of Pennsylvania Press, 1995), 66.

39. Quoted in Smith, *Power of Women,* 66.

40. Quoted in Smith, *Power of Women,* 58.

41. Geoffrey Chaucer, *The Canterbury Tales,* ed. A. Kent Hieatt and Constance Hieatt (New York: Bantam, 1964), 213.

42. Quoted in Smith, *Power of Women,* 64.

43. Anne Rudloff Stanton, "The Psalter of Isabelle, Queen of England 1308–1330: Isabelle as the Audience," *Word and Image* 18 (2002), 1–27.

44. Madeline H. Caviness, "Patron or Matron? A Capetian Bride and a Vade Mecum for Her Marriage Bed," *Speculum* 68 (1993), 333–62.

45. Alison Stones, "Nipples, Entrails, Severed Heads, and Skin: Devotional Images for Madame Marie," in *Image and Belief,* ed. Colum Hourihane (Princeton: Index of Christian Art, Department of Art and Archaeology, Princeton University, in association with Princeton University Press, 1999), 47–70.

46. Jacqueline Musacchio, "The Rape of the Sabine Women on Quattrocento Marriage-Panels," in *Marriage in Italy, 1300–1650,* ed. Trevor Dean and K.J.P. Lowe (Cambridge: Cambridge University Press, 1998), 66–82.

47. Sandra Penketh, "Women and Books of Hours," in *Women and the Book,* 266.

48. Carol M. Meale, "'alle the bokes that I haue of latyn, englisch, and frensch': Laywomen and their Books in Late Medieval England," in *Women and Literature in Britain, 1150–1500,* ed. Meale, 2nd ed. (Cambridge: Cambridge University Press, 1996), 128–58 at 130.

49. McCash, "The Cultural Patronage of Medieval Women," 2.

50. Rosi Prieto Gilday, "The Women Patrons of Neri di Bicci," in *Beyond Isabella: Secular Women Patrons of Art in Renaissance Italy,* ed. Sherryl E. Reiss and David G. Wilkins (Kirksville, MO: Truman State University Press, 2001), 51–75.

51. McCash, "The Cultural Patronage of Medieval Women," 8–9.

52. Gilday "The Women Patrons of Neri di Bicci," 54.

53. Sekules, "Women and Art in England in the Thirteenth and Fourteenth Centuries," 45.

54. Frances A. Underhill, "Elizabeth de Burgh: Connoisseur and Patron," in *The Cultural Patronage of Medieval Women,* 266–87.

55. McCash, "The Cultural Patronage of Medieval Women," 13.

56. Catherine King, "Medieval and Renaissance Matrons, Italian-Style," *Zeitschrift fur Kunstgeschichte* 55 (1992), 372–93.

57. Genevra Kornbluth, "Richildis and her Seal: Carolingian Self-Reference and the Imagery of Power," in *Saints, Sinners, and Sisters,* 161–81.

58. Fiona Kisby, "A Mirror of Monarchy: Music and Musicians in the Household Chapel of the Lady Margaret Beaufort, Mother of Henry VII," *Early Music History* 16 (1997), 203–34.

59. McCash, "The Cultural Patronage of Medieval Women," 15.

60. Tracy Chapman Hamilton, "Queenship and Kinship in the French 'Bible Moralisée': The Example of Blanche of Castile and Vienna ÖNB 2554," in *Capetian Women,* ed. Kathleen Nolan (New York: Palgrave MacMillan, 2003), 177–208.

61. Judith K. Golden, "Images of Instruction, Marie de Bretagne, and the Life of St. Eustace as Illustrated in British Library Ms. Egerton 745," in *Insights and Interpretations: Studies in Celebration of the Eighty-Fifth Anniversary of the Index of Christian Art,*

ed. Colum Hourihane (Princeton: Princeton University in association with Princeton University Press, 2002), 60–84.

62. Anne Rudloff Stanton, "Isabelle of France and her Manuscripts, 1308–58," in *Capetian Women*, 225–52.

63. Deborah McGrady, "Reinventing the *Roman de la Rose* for a Woman Reader: The Case of Ms. Douce 195," *Journal of the Early Book Society for the Study of Manuscripts and Printing History* 4 (2001), 202–21.

64. Andrew Taylor, "Anne of Bohemia and the Making of Chaucer," *Studies in the Age of Chaucer* 19 (1997), 95–119.

SUGGESTED READING

Carr, Annemarie Weyl. "Women as Artists in the Middle Ages: 'The Dark is Light Enough'," in *Dictionary of Women Artists*. Ed. Delia Gaze. London: Fitzroy Dearborn Publishers, 1997, v. 1; 3–21.

Edwards, J. Michelle. "Women in Music to ca. 1450," in *Women and Music: A History*. Ed. Karin Pendle. 2nd ed., Bloomington: Indiana University Press, 2001, 26–53.

Grössinger, Christa. *Picturing Women in Late Medieval and Renaissance Art*. New York: Manchester University Press, 1997.

Hamburger, Jeffrey. *Nuns as Artists: The Visual Culture of a Medieval Convent*. Berkeley: University of California Press, 1997.

Klapisch-Zuber, Christiane, ed. *A History of Women, Volume II: Silences of the Middle Ages*. Cambridge: Belknap Press of Harvard University Press, 1992.

McCash, June Hall, ed. *The Cultural Patronage of Medieval Women*. Athens: University of Georgia Press, 1996.

Meale, Carol M., ed. *Women and Literature in Britain, 1150–1500*, 2nd ed. Cambridge: Cambridge University Press, 1996.

Smith, Lesley and Jane H. M. Taylor, eds. *Women and the Book: Assessing the Visual Evidence*. London: British Library, 1997.

Smith, Lesley and Jane H. M. Taylor, eds. *Women, the Book, and the Godly*. Woodbridge, U.K.: D. S. Brewer, 1995.

Smith, Lesley and Jane H. M. Taylor, eds. *Women, the Book, and the Worldly*. Woodbridge: D. S. Brewer U.K., 1995.

Smith, Susan L. *The Power of Women: A Topos in Medieval Art and Literature*. Philadelphia: University of Pennsylvania Press, 1995.

6

————— ∞∞∞ —————

Women, Power, and Authority

Most women exercised some degree of power in the Middle Ages, but few exercised authority. The distinction between these two terms is an important one. Power suggests the ability to effect a change, to get someone to do something that they would not otherwise do. A woman exercised power when she persuaded her husband to attend (or stay away from) church or to act graciously (or ungraciously) toward a neighbor. The wife of a bailiff, for instance, might tell him about crimes she had witnessed and urge him to bring charges against malefactors, while a queen might intercede between her husband and his subjects, persuading him to pardon a criminal. A woman also exercised power when she raised her children and instilled in them attitudes and behaviors that she thought appropriate. Medieval authors acknowledged women's power and often encouraged them to use it appropriately. As chapter 3 explains, priests encouraged wives to extract promises of good behavior from their husbands, and Christine de Pisan urged women to ensure that their husbands were honest and hardworking.

But authority was another story. Authority, defined as "recognized and legitimized power," was very seldom extended to women. At the manorial level, women rarely if ever obtained positions such as aletaster, juror, or bailiff; in the towns, women were excluded from city councils or positions of law enforcement such as constable; and among noblewomen and queens, women's power was usually contingent on their husbands. While noblewomen and queens sometimes found themselves standing in for their husbands (or, had their husbands died, their sons), such positions were usually only temporary. Lack of authority did not mean that women were powerless, but nor did it mean that they could rely on their power in a consistent way.[1] This chapter surveys the kinds of power and authority exercised by women at each social level.

QUEENS AND NOBLEWOMEN

Power

According to a medieval chronicler, a curious scene took place outside the walled city of Calais in 1347. The city had been besieged by the English for 11 months as part of the ongoing Hundred Years War between England and France. King Edward III of England accepted the surrender of the citizens of Calais and agreed to spare their lives on the condition that he execute six of their principal citizens (burghers) in an act of symbolic authority. Jean Froissart, the best-known historian of the Hundred Years War, supplies heart-wrenching details about the six burghers who volunteered to be sacrificed to save their families and fellow citizens. The six men were led out to Edward with halters around their necks, carrying the keys to the city. Although delighted to have taken the city, many of the English nobility were uncomfortable with Edward's decision to kill the burghers and begged the king to have mercy. He refused to listen, however, and sent for the executioner. Froissart explains what happened next:

> The Queen of England, whose pregnancy was far advanced, then fell on her knees, and with tears in her eyes implored him: "Ah! My lord, since I have crossed the sea in great danger, I have never asked you any favour. But now I humbly beg you, for the Son of the Blessed Mary and for the love of me, to have mercy on these six men!"
>
> The King looked at her for some minutes without speaking, and then said: "Ah, lady, I wish you were anywhere else but here. You have entreated me in such a way that I cannot refuse. Therefore, though I do it with great reluctance, I hand them over to you. Do as you like with them."
>
> The Queen thanked him from the bottom of her heart, and had the halters removed from their necks. She took them to her rooms, had them clothed and gave them a good dinner.[2]

How should scholars interpret such a scene? A dramatic story such as that of Queen Philippa's intervention in the fate of the burghers of Calais implies that medieval queens could sometimes have power second only to that of kings. Edward ignored his nobles when they begged him to have mercy, yet he listened to the pleas of his wife. Yet, in interceding for the burghers of Calais, Queen Philippa was playing a role long expected of medieval queens. "[M]ediatory activities," as one scholar has put it, "would comprise a large part of her job description."[3] Indeed, queens were trained to intervene and mediate between their subjects and their husbands when circumstances demanded it. They were reminded explicitly of the role model provided by the biblical Esther, a Hebrew woman who married a Persian king and intervened to save the Jews from destruction, and of the mediatory role served by the Virgin Mary. Clotild's conversion of Clovis, discussed in chapter 1, also provided a model of the way in which a queen could influence her husband for the better. The role of queens as intercessors became especially important during the high Middle Ages, exemplified by women such as Matilda of Scotland, who married the English king Henry I in 1100. Poets, chroniclers, and letter-writers of the time applauded Matilda's willingness to influence her husband for the better. Indeed, some actively encouraged her in this role. Pope Paschal II urged Matilda to "censure, entreat and chide" Henry until he agreed to the church's position on who had the right to appoint church officials. She also persuaded Henry to grant several large gifts to monasteries. Matilda clearly knew about the Esther story, since it was repeated in a number of manuscripts with which she was familiar.[4] Like Queen Philippa two and a half centuries later, she knew that she could expect to gain a certain amount of leeway and mercy from the king. And kings doubtless knew this too: while the story of Philippa's intervention emphasizes the power of the queen, the possibility remains that the scene was anticipated, or even provoked, by Edward. To spare the burghers of Calais on his own initiative might have made him look weak; to do so only at the urging of a tearful, pregnant queen might have enabled him to retain the reputation for toughness that he sought. Queens like Philippa and Matilda had power through their expected role as intercessors, yet they did not have authority, since the ultimate decision lay with the kings.

Noblewomen served as intercessors too. The popular legend of Lady Godiva may bear little resemblance to the real life of Lady Godgifu and her husband Earl Leofric, Anglo-Saxon nobles of the eleventh century. Nonetheless, the legend, which first appeared in surviving records in the thirteenth century, was in many ways more important than the reality. The earliest accounts of the story explain the events this way:

> [T]he countess Godiva, a devotee of the mother of God, desiring to free the town of Coventry from the heavy servitude of toll [taxes], often besought the earl, her husband, with earnest prayers to free the town from the said servitude and other troublesome exactions, by the guidance of Jesus Christ and his mother. The earl upbraided her for vainly seeking something so injurious to him and repeatedly forbade her to approach him again on the subject. Nevertheless, in her feminine pertinacity she exasperated her husband with her unceasing request and extorted from him the following

reply: "Mount your horse naked", he said, "and ride through the market place of the town, from one side right to the other, while the people are congregated, and when you return you shall claim what you desire". And the countess answered, "And if I will do this, will you give me your permission?" And he said, "I will." Then the countess, beloved of God, accompanied by two soldiers, as it is said, mounting her horse naked, loosed her hair from its bands, so veiling the whole of her body, and thus passing through the market place she was seen by nobody … except for her very white legs. Her journey completed, she returned rejoicing to her husband, and, as he wondered at the deed, she demanded of him what she had asked. Then Earl Leofric freed the town of Coventry and its inhabitants from the said servitude, confirming what he had done with a charter.

Subsequent chronicles repeated and elaborated on the legend. (The mention of "Peeping Tom," who peeked at her but was struck blind, was a seventeenth-century addition to the medieval tale.)[5] Medieval noblewomen may not have interceded in quite the same dramatic way as Godiva allegedly did, but she provided a model for them nonetheless. Again, Godiva's actions demonstrate her power, but they do not suggest any authority: by calling her husband's bluff, she wins concessions for the people of Coventry, but she does not have the ability to grant them tax relief in her own right.

The real eleventh-century Godiva was, according to more reliable sources, an important patron of the church. She and her husband gave money to several monasteries, including an abbey at Coventry. Noblewomen and queens often served as major donors to the church, either in their own right or alongside their husbands, and in some cases, it is clear that women were the driving force behind a couple's pious donations. As chapter 5 mentions, Duke Henry I of Silesia and his wife, Hedwig, were both listed as benefactors of several monasteries and convents, but the nuns of the convent of Trebnitz in the early thirteenth century were well aware that they owed gratitude primarily to Hedwig, who had "prevailed on her husband."[6] Similarly, the eleventh-century English historian Orderic Vitalis praised Adelaide of Le Puiset because she "continued to encourage her husband to befriend the monks and protect the poor."[7] Queens, too, exercised power through pious donations and fostering good relationships with the church. Eleanor of Provence, thirteenth-century Queen of Henry III of England, worked actively to maintain good relationships with English bishops. She joined her husband in his enthusiastic support for the cult of St. Edward the Confessor, and she served as patron and protector to several monasteries. Her efforts paid off in the ways in which she was remembered by chroniclers: as a pious and generous queen.[8] Pious donations on the part of noblewomen and queens were, in some ways, an extension of their expected role as mediators and intercessors: in persuading their husbands to give money, they interceded between the church and their husbands. Although some women were able to make donations from funds of their own, many relied on their husband's participation and approval. Noblewomen and queens also served as important patrons of artists, authors, and musicians, as outlined in chapter 5. Still, patronage of both creative and spiritual endeavors demonstrated their power, but seldom their authority.

Queens and noblewomen could often exercise a powerful influence over their children, too. Artists and authors depicting the Virgin Mary and Jesus emphasized the bond between mother and child, and medieval men such as the twelfth-century Guibert of Nogent sometimes paid testimony to the importance of their mothers in shaping their lives.[9] Louis IX of France (see below) was not unusual in relying on his mother's advice long after he gained his majority and was charged with ruling the country on his own. Adela, Countess of Blois (c. 1067–1137), had sufficient power over her sons to disinherit the eldest in favor of her second son, whom she deemed more temperamentally suited to ruling.[10] And the thirteenth-century Eleanor of Aquitaine had so much influence over her sons in their youth that she was able to incite them to rebel against their father Henry II of England. In each case, however, this power depended on the personalities of the mothers and children involved. Some mothers found that they were unable, despite their best efforts, to control the behavior of their children. Brigid of Sweden (1303–73) was repeatedly embarrassed by the antics of her son Karl, who dressed in a flashy way and conducted an affair with Joanna, Queen of Naples.[11] Whether acting as wives, mothers, or patrons, noblewomen and queens possessed a power that was by no means negligible.

Authority

Yet queens and noblewomen sometimes found themselves in positions of true authority, too. In rare instances, they succeeded to the crown or noble lands in their own right. More often, they served as regents or fill-ins while their sons were underage. In both situations, they found their authority scrutinized more closely than it would have been had they been male. Yet both regents and heiresses possessed a power that was acknowledged and legitimized, even if it was vulnerable.

The primary goal of regents was, in most cases, to protect the succession for their sons. Berenguela, queen to Alfonso IX of León, for example, had to use all her wits to ensure that her son Fernando succeeded to Castile. Berenguela was the sister of Enrique I of Castile, and—upon Enrique's death in 1217—she secured the kingdom for her son by concealing her brother's death from her husband, Alfonso, until Fernando's position was accepted. Berenguela also protected Fernando by arranging strategic marriages for him. Two years after his succession, she married him to Beatrice of Swabia, a move that allied Castile to the Holy Roman Empire. After Beatrice died, she found Fernando a second wife, Jeanne, daughter of the Count of Ponthieu.[12] Berenguela's sister, Blanche of Castile, is even better known for the ways in which she protected her children's inheritance. Married in 1200 to the future Louis VIII of France, Blanche bore 12 children, of whom 4 were still-born or died soon after birth. When Louis VIII died after a reign of only three years, Blanche found herself regent to the 12-year-old Louis IX in a country fraught with political tensions and rebellious nobles. Despite such odds stacked against her, Blanche managed to cling to power on her son's behalf. She negotiated, maneuvered, uncovered plots against her son's life, and even led armies against her enemies both within France and without in her successful efforts to retain the kingdom for her son. Like her sister, Blanche arranged marriages for her children as part of a broader strategy of securing alliances and ensuring that she passed the kingdom intact to her children. Adela, Countess of Blois, mentioned above, arranged marriages for her sons in a similarly strategic way during the many years that her husband was either absent or dead.

The position of regent was, however, a temporary one expiring when the heir came of age. Although regents might continue to exercise power if their children chose to seek their advice, they lost their authority. Margaret of Denmark serves as an example of a queen who retained power despite the loss of official authority. Margaret had adopted Eric, her grandnephew, as her heir after her son Olaf died in 1387. Although Eric held the title of king, Margaret continued to make decisions and to instruct him in the ways of diplomacy. A secret document sent by Margaret to Eric in 1405, when Eric was 23, shows the ways in which a medieval queen might tutor her charge:

> When you meet the Norwegians you must give them a drink of the good German beer which I have sent in advance…At the first meeting it is important to create a friendly atmosphere. If Sir Ogmund or somebody else invites you to be his guest, you should eat with them, and if anyone, man or woman, young or old, wants to give you a gift, you must receive it thankfully, even if the gift be very humble; people might misunderstand a rejection and become angry.[13]

The extent of Margaret's advice might even be considered micro-management, yet no evidence exists to suggest that Eric resented the advice of his great-aunt.

Indeed, regents sometimes proved reluctant to relinquish their positions. Queen Melisende, who ruled the Kingdom of Jerusalem on behalf of her son Baldwin between 1143 and 1145, ignored the date when Baldwin was due to come of age and continued to rule in her own name. It took seven years before Baldwin had the power to assert his right to rule. Dowager duchesses could prove equally frustrating to their sons. In late medieval England, conventions of dower meant that one-third of a man's property at the time of his death went to his wife (previously, it had been one-third of his property at the time of marriage). In addition, some couples made use of a new type of marriage contract known as a *jointure*, which stipulated that the surviving partner in a marriage could use the estates (although not sell them) for the rest of their lives. If his mother lived for a long time after his father's death, therefore, a nobleman's inheritance could be delayed. After the death of Hugh Willoughby in 1448, for instance, his son Richard had to wait almost 50 years for the death of Margaret Freville, Richard's stepmother and Hugh's wife. Richard had the right to exercise authority in the form of holding courts and employing knights, but his economic position made it harder for him to do so. Margaret, on the other hand, held economic power through the use of her dower.[14]

Women exercised authority not only when their husbands had died but also, sometimes, during their husbands' temporary absences. The kings of Aragon in the late Middle Ages, for instance, were often on the road, traveling to far-flung reaches of the kingdom or visiting allies elsewhere. In their absence, their queens governed as lieutenants, and their rule was generally accepted by nobles and populace alike.[15] Noblewomen, too, could serve as official or unofficial replacements for their husbands. Adela of Blois ruled with the authority of a count during the absence of her husband, Stephen-Henry, on crusade. This authority enabled her to collect revenues from the proceeds of fairs, send knights to support the king, defend her vassals, and settle property disputes in her court.[16] Women from the gentry (the lesser nobility) carried out the same kinds of responsibilities on a smaller scale: during John Paston's frequent absences at parliament, on business, or in prison, he left his wife Margaret to run the estate. Margaret defended the family castle when it was attacked, participated in the family's long-running lawsuit against Sir John Fastolf, and tried to arrange appropriate marriages for her children.[17]

In unusual circumstances, a woman inherited a throne, title, or position in her own right rather than due to the death or absence of her husband. Isabella de Clifford and her sister Idonea de Leyburn, for example, inherited the office of sheriff of Westmorland (England) from their father. While their respective husbands assumed the office while they were alive, Isabella and Idonea themselves took it over once they became widows. They appointed under-sheriffs to do most of the day-to-day work involved, but they did become directly involved on occasion. In 1286, for example, Isabella appeared in person at the borough court of Appleby to deliver a writ ordering the court to cease hearing a murder case. At issue was the matter of jurisdiction:

Isabella and Idonea apparently felt that the borough court was overreaching its authority in trying men for murder, a matter that ought to have been considered in the royal courts and overseen by themselves as co-sheriffs. Isabella and Idonea were unable to perform the office of sheriff when they were single or married, but their widowhood enabled them the unusual opportunity of doing so.[18] At least two other women acted as sheriffs in thirteenth-century England, too: Nicola de la Haye of Lincoln and Ela, widow of William Longespee, in Wiltshire.[19] The authority exercised by Isabella, Idonea, Nicola de la Haye, and Ela was unusual, occasioned as it was by their positions as heiresses and widows, but it was significant.

Women occasionally succeeded as queens in their own right, too, although this was again highly unusual. Between 1100 and 1500, more than a dozen women succeeded to thrones in Scotland, Léon-Castile, Navarre, Aragon, Sicily, Naples, Hungary, Poland, and the Scandinavian states of Sweden, Norway, and Denmark. In several of these cases, however, the queens were girls and it was clear that nobles expected the real power to reside with their future husbands. Margaret of Norway, queen of Scotland between 1286 and 1290, for example, inherited the throne from her grandfather at the age of three years. Margaret died four years later (prompting a succession crisis in Scotland), but it was not before the English king Edward I, the guardians of Scotland, and Margaret's father (King Erik of Norway) had entered negotiations to marry Margaret to Edward's son. Maria of Sicily was similarly regarded as a political pawn. Aged 15 when her father died in 1377, Maria's authority was seriously undermined by disputes between Sicilian and Catalonian nobles. Maria was captured by relatives from her father's side of the family and forced to marry her nephew, Martin the Younger of Aragon. Maria and Martin eventually returned to Sicily and ruled jointly. Maria thus eventually gained the throne, but she did so only after struggling with her relatives, and her authority was compromised to some degree by the fact that she shared power with her husband.

Indeed, some female claimants to thrones, like Beatrix of Portugal, never succeeded. Beatrix was the only child of her father, King Fernâo, upon his death in 1383. Not long before his death, however, she had been married to the king of Castile, and Portuguese nobles feared that the Castilian king would not rule their country well. They thus chose Fernâo's illegitimate brother to rule in her place.[20] Matilda of England (usually known as the Empress Matilda) faced a similar reception on the death of her father in 1135. After Matilda's brother was killed, Matilda's father, Henry I, had had his chief nobles acknowledge Matilda as his heir. However, Matilda's second husband, Geoffrey of Anjou, was unpopular with the English nobility, so after Henry I died they appointed Matilda's cousin Stephen in her place. Women like Matilda and Beatrix thus lost their positions as queens because of fears about their husbands.

The Empress Matilda (1101–1169) holding a charter, from a four-teenth-century English manuscript. © British Library, London, UK/ © British Library Board. All Rights Reserved/The Bridgeman Art Library

A few queens were more successful. Æthelflæd, for instance, ruled the Anglo-Saxon kingdom of Mercia from about 910 to 918, building fortresses and defending her people against the Vikings. Æthelflæd recaptured cities that the Vikings had taken, organized kingdoms into defensive alliances, and cooperated with her brother, king of the neighboring kingdom of Wessex.[21] An equally successful queen was Isabella I of Castile, who succeeded to the throne upon the death of her half-brother in 1474. Isabella was fortunate to have the support of the Castilian nobility, and she was also fortunate in that her marriage to Ferdinand V of Aragon in 1468 augmented rather than challenged her authority in Castile. Indeed, according to the terms of her marriage settlement, Isabella retained sovereignty over Castile throughout her lifetime. The partnership between Ferdinand and Isabella enabled them to assert their authority over the nobility and the church, win Granada from the Islamic dynasty that had ruled it for 700 years, and support cultural projects such as religious art and voyages of exploration. (There was, however, a more sinister side to their power, in particular the expulsion of all Jews and Muslims from the Spanish kingdoms and the support of the Spanish Inquisition.)

Some women, such as Isabella de Clifford, Æthelflæd, and Isabella of Castile, did indeed exercise not only power but also authority in their own right. These women were very much the exceptions to the rule, however. Far more common were queens and noblewomen who exercised authority on a temporary basis in the absence of their husbands or who, like Queen Philippa petitioning her husband to release the burghers of Calais, exercised power in the absence of authority. Examples abound of women who persuaded their husbands or sons to do something; examples of women with the authority to execute their desires themselves, however, are scarce.

PEASANT WOMEN AND TOWNSWOMEN

Noblewomen and queens were not the only women to exercise power and authority. Peasant women and townswomen, too, found ways to influence others and wield power in both the domestic and public spheres. Authority, however, was considerably more difficult for non-noble women to attain.

Power

As with other aspects of their lives, much of the domestic power of peasant women and townswomen remains undocumented. Records seldom stretch into family homes, so it is hard to ascertain the power dynamics that existed between husbands and wives, mothers and children, or brothers and sisters. Who decided, for instance, what items should be bought with household money? Who corrected the children when they misbehaved? Who was responsible for maintaining relationships with the neighbors? While few sources address these sorts of questions directly, some primary sources provide important clues.

First, fictional representations of peasant women and townswomen present them as anything but shrinking violets. The stereotypical peasant wife in ballads, plays, and stories is one who is obstreperous and even contrary. In one common medieval story, for instance, a woman falls into a river and is drowned. Her husband looks for her body, searching upstream. When asked by a friend why he searches upstream rather than downstream, he replies that his wife was too contrary to do the expected thing and that he therefore suspects her body will have pushed upstream against the current. Another story, common especially in France, told of two monsters, Bigorne and Chichefache. Bigorne was obese, due to the fact that he ate henpecked husbands and these were easy to find. His counterpart, Chichefache, however, was always hungry, since her diet was made up exclusively of meek and obedient women, and these were very hard to come by.[22] As chapter 5 discusses, many other plays, poems, and artistic representations berated women for their alleged vanity, lust, pride, and love of gossip. Misogynist as these stories and stereotypes are, they nonetheless demonstrate that real women must have had some power, because otherwise there would have been no point in ridiculing them. Literary critics and scholars of popular culture have pointed out that the subjects of most ridicule and scorn in a given culture are often among the most feared. According to this argument, medieval women must have wielded some degree of power in order to make ridiculing them worthwhile. The sheer volume of misogynist stories in which wives are portrayed as cantankerous and difficult is thus testament, in a roundabout way, to their power.

Second, advice literature and court cases often reflect an assumption that women exercised a degree of power over children, servants, and husbands. As chapter 5 explains, poems such as the English "How the Good Wife Taught her Daughter" and the German "Die Winsbeckin" poems depict mothers instructing their daughters. Christine de Pisan, the important fourteenth- to fifteenth-century author, also assumes that peasant women and townswomen asserted power over their husbands. She advises them to urge their husbands to be diligent, thrifty, honest, and law-abiding.[23] Moreover, many households—even those of relatively modest status— included servants and apprentices (see chapter 2), and they were certainly expected to follow the commands of their mistresses. Occasional court cases attest to circumstances in which the relationship between mistresses and servants went wrong. Joan, wife of William atte Hall, was judged in 1373 to be within her rights administering a slap to her servant Denise if she disobeyed orders or neglected her work. On the other hand, Maud, wife of Henry Forner of Tottenham, was considered to have gone beyond those rights in 1393 when she assaulted her maid Juliana. Presumably the difference between the outcomes in these two cases involved the extent of force employed.[24]

Fictional literature, advice literature, and court cases thus imply that women possessed some degree of domestic power, although the extent of this power may well have varied from one household to another. But women also often possessed a degree of public power that fell short of authority. Unmarried women or married women acting as *femmes soles* (see chapter 2) could use manorial courts to bring suits against those who owed them money or had wronged them in some way. In towns, too, women were able to use the courts to pursue grievances. Scottish women, for instance, were less likely than men to bring cases before the borough courts, but they still did so sometimes. Women brought cases against others for failing to pay debts, selling poor quality goods, or causing nuisance. Effie Malcolm, for example, brought a case against the wife of David Fausid in 1491, claiming that she had paid 21 shillings and 9 pence for malt that David's wife had failed to deliver. Women also asked the courts to acknowledge their rights to property and other inheritances and to acknowledge their rights as executors of their husbands' wills and guardians of their children.[25] Women's use of the courts demonstrates their power in a public setting, even though it falls short of authority.

Rarely, women acted together in collective actions, demonstrations, and rebellions. For example, widows on the manor of Painswick (England) in 1442 raised an outcry against their lord when 11 of the 16 men he had taken with him to the war in France were killed. For the women, the heavy losses of the Painswick contingent in France meant not only the loss of their husbands but also the potential loss of their landholdings. As a result of their outcry, an inquest was held, and the Painswick widows were allowed to keep their husbands' lands. Women occasionally acted together in support of an individual woman who had been wronged, too: when a man murdered his adopted mother in Whitechapel (London) in 1429, a group of women killed him by pelting him with filth and other missiles. Similarly, a group of London women marched into parliament in 1428 to present a petition complaining that the Duke of Gloucester had deserted his wife, Jacqueline of Hainault, in the war-torn Netherlands and that he had taken a mistress.[26] Women also participated alongside men in a number of riots and rebellions. In the English Rising of 1381, for example, both male and female peasants and townspeople marched on the city of London, burned palaces, and killed important political figures associated with high taxes. Chroniclers and court records attest to the role of women both as participants and as those urging the participation of men. Julia, wife of Richard Pouchere, allegedly met up with rebels and persuaded them to break into Maidstone prison and destroy it. The court record reiterates that "Julia was a party to this and encouraged it." Another woman, Katherine Gamen, cut off the escape route of Chief Justice John Cavendish by untying the boat into which he was about to flee from a mob. The crowd was thus able to seize and kill him. And Johanna Ferrour was accused of being a leader of the revolts, responsible for arresting members of the church and ordering their execution.[27] Certainly women are outnumbered by men among rebels in 1381, but the actions of Julia, Katherine, and Johanna show that they, too, claimed the power that came with rebellion.

In rare circumstances, women participated in warfare, too. Attitudes toward female warriors changed over the course of the Middle Ages. In the early Middle Ages, direct participation by women in warfare does not seem to have been particularly unusual, as evidenced by the fact that chroniclers who mentioned female warriors did so in a matter of fact way. Thus the chronicler who mentioned the capture of Richilde of Hainault in the Battle of Cassel in 1071 did not remark further that her participation was atypical. Authors of Viking sagas also included multiple mentions of female warriors, and archaeologists' discovery of weapons in the graves of Scandinavian women strengthens the evidence for some Viking women's participation in warfare. But during the high and late Middle Ages, authors who mentioned women warriors increasingly pointed out that these women were anomalous, participating in an activity that they expected to be confined to men alone. Women warriors seem to have been more common in the period when military bands tended to be comprised of people from the same household and women could thus rely upon familial bonds. As warfare became more professional and less personal, fewer women fought directly.[28] But women could be participants in warfare without wielding arms. Women of all social statuses accompanied men on the crusades, for example: noblewomen and queens, like Eleanor of Aquitaine, sometimes treated the journey as a vacation, while those of lower status were more likely to serve as laundresses, cooks, or prostitutes. Chroniclers describe women carrying water, both for drinking and filling moats, and using their knives to hack the heads off prisoners. In some cases, women did join the rank and file soldiers and fight directly, their bodies hidden by their helmets and uniforms, although the extent to which this occurred is hard to gauge.[29]

The best-known example of a medieval woman warrior, Joan of Arc, was a peasant girl from Domrémy (France) whose mystical visions caused her to lead the French army briefly against the English during the Hundred Years War. Joan's role in inspiring the French helped them to win a series of victories between May and August 1429. In her last known work, written in July 1429, when Joan's popularity was at its peak, Christine de Pisan commemorated her achievements:

> Oh! What honor for the female sex! It is perfectly obvious that God has special regard for it when all these wretched people who destroyed the whole kingdom—now recovered and made safe by a woman, something that 5000 men could not have done—and the traitors [have been] exterminated. Before the event they would scarcely have believed this possible. A little girl of sixteen (isn't this something quite supernatural?) who does not even notice the weight of the arms she bears—indeed her whole upbringing seems to have prepared her for this, so strong and resolute is she! And her enemies go fleeing before her, not one of them can stand up to her. She does this in full view of everyone, and drives her enemies out of France, recapturing castles and towns. Never did anyone see greater strength, even in hundreds of thousands of our men! And she is the supreme captain of our brave and able men.[30]

But the tide turned soon after Christine's words of admiration: Joan's troops were unable to retake Paris, and Joan herself was captured in May 1430. The French did little to rescue her, and the English tried her and condemned her to death. She was burned alive in Rouen in May 1431. Joan's position as temporary leader of the French armies bridges the gap between power and authority. Her role was sanctioned and encouraged by the Dauphin (heir to the French throne), especially since Joan's victories enabled him to be crowned as Charles VII. Yet the extent of her authority was never made clear, and the French quickly abandoned her once her power started to wear thin. Joan of Arc's brief popularity was certainly enabled by broader social trends, such as the increase in female mysticism outlined in chapter 1 and the ongoing conflict between the English and the French, yet Joan was in many ways an anomaly.

A more mundane type of female power took the form of female companionship outside the home. Women gathered together around the bed of women in childbirth and continued to keep the new mother company in the weeks following the birth. They also gathered together in marketplaces, either as sellers or purchasers of goods, and in social settings, such as taverns or the homes of friends. Male suspicion of occasions on which women gathered is again testimony to the power of such gatherings. Ballads that ridiculed women sharing secrets and gossip suggest a degree of concern about the subversive nature of female companionship. One such poem from the fifteenth-century begins thus:

> [L]isten to me
> Two words or three,
> And hearken to my song;
> And I shall tell you a tale,
> How ten wives sat at the nale [ale house]
> And no man them among [no man sat among them].[31]

The narrator of the ballad goes on to explain how these 10 women ridiculed their husbands, making particular fun of their poor sexual prowess. Other stories and poems emphasized the dangers of all-female gatherings too: two early sixteenth-century poems by the Scots poet William Dunbar, for example, detail conversations in which women discuss ways to alleviate the stresses of marriage and gain mastery over their husbands. In "The Two Gossips," two gossips sit drinking wine and chattering on the first day of Lent. One woman advises the other to relieve her irritation at the hardship of fasting for Lent by venting her wrath on her husband. In "The Treatise of the Two Married Women and the Widow," gossiping women complain about their husbands and listen to the widow's description of how her life is better since her husband died. The widow explains that her apparent grief at her husband's death is purely for show, and that she keeps a water-filled

Joan of Arc (1412–31) from a French manuscript of c. 1505. © Musée Dobrée, Nantes, France/The Bridgeman Art Library

sponge within her cloak so as to wet her face and simulate tears if she happens to meet an old friend of her husband.[32] Female companionship thus possessed a power that was often feared.

Peasant women and townswomen, therefore, exercised power both within and beyond their own homes. Within their households, they demanded a degree of power over husbands, servants, and children (although the extent of their power certainly varied from one household to the next), and within their villages and towns they claimed power through their use of the courts, companionship with other women, and—occasionally—collective action and participation in warfare.

Authority

Yet, despite this power, ordinary women very seldom occupied positions of authority, or recognized and legitimized power. Women's exclusion from authority was often quite deliberate, justified on the basis of their sex, since it was thought that women were, by nature, unfit to govern. Their exclusion even extended to matters on which one might think women would best be suited to exercise authority. Women made most of the ale in medieval society, for instance, yet they were almost never appointed as aletasters to check on the quality of that ale; instead, that position was assigned to men. In Cologne (Germany), the silkmaking trade was exclusively controlled by women, yet their guild was run by men.[33] Although women occasionally occupied positions of authority, as outlined below, those positions were very much the exception to the rule.

Rarely, a woman occupied a position of authority when she served as a so-called pledge for another woman or for a man in a manorial or borough court (see chapter 4 for further discussion of pledging). Pledging, similar to the modern system of posting bail, meant that she was liable to pay a fine if the person whom she had pledged did not show up at the next court date or failed to pay his or her own fine. Most women who stood as pledges were widows, reflecting the fact that widows had more control over their own money, and many of these widows were pledging for their own children. In other words, they were occupying the position that their children's father might have held, had he still been alive. Pledging by women was, however, rare. On the manor of Brigstock (England), only 24 women served as pledges in the thousands of cases recorded in surviving court records between 1287 and 1348. At least 14 of these 24 women were widows.[34] In the town of Middlewich (England), only four women served as pledges in surviving court records between 1413 and 1443.[35] In the Scottish borough of Stirling, a woman stood pledge for her mother in 1529, but this kind of occurrence was extremely rare.[36] In other jurisdictions, no woman ever served as a pledge, perhaps reflecting an unwritten community custom that barred women from this position.

Women also held positions of minor authority within their local parishes. Some served as wax collectors, collecting a few pennies from each household to pay for the church's candles. In a period before electric light, candles were the only means of artificial lighting, and they also possessed a spiritual significance. At Easter, for instance, churches typically burned large candles that might weigh 14 pounds or more. Other women served as wardens of parish guilds (organizations that participated in charitable work and often helped to maintain altars within churches). In England, membership in parish guilds was often organized by sex and marital status, so that the wives might belong to one guild, the unmarried women to another, the young men to a third, and so on. Each guild was headed by a warden, and women typically assumed leadership of their own guilds. Serving as a guild warden might require one to lead fund-raising efforts, organize special functions and charitable events, and arrange rosters for ensuring the cleaning of the church and maintenance of altars.

Occasionally, women served as churchwardens for their local parishes. This position was an important one, since churchwardens were responsible for overseeing the maintenance of the church and courtyard and for reporting to the bishop on both the physical condition of the church and on the moral condition of the priest and parishioners. Execution of these tasks thus involved raising money, employing builders and other craftspeople, and appearing before the bishop as he visited the parish. Churchwardens tended to be drawn from among the richer peasants and townspeople; occasionally, members of the gentry or even nobility served in the office, too. Scholars have found records of about 25 women who became churchwardens in English parishes between 1425 and 1547. In several of these cases, female churchwardens were widows replacing a husband who had died while he held the position. For instance, Katherine Firthe assumed the position of churchwarden for the parish of St. Nicholas Shambles in London after her husband John died in 1473, three months into his term of office. In other places, the position rotated among a small group of families, and widows might replace a husband when their family's term came up in the rotation. Women of higher social status were more likely to serve in their own right rather than as substitutes for deceased husbands. Dame Isabel Newton of Yatton (England) became churchwarden in 1496. Her husband, John, had died a decade earlier, and Isabel used her position of churchwarden to help her supervise construction of a new chapel to which her husband's remains would be transferred.[37] Women's roles within their local parishes could occasionally, therefore, lead to positions of authority as well as power.

Instances in which peasant women and townswomen held positions of authority are thus few and far between. Yet such women were by no means powerless. Indeed, some historians have hypothesized that gender differences were less obvious among men and women of lower social status than they were between men and women of higher social status. Other historians have disagreed, arguing that gender gaps were equally profound at all social levels, even if these gaps took different forms. The distinction between power and authority is important. Medieval Europe saw very few women of the stature of Queen Eleanor of Aquitaine or the peasant warrior Joan of Arc. But it contained many women who found ways to influence those around them and thus exercise a degree of power.

NOTES

1. For discussion of the distinction between power and authority as they relate to medieval women, see Judith M. Bennett, "Public Power and Authority in the Medieval English Countryside," in *Women and Power in the Middle Ages,* ed. Mary Erler and Maryanne Kowaleski (Athens: University of Georgia Press, 1988), 18–36. I have modified her definition of power slightly.

2. Jean Froissart, *Chronicles,* ed. and trans. John Jolliffe (London: Harvill Press, 1967), 156–57. In fact, modern scholars have pointed out that this event cannot actually have occurred: Philippa gave birth in May 1348, so if she was pregnant in August 1347 then

she was only just so and probably did not yet know it. Whether or not the events actually took place, the story reflects expectations of medieval queens.

3. Paul Strohm, *Hochon's Arrow: The Social Imagination of Fourteenth-Century Texts* (Princeton: Princeton University Press, 1992), 102.

4. Lois L. Honeycutt, "Intercession and the High-Medieval Queen: The Esther Topos," in *Power of the Weak: Studies on Medieval Women*, ed. Jennifer Carpenter and Sally-Beth MacLean (Urbana: University of Illinois Press, 1995), 126–46.

5. "The City of Coventry: The Legend of Lady Godiva," *A History of the County of Warwick: Volume 8: The City of Coventry and Borough of Warwick* (1969), 242–47.

6. June Hall McCash, "The Cultural Patronage of Medieval Women: An Overview," in *The Cultural Patronage of Medieval Women*, ed. McCash (Athens: University of Georgia Press, 1996), 1–49, at 8–9.

7. Quoted in Amy Livingstone, "Powerful Allies and Dangerous Adversaries: Noblewomen in Medieval Society," in *Women in Medieval Western European Culture*, ed. Linda E. Mitchell (New York: Garland, 1999) 7–30 at 25.

8. John Carmi Parsons, "Piety, Power, and the Reputations of Two Thirteenth-Century English Queens," in *Women of Power I: Queens, Regents and Potentates*, ed. Theresa M. Vann (Dallas, TX: Academia Press, 1993), 107–25.

9. *Women's Lives in Medieval Europe: A Sourcebook*, ed. Emilie Amt (New York: Routledge, 1993), 142.

10. Kimberly A. LoPrete, "Adela of Blois" in *Women in the Middle Ages: An Encyclopedia*, ed. Katharina M. Wilson and Nadia Margolis (Westport, CT: Greenwood Press, 2004), 2 vols, v. 1, 5–7.

11. Clarissa W. Atkinson, *The Oldest Vocation: Christian Motherhood in the Middle Ages* (Ithaca: Cornell University Press, 1991), 177.

12. Joseph F. O'Callaghan, "The Many Roles of the Medieval Queen: Some Examples from Castile," in *Queenship and Political Power in Medieval and Early Modern Spain*, ed. Theresa Earenfight (Aldershot, U.K.: Ashgate, 2005), 21–32 at 28–29.

13. Quoted in Steinar Imsen, "Late Medieval Scandinavian Queenship," in *Queens and Queenship in Medieval Europe*, ed. Anne Duggan (Woodbridge, U.K.: Boydell Press, 1997), 53–74 at 60.

14. Colin Platt, *King Death: The Black Death and its Aftermath in Late-Medieval England* (London: University College of London Press, 1996), 57.

15. Theresa Earenfight, "Absent Kings: Queens as Political Partners in the Medieval Crown of Aragon," in *Queenship and Political Power in Medieval and Early Modern Spain*, 33–51.

16. LoPrete, "Adela of Blois."

17. *The Paston Letters: A Selection in Modern Spelling.* Ed. Norman Davis (Oxford: Oxford University Press, 1963).

18. Douglas C. Jansen, "Women and Public Authority in the Thirteenth Century," in *Women of Power I*, 91–106.

19. Judith Everard, "Public Authority and Private Rights: Women in the English Royal Court of Justice, 1196–1250," in *Sexuality and Gender in History: Selected Essays*, ed. Penelope Hetherington and Philippa Maddern (Osborne Park, Western Australia: Optima Press, 1993), 123–43 at 129.

20. Armin Wolf, "Reigning Queens in Medieval Europe: When, Where, and Why," in *Medieval Queenship*, ed. John Carmi Parsons (New York, St. Martin's Press, 1993), 169–88.

21. Katherine L. French and Allyson M. Poska, *Women and Gender in the Western Past.* 2 vols., v. 1: to 1815 (Boston: Houghton Mifflin, 2007), 156.

22. Steven M. Taylor, "Monsters of Misogyny: The Medieval French 'Dit de Chincheface' and 'Dit de Bigorne'," *Allegorica* 5 (1980), 98–124.

23. Christine de Pisan, *A Medieval Woman's Mirror of Honor: The Treasury of the City of Ladies,* trans. Charity Cannon Willard, ed. Madeleine Pelner Cosman (New York: Persea, 1989), 209–10, 219–21.

24. *Women in England, c. 1275–1525,* ed. and trans. P.J.P. Goldberg (Manchester: Manchester University Press, 1995), 94–95.

25. Elizabeth Ewan, "Scottish Portias: Women in the Courts in Mediaeval Scottish Towns," *Journal of the Canadian Historical Association* 3 (1992), 27–43, at 37–39.

26. R. A. Houlbrooke, "Women's Social Life and Common Action in England from the Fifteenth Century to the Eve of the Civil War," *Continuity and Change* 1 (1986), 171–89.

27. Sylvia Federico, "The Imaginary Society: Women in 1381," *Journal of British Studies* 40 (2001), 159–83.

28. Megan McLaughlin, "The Woman Warrior: Gender, Warfare, and Society in Medieval Europe," *Women's Studies* 17 (1990), 193–209.

29. Keren Caspi-Reisfeld, "Women Warriors during the Crusades, 1095–1254," in *Gendering the Crusades,* ed. Susan B. Edgington and Sarah Lambert (Cardiff: University of Wales Press, 2001), 94–107.

30. Christine de Pisan, "The Song of Joan of Arc," in *The Medieval Record: Sources of Medieval History,* ed. Alfred J. Andrea (Boston: Houghton Mifflin, 1997), 437–40 at 439.

31. *Jyl of Breyntford's Testament,* ed. Frederick J. Furnivall (London: Printed for private circulation, 1871), 29–33. Modernization of the text is mine.

32. William Dunbar, *The Poems of William Dunbar,* ed. William MacKay MacKenzie (Edinburgh: Porpoise Press, 1932), 84, 85–97.

33. Martha C. Howell, "Citizenship and Gender: Women's Political Status in Northern Medieval Cities," in *Women and Power in the Middle Ages,* 37–60 at 38.

34. Bennett, "Public Power and Authority in the Medieval English Countryside," 25.

35. The National Archives: Public Record Office SC2 156/3–7; *A Middlewich Chartulary,* Part 1, ed. Joan Varley, Chetham Society Publications, new series, v. 105 (1941); *A Middlewich Chartulary,* Part 2, ed. Joan Varley and James Tait, Chetham Society Publications, new series, v. 108 (1944).

36. Ewan, "Scottish Portias," 30, n. 12.

37. Katherine L. French, 'Women Churchwardens in Late Medieval England," in *The Parish in Late Medieval England,* ed. Clive Burgess and Eamon Duffy (Donington, U.K.: Shaun Tyas, 2006), 302–21.

SUGGESTED READING

Carpenter, Jennifer and Sally-Beth MacLean, eds. *Power of the Weak: Studies on Medieval Women.* Urbana: University of Illinois Press, 1995.

Duggan, Anne, ed. *Queens and Queenship in Medieval Europe.* Woodbridge, U.K.: Boydell Press, 1997.

Earenfight, Theresa. *Queenship and Political Power in Medieval and Early Modern Spain.* Aldershot, U.K.: Ashgate, 2005.

Erler, Mary C. and Maryanne Kowaleski, eds. *Gendering the Master Narrative: Women and Power in the Middle Ages.* Ithaca: Cornell University Press, 2003.

Erler, Mary C. and Maryanne Kowaleski, eds. *Women and Power in the Middle Ages.* Athens: University of Georgia Press, 1988.

Houlbrooke, R. A. "Women's Social Life and Common Action in England from the Fifteenth Century to the Eve of the Civil War," *Continuity and Change* 1 (1986): 171–89.

McLaughlin, Megan. "The Woman Warrior: Gender, Warfare, and Society in Medieval Europe," *Women's Studies* 17 (1990): 193–209.

Meek, Christine, and Catherine Lawless, eds. *Studies on Medieval and Early Modern Women: Pawns or Players?* (Dublin: Four Courts Press, 2003).

Parsons, John Carmi, ed. *Medieval Queenship.* New York, St. Martin's Press, 1993.

Vann, Theresa M., ed. *Women of Power I: Queens, Regents and Potentates.* Dallas, TX: Academia Press, 1993.

Wheeler, Bonnie and Charles T. Wood, eds. *Fresh Verdicts on Joan of Arc.* New York: Garland, 1996.

Selected Bibliography

Adams, Carol. *From Workshop to Warfare: The Lives of Medieval Women.* Cambridge: Cambridge University Press, 1983.

Ahmed, Leila. *Women and Gender in Islam: Historical Roots of a Modern Debate.* New Haven: Yale University Press, 1992.

Amt, Emilie, ed. *Women's Lives in Medieval Europe: A Sourcebook.* New York: Routledge, 1993.

Anderson, Bonnie S. and Judith P. Zinsser. *A History of Their Own: Women in Europe from Prehistory to the Present.* Revised edition. 2 vols. New York: Oxford University Press, 2000.

Archer, Robert. *The Problem of Woman in Late-Medieval Hispanic Literature.* Woodbridge, U.K.: Tamesis, 2005.

Ashley, Kathleen M. and Robert L. A. Clark, eds. *Medieval Conduct.* Minneapolis: University of Minnesota Press, 2001.

Ashley, Kathleen M. and Pamela Sheingorn, eds. *Interpreting Cultural Symbols: Saint Anne in Late Medieval Society.* Athens: University of Georgia Press, 1990.

Atkinson, Clarissa. *Mystic and Pilgrim: The Book and the World of Margery Kempe.* Ithaca: Cornell University Press, 1983.

———. *The Oldest Vocation: Christian Motherhood in the Middle Ages.* Ithaca: Cornell University Press, 1991.

———. "'Precious Balsam in a Fragile Glass': The Ideology of Virginity in the Later Middle Ages." *Journal of Family History* 8 (1983): 131–43.

Baker, Derek and Rosalind M. T. Hill, eds. *Medieval Women.* Oxford: Blackwell, 1978.

Bardsley, Sandy. *Venomous Tongues: Speech and Gender in Late Medieval England.* Philadelphia: University of Pennsylvania Press, 2006.

Bartlett, Anne Clark. *Male Authors, Female Readers: Representation and Subjectivity in Middle English Devotional Literature.* Ithaca: Cornell University Press, 1995.

———. ed. *Vox Mystica: Essays on Medieval Mysticism in Honor of Valerie Lagorio.* Cambridge: D. S. Brewer, 1995.

Barratt, Alexandra, ed. *Women's Writing in Middle English.* London: Longman, 1992.

Barron, Caroline M. and Anne F. Sutton, eds. *Medieval London Widows, 1300–1500.* London: Hambledon Press, 1994.

Baskin, Judith R. ed. *Jewish Women in Historical Perspective.* Detroit: Wayne State University Press, 1991.

Beer, Frances. *Women and Mystical Experience in the Middle Ages.* Woodbridge, U.K.: Boydell Press, 1992.

Bennett, Judith M. *Ale, Beer and Brewsters in England: Women's Work in a Changing World, 1300–1600.* New York: Oxford University Press, 1996.

———. "History that Stands Still: Women's Work in the European Past." *Feminist Studies* 14 (1998): 269–83.

———. *A Medieval Life: Cecilia Penifader of Brigstock, c. 1295–1344.* Boston: McGraw-Hill College, 1999.

———. *Medieval Women in Modern Perspective.* Washington, D.C.: American Historical Association, 2000.

———. "Theoretical Issues: Confronting Continuity." *Journal of Women's History* 9 (1997): 73–94.

———. *Women in the Medieval English Countryside: Gender and Household in Brigstock before the Plague.* New York: Oxford University Press, 1987.

Bennett, Judith M. and Amy M. Froide, eds. *Singlewomen in the European Past, 1250–1800.* Philadelphia: University of Pennsylvania Press, 1999.

Bennett, Judith M. and C. Warren Hollister. *Medieval Europe: A Short History,* 10th ed. Boston: McGraw Hill, 2006.

Bennett, Judith M. et al. eds. *Sisters and Workers in the Middle Ages.* Chicago: University of Chicago Press, 1989.

Berman, Constance H. ed. *Women and Monasticism in Medieval Europe: Sisters and Patrons of the Cistercian Reform.* Kalamazoo, MI: Medieval Institute Publications, 2002.

Berman, Constance H. and Charles W. Connell, eds. *The Worlds of Medieval Women: Creativity, Influence, Imagination.* Morgantown: West Virginia University Press, 1985.

Bitel, Lisa M. *Land of Women: Tales of Sex and Gender from Early Ireland.* Ithaca, NY: Cornell University Press, 1996.

———. *Women in Early Medieval Europe, 400–1100.* Cambridge: Cambridge University Press, 2002.

Blamires, Alcuin. *The Case for Women in Medieval Culture.* Oxford: Clarendon Press, 1997.

Blamires, Alcuin, Karen Pratt and C. W. Marx, eds. *Women Defamed and Women Defended: An Anthology of Medieval Texts.* Oxford: Clarendon Press, 1992.

Bloch, R. Howard. *Medieval Misogyny and the Invention of Western Romantic Love.* Chicago: University of Chicago Press, 1991.

Blumenfeld-Kosinski, Renate. *Not of Woman Born: Representations of Caesarean Birth in Medieval and Renaissance Culture.* Ithaca: Cornell University Press, 1990.

Bolton, Brenda and Susan Mosher Stuard, eds. *Women in Medieval Society.* Philadelphia: University of Pennsylvania, 1976.

Bornstein, Daniel and R. Rusconi, eds. *Women and Religion in Medieval and Renaissance Italy.* Chicago: University of Chicago Press, 1996.

Bornstein, Diane, ed. *Ideals for Women in the Works of Christine de Pizan.* Detroit, MI: Fifteenth Century Symposium, 1981.

———. *The Lady in the Tower: Medieval Courtesy Literature for Women.* Hamden, CT: Archon Books, 1983.

Bowers, Jane and Judith Tick, eds. *Women Making Music: The Western Arts Tradition, 1150–1950.* Urbana: University of Illinois Press, 1986.

Brasher, Sally Mayall. *Women of the Humiliati: A Lay Religious Order in Medieval Civic Life.* New York: Routledge, 2003.

Bridenthal, Renate and Claudia Koonz, eds. *Becoming Visible: Women in European History.* Boston: Houghton Mifflin, 1977.

Brink, Jean R. ed. *Female Scholars: A Tradition of Learned Women before 1800.* Montréal: Eden's Press Women's Publications, 1980.

Brooke, C.N.L. *The Medieval Idea of Marriage.* Oxford: Oxford University Press, 1989.

Brown, Peter. *The Body and Society: Men, Women and Sexual Renunciation in Early Christianity.* New York: Columbia University Press, 1988.

Brubaker, Leslie and Julia M. H. Smith, eds. *Gender in the Early Medieval World: East and West, 300–900.* Cambridge: Cambridge University Press, 2004.

Bruckner, Matilda Tomaryn, Laurie Shepard and Sarah White, eds. *Songs of the Women Troubadours.* New York: Garland, 2000.

Brundage, James A. *Law, Sex and Christian Society in Medieval Europe.* Chicago: University of Chicago Press, 1987.

Bullough, Vern L. and James A. Brundage, eds. *A Handbook of Medieval Sexuality.* New York: Garland, 1996.

Bullough, Vern L. and James A. Brundage. *Sexual Practices and the Medieval Church.* Buffalo, NY: Prometheus Books, 1982.

Bynum, Caroline Walker. *Fragmentation and Redemption: Essays on Gender and the Human Body in Medieval Religion.* Cambridge: MIT Press, 1991.

———. *Holy Feast and Holy Fast: The Religious Significance of Food to Medieval Women.* Berkeley: University of California Press, 1987.

———. *Jesus as Mother: Studies in the Spirituality of the High Middle Ages.* Berkeley: University of California Press, 1982.

Carpenter, Jennifer and Sally-Beth MacLean, eds. *Power of the Weak: Studies on Medieval Women.* Urbana: University of Illinois Press, 1995.

Chance, Jane. *Woman as Hero in Old English Literature.* New York: Syracuse University Press, 1986.

Charles, Lindsey and Lorna Duffin, eds. *Women and Work in Pre-Industrial England.* London: Croom Helm, 1985.

Cherewatuk, Karen and Ulrike Wiethaus, eds. *Dear Sister: Medieval Women and the Epistolary Genre.* Philadelphia: University of Pennsylvania Press, 1993.

Chibnall, Marjorie. *The Empress Matilda: Queen Consort, Queen Mother and Lady of the English.* Oxford: Blackwell, 1992.

Classen, Albrecht, ed. and trans. *Late Medieval German Women's Poetry: Secular and Religious Songs.* Rochester, NY: D. S. Brewer, 2004.

Collis, Louise. *Memoirs of a Medieval Woman: The Life and Times of Margery Kempe.* New York: Crowell, 1964.

Condren, Mary. *The Serpent and the Goddess: Women, Religion and Power in Celtic Ireland.* San Francisco: Harper and Row, 1989.

Connor, Carolyn L. *Women of Byzantium.* New Haven: Yale University Press, 2004.

Coss, Peter R. *The Lady in Medieval England, 1000–1500.* Mechanicsburg, PA: Stackpole Books, 1998.

Crawford, Anne, ed. *Letters of Medieval Women.* Stroud: Sutton, 2002.

Damico, Helen and Alexandra Hennessey Olsen, eds. *New Readings on Women in Old English Literature.* Bloomington: Indiana University Press, 1990.

D'Arcens, Louise and Juanita Feros Ruys, eds. *Maistresse of my Wit: Medieval Women, Modern Scholars.* Turnhout, Belgium: Brepols, 2004.

Davids, Adelbert, ed. *The Empress Theophano: Byzantium and the West at the Turn of the Millennium.* Cambridge: Cambridge University Press, 1995.

Dean, Trevor and K.J.P. Lowe, eds. *Marriage in Italy, 1300–1650.* Cambridge: Cambridge University Press, 1998.

de Pisan, Christine. *A Medieval Woman's Mirror of Honor: The Treasury of the City of Ladies.* Edited by Madeleine Pelner Cosman. Translated by Charity Cannon Willard. Tenafly, N.J.: Bard Hall Press; New York: Persea Books, 1989.

de Voragine, Jacobus. *Women of the Gilte Legende: A Selection of Middle English Saints Lives.* Translated by Larissa Tracy. Cambridge: D. S. Brewer, 2003.

Dillard, Heath. *Daughters of the Reconquest: Women in Castilian Town Society, 1100–1300.* Cambridge: Cambridge University Press, 1984.

Dinshaw, Carolyn and David Wallace, eds. *The Cambridge Companion to Medieval Women's Writing.* Cambridge: Cambridge University Press, 2003.

Dockray-Miller, Mary. *Motherhood and Mothering in Anglo-Saxon England.* New York: St. Martin's Press, 2000.

Dor, Juliette, Lesley Johnson and Jocelyn Wogan-Browne, eds. *New Trends in Feminine Spirituality: The Holy Women of Liège and Their Impact.* Turnhout, Belgium: Brepols, 1999.

Dronke, Peter. *Women Writers of the Middle Ages: A Critical Study of Texts from Perpetua to Marguerite Porete.* Cambridge: Cambridge University Press, 1984.

Duby, Georges. *The Knight, the Lady and the Priest: The Making of Modern Marriage in Medieval France.* Translated by B. Bray. New York: Pantheon Books, 1983.

———. *Medieval Marriage: Two Models from Twelfth-Century France.* Baltimore: Johns Hopkins University Press, 1978.

———. *Women of the Twelfth Century.* Chicago: University of Chicago Press, 1997–8.

Dunnigan, Sarah, C. Marie Harker and Evelyn S. Newlyn, eds. *Woman and the Feminine in Medieval and Early Modern Scottish Writing.* New York: Palgrave Macmillan, 2004.

Duggan, Anne, ed. *Queens and Queenship in Medieval Europe.* Woodbridge, U.K.: Boydell Press, 1997.

Dyas, Dee, Valerie Edden and Roger Ellis, eds. *Approaching Medieval English Anchoritic and Mystical Texts.* Woodbridge, U.K.: D. S. Brewer, 2005.

Earenfight, Theresa, ed. *Queenship and Political Power in Medieval and Early Modern Spain.* Aldershot, U.K.: Ashgate, 2005.

Echols, Annie and Marty Williams. *An Annotated Index of Medieval Women.* New York: M. Wiener, 1992.

Edgington, Susan and Sarah Lambert, eds. *Gendering the Crusades.* New York: Columbia University Press, 2002.

Edwards, Robert and Vickie L. Ziegler, eds. *Matrons and Marginal Women in Medieval Society.* Woodbridge, U.K.: Boydell Press, 1995.

Elkins, S. *Holy Women in Twelfth Century England.* Chapel Hill: University of North Carolina Press, 1988.

Elliott, Dyan. *Spiritual Marriage: Sexual Abstinence in Medieval Wedlock.* Princeton: Princeton University Press, 1993.

Ennen, Edith. *The Medieval Woman.* Oxford: Blackwell, 1989.

Erler, Mary Carpenter. *Women, Reading and Piety in Late Medieval England.* Cambridge: Cambridge University Press, 2002.

Erler, Mary Carpenter and Maryanne Kowaleski, eds. *Gendering the Master Narrative: Women and Power in the Middle Ages.* Ithaca: Cornell University Press, 2003.

———.*Women and Power in the Middle Ages.* Athens: University of Georgia Press, 1988.

Evans, Ruth and Lesley Johnson, eds. *Feminist Readings in Middle English Literature: The Wife of Bath and all her Sect.* London: Routledge, 1994.

Evergates, Theodore. *Aristocratic Women in Medieval France.* Philadelphia: University of Pennsylvania Press, 1990.

Ewan, Elizabeth. "Scottish Portias: Women in the Courts in Mediaeval Scottish Towns," *Journal of the Canadian Historical Association* 3 (1992): 27–43.

Ewan, Elizabeth and Maureen M. Meikle, eds. *Women in Scotland: c. 1100–c. 1750.* East Linton, U.K.: Tuckwell Press, 1999.

Fanous, Samuel and Henrietta Leyser, eds. *Christina of Markyate: A Twelfth-Century Holy Woman.* London: Routledge, 2005.

Farmer, Sharon A. *Surviving Poverty in Medieval Paris: Gender, Ideology and the Daily Lives of the Poor.* Ithaca: Cornell University Press, 2002.

Farmer, Sharon A. and Carol Braun Pasternack, eds. *Gender and Difference in the Middle Ages.* Minneapolis: University of Minnesota Press, 2003.

Fell, Christine E. *Women in Anglo-Saxon England and the Impact of 1066.* Bloomington: Indiana University Press, 1984.

Ferrante, Joan M. *To the Glory of Her Sex: Women's Roles in the Composition of Medieval Texts.* Bloomington: Indiana University Press, 1997.

Fiero, Gloria K. Wendy Pfeffer and Mathé Allain, ed. and trans. *Three Medieval Views of Women.* New Haven: Yale University Press, 1989.

Fildes, Valerie, ed. *Women as Mothers in Pre-Industrial England: Essays in Memory of Dorothy McLaren.* London: Routledge, 1989.

Finch andrew. "Women and Violence in the Later Middle Ages: The Evidence of the Officialty of Cerisy," *Continuity and Change* 7 (1992): 23–45.

Finke, Laurie. *Women's Writing in English: Medieval England.* London: Longman, 1999.

Flanagan, Sabina. *Hildegard of Bingen, 1098–1179: A Visionary Life.* London: Routledge, 1989.

Foot, Sarah. *Veiled Women I: The Disappearance of Nuns from Anglo-Saxon England.* Aldershot, U.K.: Ashgate, 2000.

———. *Veiled Women II: Female Religious Communities in England, 871–1066.* Aldershot, U.K.: Ashgate, 2000.

Forsyth, Ilene H. *The Throne of Wisdom: Wood Sculptures of the Madonna in Romanesque France.* Princeton: Princeton University Press, 1972.

Fradenburg, Louise Olga, ed. *Women and Sovereignty.* Edinburgh: Edinburgh University Press, 1992.

Fradenburg, Louise Olga and Carla Freccero, eds. *Premodern Sexualities.* New York: Routledge, 1995.

French, Katherine L. *The People of the Parish: Community Life in a Late Medieval English Diocese.* Philadelphia: University of Pennsylvania Press, 2001.

French, Katherine L. and Allyson M. Poska. *Women and Gender in the Western Past.* 2 vols. v. 1: to 1815. Boston: Houghton Mifflin, 2007.

Gadol, Joan Kelly. "Did Women have a Renaissance?" Reprinted in *Feminism and Renaissance Studies,* ed. Lorna Hutson. New York: Oxford University Press, 1999.

Garber, Rebecca L. R. *Feminine Figurae: Representations of Gender in Religious Texts by Medieval German Women Writers, 1100–1375.* New York: Routledge, 2003.

Garland, Lynda, ed. *Byzantine Women: Varieties of Experience 800–1200.* Aldershot, U.K.: Ashgate, 2006.

Gathercole, Patricia May. *The Depiction of Women in Medieval French Manuscript Illumination.* Lewiston, NY: Edwin Mellen Press, 1995.

Gies, Frances and Joseph Gies. *Marriage and the Family in the Middle Ages.* New York: Harper & Row, 1987.

———. *Women in the Middle Ages.* New York: Crowell, 1978.

Gilchrist, Roberta. *Gender and Material Culture: The Archaeology of Religious Women.* London: Routledge, 1994.

Gilchrist, Roberta and Marilyn Oliva. *Religious Women in Medieval East Anglia: History and Archaeology c. 1100–1540.* Norwich: Centre of East Anglian Studies, University of East Anglia, 1993.

Gold, Penny Schine. *The Lady and the Virgin: Image, Attitude and Experience in Twelfth-Century France.* Chicago: University of Chicago Press, 1985.

Goldberg, P.J.P. *Women, Work and Life Cycle in a Medieval Economy: Women in York and Yorkshire.* Oxford: Clarendon Press, 1992.

———. ed. *Woman is a Worthy Wight: Women in English Society c. 1200–1500.* Wolfeboro Falls, NH: Alan Sutton, 1992.

———. ed. *Women in England, c. 1275–1525: Documentary Sources.* Manchester: University of Manchester Press, 1995.

Gravdal, Kathryn. *Ravishing Maidens: Writing Rape in Medieval French Literature and Law.* Philadelphia: University of Pennsylvania Press, 1991.

Green, Monica. *Women's Healthcare in the Medieval West: Texts and Contexts.* Aldershot, U.K.: Ashgate, 2000.

———. "Women's Medical Practice and Health Care in Medieval Europe." *Signs* 14 (1988–9): 434–73.

Grössinger, Christa. *Picturing Women in Late Medieval and Renaissance Art.* New York: Manchester University Press, 1997.

Grossman, Avraham. *Pious and Rebellious: Jewish Women in Medieval Europe.* Waltham, MA: Brandeis University Press, 2004.

Hall, Dianne. *Women and the Church in Medieval Ireland, c. 1140–1540.* Dublin: Four Courts Press, 2003.

Hallissy, Margaret. *Clean Maids, True Wives, Steadfast Widows: Chaucer's Women and Medieval Codes of Conduct.* Westport, CT: Greenwood Press, 1993.

Hambly, Gavin R. G. ed. *Women in the Medieval Islamic World: Power, Patronage and Piety.* New York: St. Martin's Press, 1998.

Hamburger, Jeffrey. *Nuns as Artists: The Visual Culture of a Medieval Convent.* Berkeley: University of California Press, 1997.

———. *The Visual and the Visionary: Art and Female Spirituality in Late Medieval Germany.* New York: Zone Books, 1998.

Hanawalt, Barbara A. *Growing Up in Medieval London: The Experience of Childhood in History.* New York: Oxford University Press, 1995.

———. *The Ties that Bound: Peasant Families in Medieval England.* New York: Oxford University Press, 1986.

———. ed. *Women and Work in Preindustrial Europe.* Bloomington: Indiana University Press, 1986.

Harrison, Dick. *The Age of Abbesses and Queens: Gender and Political Culture in Early Medieval Europe.* Lund, Sweden: Nordic Academic Press, 1998.

Herlihy, David. *Opera Muliebria: Women and Work in Medieval Europe*. Philadelphia: Temple University Press, 1990.

———. *Women in Medieval Society*. Houston, TX: University of St. Thomas, 1971.

Herrin, Judith. *Women in Purple: Rulers of Medieval Byzantium*. Princeton: Princeton University Press, 2001.

Hollis, Stephanie. *Anglo-Saxon Women and the Church: Sharing a Common Fate*. Woodbridge, U.K.: Boydell Press, 1992.

Holloway, Julia Bolton, Constance S. Wright and Joan Bechtold, eds. *Equally in God's Image: Women in the Middle Ages*. New York: P. Lang, 1990.

Hotchkiss, Valerie R. *Clothes make the Man: Female Cross Dressing in Medieval Europe*. New York: Garland, 1996.

Howell, Margaret. *Eleanor of Provence: Queenship in Thirteenth-Century England*. Oxford: Blackwell, 1998.

Howell, Martha C. *Women, Production and Patriarchy in Late Medieval Cities*. Chicago: University of Chicago Press, 1986.

Jewell, Helen M. *Women in Dark Age and Early Medieval Europe, c. 500–1200*. Basingstoke, U.K.: Palgrave Macmillan, 2007.

———. *Women in Late Medieval and Reformation Europe, 1200–1550*. Basingstoke, U.K.: Palgrave Macmillan, 2007.

———. *Women in Medieval England*. Manchester: Manchester University Press, 1996.

Jesch, Judith. *Women in the Viking Age*. Woodbridge, U.K.: Boydell Press, 1991.

Jochens, Jenny. *Old Norse Images of Women*. Philadelphia: University of Pennsylvania Press, 1996.

———. *Women in Old Norse Society*. Ithaca: Cornell University Press, 1995.

Johns, Susan M. *Noblewomen, Aristocracy and Power in the Twelfth-Century Anglo-Norman Realm*. Manchester: Manchester University Press, 2003.

Johnson, Penelope D. *Equal in Monastic Profession: Religious Women in Medieval France*. Chicago: Chicago University Press, 1991.

Jones, Malcolm. "Folklore Motifs in Late Medieval Art, II: Sexist Satire and Popular Punishments." *Folklore* 101 (1990): 69–87.

Jones, Michael K. and Malcolm G. Underwood. *The King's Mother: Lady Margaret Beaufort, Countess of Richmond and Derby*. Cambridge: Cambridge University Press, 1992.

Jordan, Erin L. *Women, Power and Religious Patronage in the Middle Ages*. New York: Palgrave Macmillan, 2006.

Jordan, William Chester. *Women and Credit in Pre-Industrial and Developing Societies*. Philadelphia: University of Pennsylvania Press, 1993.

Kanner, Barbara, ed. *The Women of England: From Anglo-Saxon Times to the Present: Interpretive Bibliographical Essays*. Hamden, CT: Archon Books, 1979.

Karras, Ruth Mazo. *Common Women: Prostitution and Sexuality in Medieval England*. New York: Oxford University Press, 1996.

Kelly, Amy Ruth. *Eleanor of Aquitaine and the Four Kings*. Cambridge: Harvard University Press, 1950.

Kempe, Margery. *The Book of Margery Kempe*, ed. B. A. Windeatt. New York: Viking Penguin, 1985.

Kibler, William W. ed. *Eleanor of Aquitaine: Patron and Politician*. Austin: University of Texas Press, 1976.

Kieckhefer, R. *European Witch Trials: Their Foundations in Popular and Learned Culture, 1300–1500*. Berkeley: University of California Press, 1976.

Kirshner, Julius and Suzanne F. Wemple, eds. *Women of the Medieval World: Essays in Honor of John H. Mundy.* Oxford: Blackwell, 1985.

Kittell, Ellen E. and Mary A. Suydam, eds. *The Texture of Society: Medieval Women in the Southern Low Countries.* New York: Palgrave Macmillan, 2004.

Klapisch-Zuber, Christiane. *Women, Family and Ritual in Renaissance Italy.* Chicago: University of Chicago Press, 1985.

———. ed. *Silences of the Middle Ages,* vol. II of *A History of Women in the West.* Edited by Georges Duby and Michelle Perrot. Cambridge: Belknap Press of Harvard University Press, 1992.

Krueger, Roberta. *Women Readers and the Ideology of Gender in Old French Verse Romance.* Cambridge: Cambridge University Press, 1993.

Krug, Rebecca. *Reading Families: Women's Literate Practice in Late Medieval England.* Ithaca: Cornell University Press, 2002.

Labalme, Patricia H. ed. *Beyond their Sex: Learned Women of the European Past.* New York: New York University Press, 1980.

LaBarge, Margaret Wade. *A Small Sound of the Trumpet: Women in Medieval Life.* Boston: Beacon Press, 1986.

Ladurie, Emmanuel LeRoy. *Montaillou: The Promised Land of Error.* Translated by B. Bray. New York: Vintage Books, 1979.

Laiou, Angeliki E. *Gender, Society and Economic Life in Byzantium.* Aldershot, U.K.: Variorum, 1992.

———, ed. *Consent and Coercion to Sex and Marriage in Ancient and Medieval Societies.* Washington, D.C.: Dumbarton Oaks Research Library and Collection, 1993.

Larrington, Carolyne, ed. *Women and Writing in Medieval Europe: A Sourcebook.* London: Routledge, 1995.

Lanz, Eukene Lacarra, ed. *Marriage and Sexuality in Medieval and Early Modern Iberia.* New York: Routledge, 2002.

Lawler, Jennifer. *Encyclopedia of Women in the Middle Ages.* Jefferson, NC: McFarland, 2001.

Laynesmith, J. L. *The Last Medieval Queens: English Queenship 1445–1503.* Oxford: Oxford University Press, 2004.

Lees, Clare A. ed. *Medieval Masculinities: Regarding Men in the Middle Ages.* Minneapolis: University of Minnesota Press, 1994.

Levin, Carole and Jeanie Watson, eds. *Ambiguous Realities: Women in the Middle Ages and Renaissance.* Detroit: Wayne State University Press, 1987.

Levin, Carole, et al. eds. *Extraordinary Women of the Medieval and Renaissance World: A Biographical Dictionary.* Westport, CT: Greenwood Press, 2000.

Lewis, Gertrud Jaron. *By Women, For Women, About Women: The Sister-books of Fourteenth-Century Germany.* Toronto: Pontifical Institute of Mediaeval Studies, 1996.

Lewis, Katherine, Noël James Menuge and Kim M. Phillips, eds. *Young Medieval Women.* New York: St. Martin's Press, 1999.

Leyser, Henrietta. *Medieval Women: A Social History of Women in England, 450–1500.* New York: St. Martin's Press, 1995.

Liss, Peggy K. *Isabel the Queen: Life and Times.* New York: Oxford University Press, 1992.

Lomperis, Linda and Sarah Stanbury, eds. *Feminist Approaches to the Body in Medieval Literature.* Philadelphia: University of Pennsylvania Press, 1993.

Lucas, Angela, ed. *Women in the Middle Ages: Religion, Marriage and Letters.* New York: St. Martin's Press, 1983.

Martin, Priscilla. *Chaucer's Women: Nuns, Wives and Amazons.* Iowa City: University of Iowa Press, 1990.

Mate, Mavis E. *Women in Medieval English Society.* Cambridge: Cambridge University Press, 1990.

Matter, E. Ann and John Wayland Coakley, eds. *Creative Women in Medieval and Early Modern Italy: A Religious and Artistic Renaissance.* Philadelphia: University of Pennsylvania Press, 1994.

McCash, June Hall, ed. *The Cultural Patronage of Medieval Women.* Athens: University of Georgia Press, 1996.

McClanan, Anne L. and Karen Rosoff Encarnación, eds. *The Material Culture of Sex, Procreation and Marriage in Premodern Europe.* New York: Palgrave MacMillan, 2002.

McDonnell, E. W. *The Beguines and Beghards in Medieval Culture.* New Brunswick, NJ: Rutgers University Press, 1954.

McEntire, Sandra J. ed. *Margery Kempe: A Book of Essays.* New York: Garland, 1992.

McItnyre, Cathy Jorgensen, ed. *Medieval Family Roles: A Book of Essays.* New York: Garland, 1996.

McNamara, Jo Ann. *Sisters in Arms: Catholic Nuns through Two Millennia.* Cambridge: Harvard University Press, 1996.

McNamara, Jo Ann and John E. Halborg, eds. *Sainted Women of the Dark Ages.* Durham, NC: Duke University Press, 1992.

McSheffrey, Shannon. *Gender & Heresy: Women and Men in Lollard Communities, 1420–1530.* Philadelphia: University of Pennsylvania Press, 1995.

Meale, Carol M. ed. *Women and Literature in Britain, 1150–1500.* Cambridge: Cambridge University Press, 1993.

Meek, Christine, ed. *Women in Renaissance and Early Modern Europe.* Dublin: Four Courts Press, 2000.

Meek, Christine and Catherine Lawless, eds. *Studies on Medieval and Early Modern Women: Pawns or Players?* Dublin: Four Courts Press, 2003.

———. *Studies on Medieval and Early Modern Women: Victims or Viragos?* Dublin, Ireland: Four Courts Press, 2005.

Meek, Christine and Katherine Simms. *The Fragility of her Sex?: Medieval Irishwomen in their European Context.* Dublin: Four Courts Press, 1996.

Menuge, Noël James, ed. *Medieval Women and the Law.* Woodbridge, U.K.: Boydell Press, 2000.

Millett, Bella and Jocelyn Wogan-Browne, eds. *Medieval English Prose for Women: Selections from the Katherine Group and Ancrene Wisse.* Oxford: Clarendon Press, 1990.

Mirrer, Louise, ed. *Upon my Husband's Death: Widows in the Literature and Histories of Medieval Europe.* Ann Arbor: University of Michigan Press, 1992.

———. *Women, Jews and Muslims in the Texts of Reconquest Castile.* Ann Arbor: University of Michigan Press, 1996.

Mitchell, Linda Elizabeth. *Portraits of Medieval Women: Family, Marriage and Politics in England, 1225–1350.* New York: Palgrave MacMillan, 2003.

———. ed. *Women in Medieval Western European Culture.* New York: Garland, 1999.

Mooney, Catherine, ed. *Gendered Voices: Medieval Saints and Their Interpreters.* Philadelphia: University of Pennsylvania Press, 1999.

Morewedge, Rosmarie T. ed. *The Role of Woman in the Middle Ages.* Albany: State University of New York Press, 1975.

Morris, Bridget. *St. Birgitta of Sweden.* Woodbridge, U.K.: Boydell Press, 1999.

Morris, Katherine. *Sorceress or Witch?: The Image of Gender in Medieval Iceland and Northern Europe.* Lanham, MD: University Press of America, 1991.

Mulder-Bakker, Anneke B. *Lives of the Anchoresses: The Rise of the Urban Recluse in Medieval Europe.* Trans. Myra Heerspink Scholz. Philadelphia: University of Pennsylvania Press, 2005.

———. ed. *Sanctity and Motherhood: Essays on Holy Mothers in the Middle Ages.* New York: Garland, 1995.

———. ed. *Seeing and Knowing: Women and Learning in Medieval Europe 1200–1550.* Turnhout, Belgium: Brepols, 2004.

Mulder-Bakker, Anneke B. and Jocelyn Wogan-Browne. *Household, Women and Christianities in Late Antiquity and the Middle Ages.* Turnhout, Belgium: Brepols, 2005.

Neel, Carol, ed. *Medieval Families: Perspectives on Marriage, Household and Children.* Toronto: University of Toronto Press, 2004.

Newman, Barbara. *From Virile Woman to Woman Christ: Studies in Medieval Religion and Literature.* Philadelphia: University of Pennsylvania Press, 1995.

———. *God and the Goddesses: Vision, Poetry and Belief in the Middle Ages.* Philadelphia: University of Pennsylvania Press, 1995.

Nicholas, David. *The Domestic Life of a Medieval City: Women, Children and the Family in Fourteenth Century Ghent.* Lincoln: University of Nebraska Press, 1985.

Nichols, John A. and Lillian Thomas Shank, eds. *Medieval Religious Women,* vols. 1–3. Kalamazoo, MI: Cistercian Publications, 1984–7.

Nicol, Donald MacGillivray. *The Byzantine Lady: Ten Portraits, 1250–1500.* Cambridge: Cambridge University Press, 1994.

Noffke, Suzanne. *Catherine of Siena: Vision Through a Distant Eye.* Collegeville, MN: Liturgical Press, 1996.

Nolan, Kathleen, ed. *Capetian Women.* New York: Palgrave Macmillan, 2003.

Oliva, M. *The Convent and the Community in Late Medieval England: Female Monasteries in the Diocese of Norwich, 1350–1540.* Woodbridge, U.K.: Boydell Press, 1998.

Orme, Nicholas. *Medieval Children.* New Haven: Yale University Press, 2001.

Otis, Leah. *Prostitution in Medieval Society: The History of an Urban Institution in Languedoc.* Chicago: University of Chicago Press, 1985.

Paden, W. D. ed. *The Voice of the Trobairitz: Perspectives on the Women Troubadours.* Philadelphia: University of Pennsylvania Press, 1989.

Parsons, John Carmi, ed. *Eleanor of Castile: Queen and Society in Thirteenth-Century England.* New York: St. Martin's Press, 1995.

———. ed. *Medieval Queenship.* New York: St. Martin's Press, 1993.

Parsons, John Carmi and Bonnie Wheeler, eds. *Medieval Mothering.* New York: Garland, 1996.

Partner, Nancy F. ed. *Studying Medieval Women: Sex, Gender, Feminism.* Cambridge, MA: Medieval Academy of America, 1993.

Pendle, Karin, ed. *Women and Music: A History.* 2nd ed. Bloomington: Indiana University Press, 2001.

Perfetti, Lisa Renée. *Women and Laughter in Medieval Comic Literature.* Ann Arbor: University of Michigan Press, 2003.

Pernoud, Régine. *Women in the Days of Cathedrals.* San Francisco: Ignatius Press, 1998.

Peters, Christine. *Patterns of Piety: Women, Gender and Religion in Late Medieval and Reformation England.* Cambridge: Cambridge University Press, 2002.

Petroff, Elizabeth. *Body and Soul: Essays on Medieval Women and Mysticism.* New York: Oxford University Press, 1994.

———. ed. *Medieval Women's Visionary Literature.* New York: Oxford University Press, 1989.

Phillips, Kim M. *Medieval Maidens: Young Women and Gender in England, 1270–1540.* Manchester: Manchester University Press, 2003.

Plummer, John F. ed. *Vox Feminae: Studies in Medieval Woman's Songs.* Kalamazoo, MI: Medieval Institution Publications, 1981.

Potkay, Monica Brzezinski and Regula Meyer Evitt. *Minding the Body: Women and Literature in the Middle Ages, 800–1500.* London: Twayne Publishers, 1997.

Power, Eileen Edna. *Medieval Women.* Cambridge: Cambridge University Press, 1975.

Raguin, Virginia Chieffo and Sarah Stanbury, eds. *Women's Space: Patronage, Place and Gender in the Medieval Church.* Albany, NY: State University of New York Press, 2005.

Ranft, Patricia. *Women and the Religious Life in Premodern Europe.* New York: St. Martin's Press, 1996.

Renevey, Denis and Christina Whitehead, eds. *Writing Religious Women: Female Spiritual and Textual Practices in Late Medieval England.* Cardiff: University of Wales Press, 2000.

Riches, Samantha J. E. and Sarah Salih, eds. *Gender and Holiness: Men, Women and Saints in Late Medieval Europe.* London: Routledge, 2002.

Roberts, Anna, ed. *Violence Against Women in Medieval Texts.* Gainesville, FL: University Press of Florida, 1998.

Robertson, Elizabeth Ann. *Early English Devotional Prose and the Female Audience.* Knoxville: University of Tennessee Press, 1990.

Rose, Mary Beth, ed. *Women in the Middle Ages and the Renaissance: Literary and Historical Perspectives.* Syracuse, NY: Syracuse University Press, 1986.

Rosenthal, Joel Thomas, ed. *Medieval Women and the Sources of Medieval History.* Athens: University of Georgia Press, 1990.

Rossiaud, Jacques. *Medieval Prostitution.* Oxford: Blackwell, 1998.

Rousseau, Constance M. and Joel T. Rosenthal, eds. *Women, Marriage and Family in Medieval Christendom: Essays in Memory of Michael M. Sheehan, C.S.B.* Kalamazoo, MI: Medieval Institute Publications, 1998.

Russell, J. B. *Witchcraft in the Middle Ages.* Ithaca: Cornell University Press, 1972.

Schaus, Margaret, ed. *Women and Gender in Medieval Europe: An Encyclopedia.* New York: Routledge, 2006.

Scheepsma, Wybren. *Medieval Religious Women in the Low Countries: The "Modern Devotion," the Canonesses of Windesheim and their Writings.* Translated by David F. Johnson. Woodbridge, U.K.: Boydell Press, 2004.

Schulenburg, Jane Tibbetts. *Forgetful of Their Sex: Female Sanctity and Society, ca. 500–1100.* Chicago: University of Chicago Press, 1998.

Schutte, Anne Jacobson, Thomas Kuehn and Silvana Seidel Menchi, eds. *Time, Space and Women's Lives in EarlyModern Europe.* Kirksville, MO: Truman State University Press, 2001.

Scott-Stokes, Charity, ed. *Women's Books of Hours in Medieval England.* Woodbridge, U.K.: D. S. Brewer, 2006.

Shahar, Shulamith. *The Fourth Estate: A History of Women in the Middle Ages.* London: Methuen, 1983.

Sheehan, Michael M. *Marriage, Family and Law in Medieval Europe.* Toronto: University of Toronto Press, 1996.

Sheils W. J. and D. Wood, eds. *Women in the Church*. Oxford: Blackwell, 1990.

Simons, Walter. *Cities of Ladies: Beguine Communities in the Medieval Low Countries, 1200–1565*. Philadelphia: University of Pennsylvania Press, 2001.

Skinner, Patricia. *Women in Medieval Italian Society, 500–1200*. Harlow, England: Pearson Education, 2001.

Smith, Lesley and Jane H. M. Taylor, eds. *Women and the Book: Assessing the Visual Evidence*. London: British Library, 1996.

——. *Women, the Book and the Godly: Selected Proceedings of the St. Hilda's Conference, 1993*. Woodbridge, U.K.: D. S. Brewer, 1995.

——. *Women, the Book and the Worldly: Selected Proceedings of the St. Hilda's Conference, 1993*. Woodbridge, U.K.: D. S. Brewer, 1995.

Smith, Susan L. *The Power of Women: A Topos in Medieval Art and Literature*. Philadelphia: University of Pennsylvania Press, 1995.

Stafford, Pauline. *Gender, Family and the Legitimation of Power: England from the Ninth to Early Twelfth Century*. Aldershot, U.K.: Ashgate/Variorum, 2006.

——. *Queen Emma and Queen Edith: Queenship and Women's Power in Eleventh-Century England*. Oxford: Blackwell, 1997.

——. *Queens, Concubines and Dowagers: The King's Wife in the Early Middle Ages*. Athens, GA.: University of Georgia Press, 1983.

Stone, Marilyn and Carmen Benito-Vessels, eds. *Women at Work in Spain: From the Middle Ages to Early Modern Times*. New York: Peter Lang, 1998.

Stuard, Susan Mosher, ed. *Women in Medieval History and Historiography*. Philadelphia: University of Pennsylvania Press, 1987.

Sutherland, Elizabeth. *Five Euphemias: Women in Medieval Scotland, 1200–1420*. New York: St. Martin's Press, 1999.

Swabey, Fiona. *Medieval Gentlewoman: Life in a Gentry Household in the Later Middle Ages*. New York: Routledge, 1999.

Thiébaux, Marcelle, ed. *The Writings of Medieval Women: An Anthology*. New York: Garland, 1994.

Thompson, Sally. *Women Religious: The Founding of English Nunneries after the Norman Conquest*. Oxford: Clarendon Press, 1991.

Uitz, Erika. *The Legend of Good Women: Medieval Women in Towns and Cities*. Mount Kisco, NY: Moyer Bell, 1990.

Underhill, Frances A. *For Her Good Estate: The Life of Elizabeth de Burgh*. New York: St. Martin's Press, 1999.

van Houts, Elisabeth, ed. *Medieval Memories: Men, Women and the Past, 700–1300*. Harlow, U.K.: Longman, 2001.

Vann, Theresa M. ed. *Women of Power I: Queens, Regents and Potentates*. Dallas, TX: Academia Press, 1993.

Venarde, Bruce. *Women's Monasticism and Medieval Society: Nunneries in France and England, 890–1215*. Ithaca: Cornell University Press, 1997.

Voaden, R. *God's Words, Women's Voices: The Discernment of Spirits in the Writing of Late-Medieval Women Visionaries*. Woodbridge, U.K.: York Medieval Press, 1999.

——. ed. *Prophets Abroad: The Reception of Continental Holy Women in Late-Medieval England*. Woodbridge, U.K.: D. S. Brewer, 1996.

Wada, Yoko, ed. *A Companion to Ancrene Wisse*. Woodbridge, U.K.: D. S. Brewer, 1996.

Walker, Sue Sheridan, ed. *Wife and Widow in Medieval England*. Ann Arbor: University of Michigan Press, 1993.

Ward, Jennifer C. *English Noblewomen in the Later Middle Ages.* London: Longman, 1992.

——. ed. *Women in Medieval Europe, 1200–1500.* London: Longman, 2002.

——. *Women of English Nobility and Gentry, 1066–1500.* Manchester: Manchester University Press, 1995.

Warner, Marina. *Alone of All Her Sex: The Myth and Cult of the Virgin Mary.* London: Weidenfeld & Nicholson, 1976.

Warren, Nancy Bradley. *Spiritual Economies: Female Monasticism in Later Medieval England.* Philadelphia: University of Pennsylvania Press, 2001.

Watt, Diane, ed. *Medieval Women in their Communities.* Toronto: University of Toronto Press, 1997.

——. ed. *The Paston Women: Selected Letters.* Rochester: D. S. Brewer, 2004.

——. *Secretaries of God: Women Prophets in Late Medieval and Early Modern England.* Woodbridge, U.K.: D. S. Brewer, 1997.

Weightman, Christine B. *Margaret of York, Duchess of Burgundy 1446–1503.* New York: St. Martin's Press, 1989.

Wemple, Suzanne Fonay. *Women in Frankish Society: Marriage and the Cloister, 500 to 900.* Philadelphia: University of Pennsylvania Press, 1981.

Wheeler, Bonnie and Charles T. Wood, eds. *Fresh Verdicts on Joan of Arc.* New York: Garland, 1996.

Whitaker, Muriel, ed. *Sovereign Lady: Essays on Women in Middle English Literature.* New York: Garland, 1995.

Wiesner, Merry E. *Working Women in Renaissance Germany.* New Brunswick, NJ: Rutgers University Press, 1986.

Wiethaus, Ulrike, ed. *Maps of Flesh and Light: The Religious Experience of Medieval Women Mystics.* Syracuse, NY: Syracuse University Press, 1993.

Williams, Marty and Anne Echols. *Between Pit and Pedestal: Women in the Middle Ages.* Princeton, NJ: Markus Wiener Publishers, 1994.

Wilson, Katharina M. ed. *Medieval Women Writers.* Athens: University of Georgia Press, 1984.

Wilson, Katharina M. and Nadia Margolis, eds. *Women in the Middle Ages: An Encyclopedia.* Westport, CT: Greenwood Press, 2004.

Winstead, Karen A. *Virgin Martyrs: Legends of Sainthood in Late Medieval England.* Ithaca: Cornell University Press, 1997.

Winston-Allen, Anne. *Convent Chronicles: Women Writing about Women and Reform in the Late Middle Ages.* University Park, PA: Pennsylvania State University Press, 2004.

Wogan-Browne, Jocelyn. *Saints' Lives and Women's Literary Culture, c. 1150–1300: Virginity and Its Authorizations.* Oxford: Oxford University Press, 2001.

Wogan-Browne, Jocelyn, et al. eds. *Medieval Women: Texts and Contexts in Late Medieval Britain: Essays for Felicity Riddy.* Turnhout, Belgium: Brepols, 2000.

Wood, Diana, ed. *Women and Religion in Medieval England.* Oxford: Oxbow Books, 2003.

Wood, Jeryldene. *Women, Art and Spirituality: The Poor Clares of Early Modern Italy.* Cambridge: Cambridge University Press, 1996.

Woolgar, C. M. *The Great Household in Late Medieval England.* New Haven: Yale University Press, 1999.

Zum Brunn, Emilie and Georgette Epiney-Burgard, eds. *Women Mystics in Medieval Europe.* New York: Paragon House, 1989.

Index